THE CONTESTED STATE

American Foreign Policy and Regime Change in the Philippines

Amy Blitz

ROWMAN & LITTLEFIELD PUBLISHERS, INC.
Lanham • Boulder • New York • Oxford

ROWMAN & LITTLEFIELD PUBLISHERS, INC.

Published in the United States of America
by Rowman & Littlefield Publishers, Inc.
4720 Boston Way, Lanham, Maryland 20706
http://www.rowmanlittlefield.com

12 Hid's Copse Road, Cumnor Hill, Oxford OX2 9JJ, England

British Library Cataloguing in Publication Information Available

Library of Congress Cataloging-in-Publication Data

Blitz, Amy
      The Contested State : American Foreign Policy and regime change in the
Phillipines / by Amy Blitz.
         p. cm.
      Includes bibliographical references and index.
      ISBN 0-8476-9934-X (alk. paper)—ISBN 0-8476-9935-8 (pbk. : alk. paper)
         1. United States—Foreign relations—Philippines. 2. Philippines—Foreign
relations—United States. 3. Imperialism—United States—History—20th century.
4. Philippines—Politics and government. 5. Authoritarianism—Philippines—History—
20th century. 6. Democracy—Philippines—History—20th century. I. Title.

E183.8.P6 B57 2000
327.730599'09'04—dc21   00-029084

Printed in the United States of America

♾™ The paper used in this publication meets the minimum requirements of American
National Standard for Information Sciences—Permanence of Paper for Printed Library
Materials, ANSI/NISO Z39.48-1992.

THE CONTESTED STATE

For my parents

Contents

Acknowledgments   ix

1. The Sword and the Cross:
   Spanish Foundations of U.S. Colonialism   1

2. Conquest and Coercion:
   Early U.S. Colonialism, 1899–1916   31

3. Colonialism amid Crises:
   The Road to Independent Democracy, 1917–1946   57

4. The Transition to "One-Man Democracy," 1946–1972   81

5. "Salvaging" Democracy: The Impact of Authoritarian Rule
   1972–1983   117

6. People Power: The Transition from Marcos to Aquino,
   1983–1986   157

7. The Contested State: Transnational Sources of Regime Change   193

References   215

Index   227

About the Author   237

Acknowledgments

I n the Philippines, it's called "Bayanihan" —a cooperative community effort to move a house, harvest rice, or, in this case, write a book. This project has been blessed with many strong backs and hearty spirits. First and foremost are my parents, Sandy and Mel Blitz, who have taught me by example the power of love and laughter as well as a passion for excellence. Thank you for always encouraging me to dream and for your unflagging support throughout my journey. It is to you that this book is dedicated. Thanks also to my brother Jeff for always teaching me to look at the world a little differently and for endless witticisms and insights.

I have a special debt of gratitude as well to a few key mentors throughout the research and writing phases of the book. Thanks first to Jonathan Fox for being such a kind, incisive, and inspiring advisor throughout my graduate studies at M.I.T.; for crucial help in developing the methodology, theoretical model, and detailed aspects of the story; and, most importantly, for teaching me not just about political science but also about commitment and always striving to bridge academia with action. Thanks also to Steve Van Evera for vital input on the methodological, theory-building and international relations elements of the book and for imparting to me a devotion to relevance as well as research. And to Steve Miller for teaching me the craft and discipline of writing day by day and for contributing to the international security and foreign policy aspects of the book.

I am also grateful to the many professors at M.I.T. and Harvard who guided me along the way and shone a light for me by example. Thanks, in particular, to Marvin Kalb, Willard Johnson, Charles Stewart, Myron Weiner, Josh Cohen, Ken Oye, Lincoln Bloomfield, and Michael Piore.

I have another special debt of gratitude to my friends. Thanks especially to Carla DeLuca-Wardwell, Pamela D'Angelo Hagey, Ewell Hopkins, Yolanda Nunley, and Valerie Ruccia Eagan, for teaching me continuity and the joy of old friends, and for sustaining me throughout this project. And to Ali Webb, Liesl Wilhardt, and Janet Lee for helping to build a place throughout my graduate studies that will always feel like home. I would also like to thank my colleagues and friends at M.I.T. and Harvard for intellectual and moral support throughout the graduate studies that led me here. Thanks, in particular, to Joanne Kauffman for going over rough drafts of chapters, Dale Murphy for helping with the data analysis, and James Rosberg and Pablo Policzer for insights into the theoretical framework. And to Karen Motley, Joanna Spear, David Mussington, David Guston, Joanne Mahoney, and Karen Rothschild Cavenaugh, a "paragon of palindromes" and friendship at Harvard's Belfer Center for Science and International Affairs during the writing phase of the book.

The story told here has many heroes and I feel truly privileged for the time and insights some of these heroes so generously shared with me, in particular, Corazon Aquino; Senator Richard Lugar and his aide Andy Semmel; Ambassador Stephen Bosworth, Scott Butcher, Tom Daughton, Sau Ching Yip, Wendy Silverman, and George Lister, all of the State Department; Warren Hoge, Leslie Gelb, and Seth Mydans, all of the *New York Times*; Pete Carey of the *San Jose Mercury News*; and Walden Bello and John Gershman of the Institute for Food and Development Policy. Thanks also to Philippe Schmitter and Teri Karl of Stanford University for theoretical insights, Lela Garner Noble for a view into the Muslim conflict in the Philippines, Boone Schirmer for both personal and scholarly insights into the history of American lobbying for Philippine autonomy, and Richard Solomon for insights into the U.S. foreign policymaking process. An anonymous reviewer also provided valuable feedback prior to final editing for publication. Thank you for your time and insights.

There were many unsung heroes as well who gave me a glimpse of true courage—borne of compassion and commitment—during the last months of the Marcos regime. I would like to thank especially Pem Catalla, Inday Fernandez, Jo Jo Pastores, Puri Matsura, Fely Suner and Eva Duenas. Thanks also to Genara Banzon for artistically and joyfully bringing the Philippines to life here. To Ken Powelson for endless energy, enthusiasm, and intelligence, and for teaching me to fully embrace the Philippine experience, and to Jane Yudelman for teaching by example a deep respect for the development process. And to the people of Alimsog, who taught me to fish by moonlight and to appreciate the richness of their lives, I am eternally grateful. Finally, to my friend Raul Guerra, who disappeared in December 1985, you taught me courage in dark times, humor to get through them, and faith to believe in brighter times. Your light endures; it will forever challenge darkness.

Lastly, this book would not have been possible without the editorial and moral support provided by Jennifer Knerr at Rowman & Littlefield. Nor would it have been possible without the generous support provided by M.I.T.'s Political Science Department and the M.I.T. Center for International Studies, the MacArthur Foundation, the Woodrow Wilson International Center for Scholars, the Institute for the Study of World Politics, the Massachusetts Foundation for the Humanities, and Harvard's Center for Press, Politics, and Public Policy. Of course, any errors, omissions, opinions or interpretations are mine alone and do not reflect the views of any of these organizations.

In the spirit of "Bayanihan," thank you.

Chapter 1

The Sword and the Cross: Spanish Foundations of U.S. Colonialism

On February 25, 1986, Philippine President Ferdinand Marcos and his wife Imelda fled to the United States, leaving behind the infamous shoes and a twenty-year legacy of cronyism and corruption. Hours later, Corazon Aquino was swept to power on a sea of yellow confetti, launching a resurgence of democracy in the Philippines, soon followed by similar changes in the region, as well as in Latin America, Eastern Europe, and Africa.

Earlier eras have experienced waves of revolutionary transitions, such as those in Latin America in the early 1800s, and authoritarian transitions, such as those in Europe prior to World War II. And these waves of regime change have had historic, transformative effects on international alliances, on the global balance of power and so on the international system. The tendency for regime change to occur in waves suggests a connection with forces at the level of the international system, beyond the apparent accidents of history driving domestic politics. To date, however, our understanding of regime transitions has emphasized either purely international or purely domestic forces, overlooking the interactions between

1

the two. Yet interactions among domestic and international forces have not only been significant in the past; they are likely to expand dramatically in the future as the Internet and other elements of the information revolution break down communication barriers, enabling real-time information exchanges that cut across national boundaries with the click of a mouse. Chiapas revolutionaries, for example, have used the Internet to build support abroad. Another important issue often overlooked relates to the role of history. Regime change, by definition, replaces one regime with another—authoritarian with democratic, democratic with authoritarian, etc. Despite the historical connections linking regimes, however, we have tended to analyze diverse types of regime change ahistorically, and as isolated events. If recent events in the Balkans have taught us nothing more, they have certainly demonstrated the power of the past, and the continuing influence regime changes of long ago have over conflicts today.

This book is an attempt to fill the gaps in our understanding, using the Philippine story as a kind of prism for exploring the international as well as domestic sources of regime change in the context of world politics over time. The book traces the roots of both authoritarian and democratic forces in the Philippines from 1898, when the United States first took the Spanish colony as its own, through major regime changes, including the 1972 transition to martial law and the subsequent "People Power" transition to democracy in 1986. In doing so, the book emphasizes the recurring role of revolutionary opposition in the Philippines, the colonial roots of such opposition, and the two competing transnational[1] U.S.–Philippine strategies for dealing with it—one military based and essentially authoritarian, the other politically based and essentially democratic. The book describes how the two strategies evolved over time through the colonial and post-colonial eras, developing institutions, interests, and transnational alliances that transcended the domestic politics of either the United States or the Philippines, while battling for control of the Philippine state. Hence the central issue facing a chronically contested state like the Philippines and the focal question of this book: bullets or ballots? What, beyond purely domestic factors in the Philippines, accounts for the relative strength of each transnational alliance at key moments? And what broader lessons might we learn from the Philippine case regarding regime change more generally? The answer, this book demonstrates, lies in the international context within which the battle for control of the state has played out over time, spanning World War I, the Depression, World War II, and the Cold War, as well as major regime changes attending, for example, the Korean and Vietnam Wars, revolution in China, Iran and Nicaragua, and the end of the Cold War.

The book is organized chronologically. This chapter examines the Spanish legacy in the Philippines and its implications for U.S. colonial rule after 1898, particularly in establishing a land tenure system that would provide an ongoing source of revolutionary opposition in the countryside. The chapter also analyzes the debate in the United States surrounding the Spanish–American War and the processes that launched U.S. overseas imperialism. Chapter two examines the early U.S. colonial experience from the outbreak of war between U.S. forces and Filipino nationalists in 1899 through the Jones Act of 1916, in which the United States pledged eventual independence for the Philippines. Chapter three examines the continuing transnational processes that shaped Philippine institutions from 1917 through World War I, the Depression and World War II. The chapter focuses on the interplay of international, domestic United States and domestic Philippine forces that eventually ushered in the transition to Philippine independence in 1946. Chapter four describes how this independence was compromised from the start, examining the onset of the Cold War, the associated rise of the transnational authoritarian U.S.–Philippine alliance, and the transition to authoritarian rule under Marcos in 1972. Chapter five describes the impact of martial law on Philippine society from 1972 through what would prove to be a pivotal event for the Marcos regime—the 1983 assassination of opposition leader Benigno Aquino Jr. Chapter six describes the resurgence of democracy, examining the transnational forces that brought Aquino's widow to power, launching the "People Power" transition to democracy in 1986.

This transition would prove fragile, however, and would be repeatedly challenged by a series of attempted military coups against the fledgling Aquino administration. Nevertheless, democracy has survived, a success made all the more remarkable in the context of other experiments with democracy in the region, notably in China during the Tiananmen Square crisis in 1989 and in East Timor on the eve of the new millenium ten years later. Moreover, democracy has survived what could have been a difficult transition—the 1992 U.S.–Philippine agreement to remove U.S. military bases from Philippine soil. Heralded by the dramatic 1991 eruption of Mount Pinatubo, a volcano long thought to be dormant but whose ashes now buried Clark Air Force Base, the new era has likewise awakened independent Philippine democracy while demonstrating the power of seemingly insignificant forces.[2] Indeed, Mount Pinatubo might serve as a metaphor for the story that will unfold here, as political undercurrents erupt at critical moments, affecting not only the Philippines but also U.S. foreign policy and international relations more broadly. And this story offers lessons that can be applied beyond the Philippines to the enduring questions surrounding civil conflict and regime change in general, as described in brief below.

Bullets or Ballots:
A Transnational Approach to Regime Transition

The story told here will describe how regime transitions in a chronically contested state like the Philippines result from competition over time among revolutionary, authoritarian and reformist, in this case, democratic forces. In such a chronically contested state, the state's authority and institutions face on-going challenges from recurring revolutionary opposition. This is particularly prevalent in countries where social, economic and/or political structures exclude enough of the population to challenge the legitimacy of the social contract. While authoritarian groups will argue that only repression can resolve an essentially *military* problem, reformist groups will argue that repression not only fails to address an essentially *political* problem but may also fuel the militancy of the insurgency. The two groups agree on the need to avert revolution but diverge on the issue of strategy, on whether repression or reform, military force or political inclusion, in short, bullets or ballots, will stem revolutionary opposition. When authoritarian forces gain control of the political process, a transition to authoritarian rule results. When democratic forces gain control, a transition to democracy results. When neither gains control either revolution or state failure results, depending upon whether or not a viable revolutionary opposition exists. Once a regime transition occurs, moreover, it creates structures, or strengthens existing ones, and so establishes new parameters for the on-going civil conflict. For this reason, regime transitions must be understood in their historical contexts.[3]

Further, contested states and the periodic regime transitions they experience must be understood in their broader, international contexts as well. Because regime type can affect international alliances, external powers have often used transnational strategies to influence the balance of power among competing forces in a contested state while those in the contested state have often sought external allies to strengthen their position at home. These transnational strategies link segments of states and society in one nation with those in another. In this framework, the state is seen as fragmented, with each fragment potentially forming coalitions with sectors of society, and then forming alliances with similar fragments of other nations. For example, an external power may support revolutionary forces in a bid to improve its own international standing by creating a new ally with the contested state, as Libya under Qaddafi has backed Muslim insurgencies beyond its borders and the former Soviet Union communist ones throughout the Cold War. Meanwhile, the existing ally will back counter-insurgency efforts in order to protect its international standing, as well as any economic, political, strategic or other interests at stake in the event of revolution. Both the existing ally and the contested state will not behave as unitary actors, however, if their own officials dispute the use of repression versus reform. Transnational coalitions of authoritarian versus reformist forces may then mobilize and compete for control of the contested state, with implications for eventual regime type.

Each side of a transnational alliance will exchange economic, political, strategic or other resources in order to strengthen its own position. Authoritarian forces in the contested state may, for example, offer their foreign allies access to military bases in exchange for technical and/or financial assistance in counter-insurgency efforts. Similarly, reformist forces in the contested state may give their foreign allies access to political or economic resources or simply an alternative means of securing access to military bases in exchange for technical and/or financial assistance to protect democratic processes and reformist efforts. Such exchanges may be official, but may also be channeled through private organizations, including foundations, corporations or universities, or through individuals. In transnational processes involving individuals, immigration patterns will come into play as will informal information exchanges via letter, phone, fax, and, increasingly, the Internet. For example, those displaced by an authoritarian regime with foreign support may well take their cause abroad. If allowed into the foreign power backing the authoritarian regime, they may seek to influence the foreign power's policies in order to influence the domestic balance of forces back home. If these immigrants become citizens, they will further enhance their potential influence, particularly in democracies where they will be able to vote. Such transnational processes are most likely to occur, and to have an effect, when states are linked by colonial legacies, with continuing interdependencies and shared interests—economic, strategic, political, etc. In such cases, the vulnerability of the external power's interests to the domestic politics in the contested state, and vice versa, is likely to be quite strong. A fact often overlooked is the leverage the contested state will thus have vis-à-vis its former colonial power, despite even substantial power imbalances.

Finally, the relative strength of revolutionary, authoritarian, and democratic forces during moments of regime change is determined by a complex interaction of domestic, international, and ultimately transnational factors. If, for example, authoritarian forces in the foreign state are weakened, through international economic, political or strategic losses, this will reduce their capacity to support authoritarian forces abroad. Watergate and Vietnam, for example, weakened the ability of U.S. hard-liners to legitimately support their allies in Central America during the 1980s. On the other hand, if an international conflict or other event increases the relative power of authoritarian forces, as was the case for U.S. hard-liners during the first half of the Cold War, the strength of authoritarian forces in the contested state will likely grow. And this international context is often crucial to the success of any authoritarian transition in the contested state since, without a pledge of external support, the transition may not even take place. Similarly, if democratic or reformist forces in the foreign state are weakened, again through international economic, political or strategic losses, as Truman and U.S. Democrats were after the 1949 Chinese revolution, this will affect democratic or reformist forces in contested states. Thus, losses in the international arena affect the balance of forces within the foreign power, which then affects the balance of forces within the contested state. Regime change in the contested state then affects, in turn, international alliances, the global balance of power, and so the international system. It may also affect the balance of forces within the foreign power, particularly if the change is viewed as a loss to either authoritarian or democratic forces. Hence the image of the contested state as a kind of prism through which international conflicts are not only refracted but are also often redefined

In short, regime transitions in chronically contested states result from ongoing conflicts among revolutionary, authoritarian and democratic forces over time. And these domestic conflicts must be understood in their broader historical and international contexts, particularly where long-standing interdependencies encourage transnational strategies to emerge. As the Philippine experience will show, when transnational authoritarian forces gain control, through a complex interplay of international and domestic factors, a transition to military rule results. When transnational democratic forces gain control, through a similarly complex interplay of international and domestic factors, a transition to democracy results. Beyond bullets or ballots, however, as long as revolutionary opposition, or the structural conditions that create it, persists, the state will remain contested or essentially unstable as revolutionary, authoritarian and democratic forces continually battle for political control. In the Philippine case, the structural conditions for recurring revolutionary opposition trace back to the Spanish colonial era from 1521 to 1898.

The Sword and the Cross: The Spanish Colonial Era

Thus, our tale begins with an earlier Ferdinand. On March 16, 1521, Ferdinand Magellan sighted an archipelago of islands in the far reaches of the Pacific Ocean. Weeks later, on Easter Sunday, he strode ashore, planted a large wooden cross near what is now the city of Cebu, and claimed the islands for Christianity and for Spain.[4] The first European to establish contact with the islanders, Magellan quickly entered negotiations with local chief Humabon. According to an account later written by Magellan's personal aide, Antonio Pigafetta, Humabon welcomed Magellan with a delegation of his emissaries bearing rice, pigs and chickens. Humabon then converted to Christianity, signed a blood pact with Magellan and convinced roughly 2,000 of his followers to convert to Christianity as well. Soon after, however, Lapu Lapu, a chief on a nearby island and Humabon's enemy, resisted. Persuaded by Humabon to attack Lapu Lapu, Magellan and his sixty men set out on April 27 in three boatloads across the narrow strait from Cebu to the island of Mactan. But word of the plan had leaked to Lapu Lapu, who had quickly mobilized 1,500 warriors. The Spaniards were quickly overcome. Magellan covered his crew's retreat; but, left alone in battle, it would be here, on Philippine shores, that Magellan's global explorations would finally end. To make matters worse, Humabon then turned against the Spaniards, slaughtering all but a few who managed to escape.[5] It was to be more than forty years before Spain would return in full force to conquer the archipelago; but in that first clash between Lapu Lapu and Magellan, the patterns of international collaboration by some Filipinos[6] and resistance by others, both of which can be seen as strategies for dealing with local conflict, were established.

Following Magellan's defeat, additional expeditions were sent to the Philippines; but there seemed little profit to be gained there and strong winds made a return trip via the Pacific apparently impossible. For the next forty years, Spain all but ignored the archipelago Magellan had discovered, focusing instead on the Americas and the gold and silver mines there. In 1564, however, interest in the islands was rekindled—less for what the islands had to offer per se than for their strategic importance vis-a-vis the Portuguese. The real prize Spain sought were the Moluccas, the so-called Spice Islands, which Portugal had already claimed. Spanish kings had long coveted this prize; but after sending out three expeditions to try to seize the Spice Islands for Spain, King Charles V finally conceded to the Portuguese claim. In 1556, Charles V abdicated and was replaced by his son, Philip II, who reigned for the next forty-two years, during the peak of Spanish glory. Determined to undo Portuguese supremacy in the East, Philip II ordered his viceroy in Mexico to mount yet another expedition to the East, this time to reestablish Spanish control of the archipelago Magellan had earlier claimed for Spain. The islands were to serve as a base for Spanish trade and military force in the region. They were also to serve as a counterweight to the Portuguese colonies in the Moluccas as well as in Macao, from which Portugal had a monopoly over trade with China, another prize Spain sought to take from the Portuguese.[7]

Miguel Lopez de Legazpi, a Basque bureaucrat based in Mexico, was chosen to lead the Spanish expedition, while Andres de Urdaneta, an Augustinian friar and noted geographer, was chosen as navigator. Setting out in November 1564, Legazpi, with Urdaneta's guidance, charted the Pacific route from Mexico to the archipelago Magellan had discovered, establishing in the process a new, direct link between Asia and the Americas. Legazpi and his crew reached the island of Samar on February 15, 1565, and renamed the archipelago, composed of over 7,000 islands, the Philippines, in tribute to King Philip II. Legazpi then sailed on to Cebu to establish contact with Humabon's successor, Chief Tupas. Far from the newly Christianized natives Pigafetta had described, however, Legazpi found virtually no trace of Christianity among the islanders and instead faced open hostility. When talks with Tupas failed, Legazpi resorted to force, bombarding *nipa* huts with cannon fire, setting them aflame, eventually forcing the inhabitants to flee as 200 Spanish troops staged an amphibious landing to conquer the villages, which had now been reduced to rubble. Tupas's followers, unlike those of Lapu Lapu, were not well organized for battle; nor were they equipped for the superior military power of Legazpi's troops. Having conquered Cebu, Legazpi signed a blood pact with Tupas and then sent a ship back to Mexico to report to Spanish colonial authorities there of his conquest. Using an innovative northeastern route devised by Urdaneta, the Spanish ship San Pedro sailed across the Pacific toward Acapulco, discovering along the way a critical return route from Asia back to America, as well as the coast of a virgin wilderness that would come to be known as California.[8]

When news of the conquest in the Philippines reached King Philip II, he agreed to send more men and equipment. Because the islands apparently lacked spices, gold, or anything much of value, however, it was not until 1571 that King Philip II decided to formally accept the Philippines as a colony. Over the next three centuries, the Spanish colonists would establish an essentially feudal land tenure system, creating in the process a key source of revolutionary opposition and civil conflict that persists today. And in response to such political instability, the Spanish would also introduce "sword and cross" strategies that laid the foundation for subsequent transnational authoritarian and reformist strategies for managing domestic conflict.

"Under the Bells" of Spanish Colonialism

After 1571, most of the Spanish colonists arriving in the Philippines were sent from Mexico, placing the Philippines in the unusual position of being essentially a colony of a colony. While native resistance persisted, there was no centralized threat to Spanish rule as the Aztecs of Mexico or the Incas of Peru had presented, so military requirements were relatively small.[9] With few colonists and little to attract them to the countryside, the Spanish focused their attention on Manila, using the port there as a center for ship repair, shipbuilding and trade. Manila quickly became an *entrepot* for the galleon trade, with Mexican silver exchanged for goods like silk and porcelain from China and spices from the Moluccas. These goods were then brought, via Mexico, to European markets. Though Manila was the center of colonization, the rapid growth of nonfarming populations there, comprised of Spanish colonists and Indian and Chinese traders, affected the countryside as well. A primarily subsistence economy was suddenly forced to produce surpluses adequate to sustain capitalist development, something European farmers had taken centuries to achieve. Compounding the need for surpluses while reducing the numbers of agrarian producers, native Filipinos were taken periodically from their villages and their fields to work as laborers for Spain. Without mines, the need for slaves was much lower in the Philippines than in Latin America; but Spain did need labor to cut and transport timber for shipbuilding, demand for which increased during Spain's frequent periods of international warfare. For this, Spain used Filipinos in gangs of up to 8,000.[10]

Spain then added to the burdens placed on rural Filipinos by requiring all adult males to pay a tribute, essentially a tax, under an *encomienda* system. The encomienda system preserved the Spanish monarchy's ownership of colonial land, but granted colonists the right to collect tribute from the inhabitants of the land. The colonial encomiendas were not hereditary beyond the third or at most the fourth generation and were then to revert back to the monarchy. With little incentive to develop the long-term profitability of the encomiendas and with much incentive to maximize short-term gains from them, *encomenderos* frequently abused their privileges. So great were the abuses in the Antilles, in fact, that King Charles V decreed the abolition of the system in the early 1500s, though this was ignored by Hernan Cortes, who brought the system to Mexico. Legazpi, pleading the poverty of his men and the paucity of natural resources in the Philippines, then convinced King Philip II to reinstate encomiendas in the new territory. In fact, Spain eventually abolished encomiendas everywhere but in the Philippines.[11]

While conflicts among tribal groups predated Spanish conquest, as with the conflict between Humabon and Lapu Lapu, the encomiendas intensified these. Initially, the Filipino "nobility," those who came forward as chiefs, were excluded from paying tribute but were typically required to collect it. A chief who fell short of the expected amount was often publicly humiliated or killed. Others collaborated with the Spanish for personal profit, while taking bribes from villagers seeking to avoid Spain's labor conscription. Out of this early colonial policy emerged a Filipino *cacique*[12] who were responsible for collecting tributes and administering colonial policies. In return, they were exempt from paying tribute and from having to provide forced labor. In the process, Spain also intensified regional conflicts among tribal groups in areas with diverse political, economic and social identities. One notable example is that of Pampanga, a fertile region near Manila that became a critical supplier of foodstuffs to the Spanish. To secure Pampangan loyalty, the Spanish cultivated a native Pampangan elite by offering them access to Spanish markets and granting them preferential treatment under colonial rule. Based in the Pampangan town of Macabebe, the emerging native elite prospered. Select natives of Macabebe were also trained as soldiers by the Spanish military, and served a vital strategic role in Spain's wars in the Moluccas and in guarding Manila from Portuguese or other incursions. In the earliest phase of a transnational authoritarian alliance, the Macabebes were also used to quell recurring revolutionary opposition to Spanish rule, which the brutal exactions of the encomienda system and labor conscriptions fueled throughout the archipelago.[13]

In fact, by the end of the 1500s, native resistance to Spanish rule had become widespread as insurrections spread from island to island, sometimes as isolated events, sometimes as coordinated rebellions, and sometimes as conflicts among Filipinos.[14] Meanwhile, the Spanish colonists were themselves divided, as the clergy and military fought for control of the conquered territories. While the encomienda system was intended to support both the Spanish military and missionaries, because the military oversaw collection of the tax, they often took more of it for themselves than they gave to the clergy. In response, the clergy publicly assailed the abuses of the encomienda, building popular opposition to it among their followers in what may be seen as an early form of a transnational anti-authoritarian alliance centered around the Catholic Church, emphasizing non-military, in this case spiritual, solutions to peasant resistance. The clergy also raised theoretical issues regarding the king's legal and moral authority in the colonies vis-à-vis the pope. To resolve the crisis, the Synod of Manila surveyed the issues and, in 1586, upheld the friars, emphasizing the role of the clergy in governing the colony and in taming abusive Spanish military forces. The Synod also curtailed the rights of foreigners, with the exception of designated friars, to enter remote areas. Far from the church and the state, the clergy hereafter gained substantial power and many used this power to accrue vast tracts of land as well as wealth from taxes, tributes, and trade. While vestiges of a transnational anti-authoritarian alliance persisted, alliances were also reestablished between the church and the military, again combining threat and coercion, the so-called sword and cross, to subdue the native population.[15]

Ultimately, the land expansion drives of the friars made religious corporations the largest landowners in the Philippines by the end of Spanish rule.[16] As increasing numbers of native producers became dispossessed from the land, then the principal means of production and subsistence, feudal sharecropping arrangements emerged as the predominant pattern of agricultural production. The produce of the land was then appropriated as a fixed share of the harvest, as tributes, or as forcible purchase by the state at government-set prices.[17] The friars also became monopolists over the internal trade of their districts and were often powerful enough to fix the prices at which produce was bought and sold.[18] Religious corporations and other Church organizations also participated in the galleon trade, even before a royal decree in 1638 conferred upon them this right.[19] To further tighten their grip over the natives, whose villages were autonomous, the Spanish built townships, the centerpieces of which were massive stone churches named for patron saints. The towns that built up around these churches would soon help bring the native Filipinos *debajo de las campanas*, or "under the bells" of Spanish colonial authority.

Pressures on Spain and the Impact on the Philippines

Meanwhile, Spain faced international threats to its authority as well. From 1568 until the 1648 Treaty of Westphalia, Spain was at war with Holland, which had risen up against Spanish rulers there. Spain was also frequently at war with England, primarily over access to the seas and control of the periphery as well as the spread of Protestantism. From 1580 to 1640, Spain absorbed metropolitan Portugal, though the Dutch seized Portuguese colonies in the East. Despite periodic Dutch incursions into Philippine waters and other Dutch challenges to Spain, the Spanish presence in Asia grew. At its peak around 1597, the Manila trade was in fact as valuable as the official Spanish trans-atlantic trade.[20] Far from being celebrated, however, the trade was seen as a growing threat to the interests of the Spanish monarchy. In particular, independent trade between the Americas and Asia began to emerge, with Mexican and Peruvian silver being siphoned off to Asia rather than Madrid. Further, manufactured goods from Asia, which were often superior in quality and cheaper than those from Spain, were now entering Mexican and Peruvian markets directly. The Manila trade, in short, threatened to detach Mexico and Peru from their intended place as conduits for Spanish colonial trade, enabling them to emerge as independent commercial centers. To curtail this, the Spanish Crown forbade trade between Mexico and Peru after 1631 in order to close Peruvian markets to Asian goods. Serving only Mexico, the Manila trade plummeted, and the Philippines slipped back into the periphery, becoming thereafter one of Spain's poorest, most isolated colonies.[21]

As profits from trade dropped, the Chinese in Manila, known as Sangleys after the Chinese word *xang lai,* meaning "to barter and trade," were among the first to face increased abuse from the Spanish colonists, who both depended upon and feared the large Chinese population in the Philippines. Alternately tolerated and persecuted, the Chinese staged two separate rebellions against the Spaniards in the 1600s; but native troops, notably those from Macabebe, helped the Spaniards put down the revolts, leaving thousands of Chinese massacred.[22] By the mid-1600s, domestic tensions within the Philippines spread as rural areas surrounding Manila threatened to revolt. Overextended in war and in decline at home, Spain turned an increasingly heavy hand on the Philippines, using primarily authoritarian strategies to extract labor for shipbuilding as well as tribute and food supplies from the countryside. The decline in the galleon trade further exacerbated domestic tensions within the Philippines, as Spanish colonists now looked to the countryside for new sources of wealth.[23] The result, however, was a further increase in revolutionary opposition to Spanish rule. Even among the Spanish-trained Macabebes, rebellion surfaced in a 1660 revolt, the immediate cause of which was ill treatment of timber cutters. The Spanish colonial governor managed, however, to defuse the situation by exploiting divisions between the Macabebes and neighboring groups who had joined the revolt. He did this by entering the town of Macabebe with a massive show of troops and a pretense of friendliness. The Macabebes, overpowered, reciprocated the pretense. When word of the mutual cordiality spread, suspisions built among neighboring groups and the Macabebes themselves became a target of revolutionary opposition. In the agreement with Spain that followed, the Macabebes demanded and received two garrisons and then quickly silenced opposition in surrounding areas. Throughout the remaining years of Spanish colonialism, there were to be no other such revolts in Macabebe, now a loyal bastion of Spain.[24]

In other provinces, however, rebellions of the late 1600s and early 1700s marked the rise again of Church-inspired challenges to the transnational authoritarian rule, this time from native Filipinos. Though Filipinos were barred from entering the clergy, Filipino rebel leaders used Catholicism to inspire their followers, recognizing the spiritual, as well as economic and political, hold the church had by then won over the masses. Putting away the sword for the moment, "enlightened despot" and Bourbon King Charles III, hailed by the salons of Europe, tried to liberalize the church throughout the colonies from 1757 to 1788. One result for the Philippines was the emergence of a new breed of Filipino priests. In addition, Charles III liberalized colonial trade, reopening the Philippines to world markets. He also promoted the development of commercial plantation crops such as tobacco and indigo, and allowed for the establishment of *haciendas*. Unlike the encomiendas, haciendas were owned and could be passed from generation to generation, thus encouraging investment in the land.

Though the Chinese, with their access to trade and their relatively strong financial resources, were perhaps best suited to commercialize agriculture, their prospects were upset in 1762, when Britain, as part of its seven years war with Spain, captured Manila.[25] Long abused by the Spaniards, the Chinese allied with the British; but, when Spain retook Manila two years later, the British left the Chinese to the mercies of the Spanish. Many Chinese were massacred. The rest were expelled. Chinese *mestizos*, those of mixed Chinese and Filipino extraction, were now granted the right to reside in the provinces as long as they converted to Christianity. These mestizos quickly filled the commercial vacuum left by the Chinese, developing new enterprises in export agriculture and accruing vast tracts of land, becoming the second largest group of landowners after the religious corporations for the remainder of the Spanish colonial era.[26] Some Filipinos emerged too as merchants and middlemen, though most were left more alienated from the land than ever. Thus, while the commercialization of agriculture extended profits to a new elite comprised of mestizos and Filipinos, it also increased the concentration of land ownership as well as the concomitant conflicts over control of the state.[27]

Meanwhile, for Spain, the commercialization of agriculture could save neither the crown nor its colonies. As the eighteenth century drew to a close, Spain faced increased threats both at home and abroad following revolutions that rocked the foundations of European power. While the American Revolution of 1776 fired a warning shot regarding the limits of colonial taxation, sparking rebellious agitation throughout Spain's territories, the French Revolution of 1789, overthrowing a European monarchy, posed a more direct challenge to Spain's monarchy. Long-standing tensions within Spain were now ignited, and debates concerning Spanish governance exploded. By 1808, Napoleon's expansionary drives brought France's Joseph Bonaparte to the Spanish throne. The French then dissolved the monasteries in 1809, an act Spanish liberals readily accepted, viewing the Church as a barrier to progress. In response, much of the Spanish Church allied with reactionary forces led by the military, strengthening the link between the sword and the cross. For the colonies, however, the link to the peninsular monarchy was broken during the French occupation from 1808 through 1814. For the Philippines, the flow of Spanish friars to the Philippines was cut off, and vacancies filled by the new breed of Filipino priests. Moreover, the economic ties between the Philippines and Latin America were cut. By 1811, the last galleon left Manila, ending centuries of trade between Spain's Asian colony and its counterparts in the Americas.[28]

Blockades now separated the Americas from Spain as well. Though some Spanish colonists remained loyal to the Crown, others reveled in their sudden freedom from centuries of restrictive economic policies. As Latin American commerce spread, the appetite for independence among Spanish colonists and emerging native elites grew, even after the Spanish monarchy was restored in 1815. A surge of revolutions in its colonies soon exploded, leaving Spain with just Cuba, Puerto Rico and the Philippines by 1826. Now the ultraconservative King Ferdinand VII stepped in to undo the work of Charles III. When it was discovered that Latin American clergymen had contributed substantially to the emancipation of their countries from Spain, the Spanish church strengthened its ties to reactionary forces as well as to the monarchy, which now sought to reverse the economic, social, and political liberalizations in the remaining colonies. In 1826, King Ferdinand VII, suspecting Filipino priests of the kind of anti-colonial ambitions that had swept Latin America, removed the Filipino priests from their parishes.[29] Moreover, Spain extended the restrictions to Philippine-born Spaniards, or *criollos*, ousting them from their parishes as well.[30]

Meanwhile, civil conflicts persisted back home, as numerous groups including liberals, democrats, monarchists and others continued to battle for control of Spain. After 1833, the situation intensified as Spain experienced a wave of revolutionary challenges, with alternate attempts at liberalization, reaction and military juntas attending a series of political transitions. These transitions, in turn, created uncertainty and instability in the Philippines, where the colonial administration was constantly shifting. During this period, a new generation of ultraconservative friars began to reach the archipelago and, in 1849, the so-called Recollects reclaimed parishes from Filipinos and criollos in Cavite Province, located just beyond Manila. Many displaced criollo clergymen, like their earlier Latin American counterparts, decried the new policies while rallying Filipinos against Spain.[31] Responding with more sword than cross, both at home and in the Philippines, a military junta gained control of Spain in 1868 and swiftly broadened the attack on Philippine criollos in other sectors of society. One particularly incendiary decree came in 1871, when Spain annulled the privileges of several criollo army officers and non-combatants, replacing them with Spanish-born *peninsulares*.[32] Such policies further strengthened growing ties between the Philippine-born Spanish criollos and other groups, including an increasingly powerful mestizo community as well as native Filipinos.

By January 1872, the conflict exploded when an uprising led by a newly displaced criollo sergeant named Lamadrid, with about 200 native troops, staged a rebellion that eventually required two Spanish regiments to be sent to the Philippines to restore order. The Spanish regiments swiftly slaughtered the insurgents, including Lamadrid, and summarily executed other rebels in subsequent days. Spain then ordered the arrest of thirty prominent Filipino lawyers, priests and other elites, assuming without substantiating their complicity in the uprising. Worse, a popular criollo priest named Jose Burgos, who had opposed Spain's increasingly restrictive policies, was implicated in a trial widely held at the time as unfair. Together with two other priests, Mariano Gomez, then in his seventies, and Jacinto Zamora, Burgos was executed on February 17, 1872. Far from silencing the opposition, this event has been cited by Filipino nationalists as the birth of a nationalist consciousness, forging a link between criollos and Filipinos, moderates and revolutionaries, rich and poor against a common enemy, setting the stage for the next, final wave of rebellion against Spain.[33]

Nationalism and Revolution

It was Spain's eventual undoing to encourage solidarity among diverse Filipinos, and among Filipinos and criollos, by extending restrictive policies to them all, regardless of class, political views or loyalties. Such restrictions not only fed agitation against Spain, they also gave formerly divided groups a common enemy and a new sense of Filipino nationalism. And this growing sense of nationalism would strengthen markedly by the mid-1890s when two opposition movements joined forces to oust Spain. The first group emerged in 1892, when a group of elite Filipinos who came to be known as *ilustrados* or "enlightened ones" formed the Liga Filipina under the leadership of Jose Rizal. The Spanish-educated doctor, novelist, linguist and scholar had studied in Madrid and had experienced first-hand the political ferment of late nineteenth-century Spain where debates raged among monarchists, democrats, socialists, republicans and others. Rizal wanted the same freedom of political expression for his compatriots and argued for moderate reforms including Philippine integration with Spain so as to provide Filipinos the same rights as Spaniards. He also argued for improved educational, judicial and welfare systems as well as Filipino representation in the Cortes. In his irreverent novel *Noli Me Tangere*, Rizal gave voice to his anger, wickedly satirizing the excesses of the Spanish friars who controlled much of Philippine political, economic and social institutions. Angry though the voice was, it was a cry for reform in order to avert revolution. And this cry awakened growing numbers of elite Filipinos and *criollos*, fueling moderate opposition to Spain.[34]

At the same time, Andres Bonifacio, a Manila clerk with peasant roots, founded a revolutionary secret society with the remarkable, if tongue-twisting name—the "Kataastaasang Kagalanggalang na Katipunan ng mga Anak ng Bayan," or, roughly, the "Most Noble Society of the Sons and Daughters of the Country." This came to be known as simply the Katipunan. Seeking, among other things, redistribution of land, the Katipunan grew rapidly among the lower and middle classes in the region surrounding Manila, particularly among dispossessed peasants. The movement failed to develop a national stronghold, however, and was also unable to gain acceptance from the ilustrados, who condemned the Katipunan as too radical. The Katipunan did, however, gain strength in southern and central Luzon, the area surrounding Spanish forces in Manila. And on August 29, 1896, Bonifacio declared war on Spain. Although Spain was able to subdue the uprising, a young rebel named Emilio Aguinaldo waged a particularly effective battle in Cavite. When Spain subsequently arrested hundreds of Bonifacio's men as well as roughly 500 ilustrados, among them Rizal, Spain made a critical tactical error. Treating reformers and revolutionaries equally harshly, Spain further encouraged moderate and revolutionary forces to ally.[35]

And this intensified after December 30, 1896 when Rizal, who had pledged allegiance to Spain, arguing only for reforms while rejecting the radicalism of the Katipunan, was executed for treason. If the execution of the three priests in 1872 had marked the birth of Filipino nationalism, the execution of Rizal marked its call to arms. Rizal became an instant martyr and symbol of both moderate and revolutionary opposition to Spain. The emerging rationale for an alliance between the ilustrados and the Katipunan was then nudged along by Bonifacio, who forged the signatures of hundreds of elite Filipinos on the Katipunan's membership rolls and then secretly passed the list along to Spanish officials. When the Spaniards responded in a reign of terror aimed at Filipino ilustrados and Katipunan members, those remaining together with a growing base among the peasantry quickly rallied behind Bonifacio in a mounting revolt against Spain. In response, Spain introduced new ultra-hard-line policies, emptying crowded jails by executing prisoners while stepping up the campaign against the insurgents. Still, by mid-1897, Spanish leaders in Manila acknowledged they lacked sufficient resources to win the war, and urged Queen Maria Cristina to either negotiate a settlement with the revolutionaries or provide extensive reinforcements. But the Queen rebuffed both proposals, the first because she feared the Spanish clergy should she negotiate, the latter because the war Spain was waging against revolutionaries in Cuba, where fighting had broken out in 1895, was draining her resources.

Spain, however, soon found an unexpected ally—internal feuding among the Filipino revolutionaries.[36] In early 1897, Aguinaldo and Bonifacio began to compete for control of the Katipunan. By May, Aguinaldo had Bonifacio executed and assumed leadership of the revolutionary forces. This seriously weakened the Filipino movement and, soon after Bonifacio's execution, the Filipinos were forced to retreat. Aguinaldo now negotiated a settlement with Spain, which paid him P 800,000 to lay down his arms and go into exile abroad. In exchange, Spain promised Aguinaldo a series of reforms. Aguinaldo chose Hong Kong as his new base and, from there, as Spain failed to fulfill its promises of reform and as unrest continued to simmer in the Philippines, he plotted the next course of action.[37] This new course of action began to evolve in 1898, when a new international player entered the drama.

The Question of U.S. Foreign Policy: Anti-Imperialists vs. Expansionists

On May 1, 1898, Commodore George Dewey sailed into Manila harbor and quickly routed Spanish forces there in what came to be known as "the splendid little war." A less "splendid" war of U.S. conquest would follow, eventually leaving as many as half a million Filipinos dead while raising to a pitch a long-standing tension within the United States between isolationists and interventionists.[38] This tension had its roots in the American Revolution, when Britain, in defeat, granted the United States the right to the Mississippi and access to the Great Lakes. With Spain facing a newly powerful adversary for American territory, U.S. expansionists gained power. The first Spanish loss was the Louisiana Territory, which Napoleon had secretly forced Spain to cede to France. Napoleon then sold the territory in 1803 to the United States for $15 million, more than doubling the size of the new nation while further enclosing Spain's North American territories. The United States then targeted Spanish territory along the Gulf of Mexico known as West Florida and, in 1810, James Madison accepted an invitation from American rebels there to occupy lands not garrisoned by Spain. Conquest of all of Florida was completed in 1819, when the United States wrested control of it from Spain. After Mexican independence in 1821, the United States faced down a new adversary, eventually taking formerly Spanish territories from Mexico. The United States conquered Texas in 1848 after years of warfare and then, with the Treaty of Guadalupe Hidalgo signed that same year, took what are now New Mexico, Colorado, Utah, Arizona, Nevada and the land Urdaneta had discovered so long ago, California.[39]

America's territorial expansion was spurred by population pressures, a belief in "manifest destiny," and technological innovations attending the industrial revolution, which allowed for communication and transportation across ever increasing distances. Prior to the Civil War, acquisition of territory in North America had fed U.S. expansionism, but afterwards the rising industrial economy together with the lack of empty, contiguous territory made economic rather than territorial expansion the driving force behind U.S. foreign policy. The North's victory also shifted power from southern planters to northern industrialists and financiers. America now looked abroad, seeking territories in the Caribbean, Central America and the Pacific, less for their land or resources than as steppingstones to markets in Europe, Latin America and Asia. The completion of the transcontinental railway in 1869 was one factor facilitating increased trade, particularly with Asia, though the American treatment of immigrant Chinese rail workers had strained U.S. relations with China. The opening of Japan during the Meiji Restoration, beginning in 1868, was another factor facilitating trade.[40] At home, the value of U.S. manufactured goods rose from fourth in the world in the 1860s to first by 1894, almost equaling that of Great Britain, Germany and France combined.[41]

Such progress was not without cost, however. Frequent periods of economic depression and labor unrest threatened U.S. expansion from within.[42] Abolitionists, linking expansion with slavery, also clamored for restraint, as did various economic interest groups who feared competition from new territories. The isolationists, now anti-imperialists, formed a broad coalition and, through the 1880s, worked effectively through congress to check American expansionism.[43] This shifted after 1893, when the worst economic crisis and the most intense labor unrest the U.S. had yet seen reignited debates between anti-imperialists and interventionists, now expansionists. With over 600 bank failures, 156 railroads in receivership, a Treasury deficit of $69.8 million, unemployment of 20 percent of the workforce, and increasingly violent labor confrontations such as the 1894 Pullman strike, America's golden era was tarnishing.[44]

Expansionists argued that the crisis was caused by overproduction and underconsumption, that the industrial growth and enhanced efficiency of the post-Civil War era had to be met with expansions in market size. Given the limits of the domestic market, they argued, the United States must look abroad for new markets. It was this rationale that Hobson and later Lenin would cite as the driving force behind imperialism. Social Darwinists supported these claims, arguing for "survival of the fittest" in crudely racist terms. At the same time, the U.S. Navy was expanding, following the 1890 publication of Captain Alfred Mahan's important work, *The Influence of Sea Power on History*, and the authorization by congress the same year to build the nation's first battleships. Mahan had argued that national security as well as international supremacy required a strong navy, and the U.S. Congress had acquiesced. Moreover, the rise of trusts in steel, oil, sugar and other key sectors led to high concentrations of capital, and the attendant political power such concentration conferred. Core elements of the trusts, with the notable exception of Andrew Carnegie, sought overseas expansion to improve the supply of raw materials, increase their market, and sell excess goods.[45]

Despite the daunting array of pro-imperialist forces, however, the anti-imperialists continued to have a powerful voice in the debates of the period. In fact, despite their much greater wealth and power, the expansionists faced serious challenges at several critical moments. The first moment came in 1893, when Hawaiian sugar planters staged a nearly bloodless coup and offered the islands to the United States. The planters offered the islands to the United States primarily so that Hawaiian sugar could be free of U.S. tariffs and thus be more competitive with domestic U.S. beet sugar as well as Cuban cane sugar, which was closer to the major East Coast refineries. U.S. soldiers were sent to maintain order during the coup, thereby lending support to the Hawaiian planters' regime. Despite intense pressure from the planters and their U.S. allies, notably U.S. investors who accounted for nearly three quarters of the capital invested in Hawaiian sugar, newly-elected President Cleveland refused to resubmit a treaty calling for Hawaiian annexation, a treaty his predecessor, Benjamin Harrison, had sent to the U.S. Senate. In declining to seek annexation of Hawaii, Cleveland cited the "undue influence" U.S. soldiers had exerted during the coup.[46] Perhaps a more important factor, however, was the growing power of the Sugar Trust, comprised of sugar refiners, which now controlled 98 percent of the U.S. sugar trade and had given Cleveland's campaign the largest single gift in the history of American politics to that time.[47] At that moment, annexation of Hawaii would have enabled the planters to raise the price of sugar, strengthening their position vis-à-vis the Trust. By 1899, the Trust would seek annexation of Hawaii and the Philippines to bring raw sugar within new tariff walls that had raised the price of foreign sugar.[48] For now, however, the Trust's interests were aligned with those of the anti-imperialists, who prevailed at this critical juncture.

The second, more contentious moment in the conflict between anti-imperialists and expansionists came in February 1895, when insurrection against Spain broke out in Cuba. As in the Philippines, Spain's colonial policies had encouraged moderates and revolutionaries among the 800,000 white Cubans and 600,000 recently released slaves to ally. In fact, Spanish colonial authorities in Cuba had endured nine separate rebellions since 1823, and the endemic chaos worried American leaders, who watched Cuba closely throughout most of the nineteenth century. The United States had long coveted Cuba, primarily for its sugar plantations but also for its markets and harbors. American investors in Cuban sugar were also an important force both in Cuban and in American politics. As the war heated up, American exports to Cuba dropped from $20 million in 1894 to half that by 1898, while $50 million worth of American investments were similarly threatened.[49] Meanwhile in Cuba, Spain developed a harsh *reconcentrado* policy of rounding up Cubans into camps, which led to widespread human rights abuses as well as illness. As word of the reconcentrado policy and its abuses spread to the U.S., former abolitionists, liberals and anti-imperialists alike were enraged. Meanwhile, U.S. expansionists, notably Assistant Secretary of the Navy Theodore Roosevelt, Massachusetts Senator Henry Cabot Lodge and their allies in the religious, business, newspaper and other sectors, used this to persuade congress in April 1896 to support the Cuban revolutionaries. For the moment, anti-imperialists and expansionists joined forces, clamoring for intervention in Cuba.[50]

Under pressure from the United States as well as from opponents of the monarchy within Spain, Spain promised in 1897 to end the reconcentrado policy and announced plans for limited Cuban self-government. The remaining Spanish colonists in Cuba bitterly resented Spain's concessions, however, and, in January 1898, Spanish officers led a riot in Havana. U.S. interventionists now demanded that U.S. battleships be sent to support the Cuban revolutionaries. To avoid a debate on Capitol Hill, President McKinley agreed to send the battleship Maine to Havana to provide a U.S. military presence while Spain and the United States pursued diplomatic solutions. On January 25, 1898, the U.S. battleship *Maine* arrived in Havana Harbor. A tense period of negotiations among Spanish and U.S. officers followed; but on February 15, an explosion blew the Maine to pieces, instantly killing 254 men and an additional 8 who died shortly after. Though a subsequent U.S. inquiry into the source of the bombing cited a floating mine, not an overtly hostile act by Spain, the phrase "Remember the Maine! To Hell with Spain!" became the battle cry of U.S. interventionists. Among these was William Randolph Hearst, publisher of the *New York Journal*. Six months earlier, Hearst had sent Frederic Remington to Cuba to report on the hostilities there. When Remington had cabled back that there would be no war and had asked to return home, Hearst reportedly sent a reply now famous in the annals of U.S. journalism. "Please Remain," Hearst cabled, "You Furnish the Pictures and I'll Furnish the War."[51] Whatever he was able to accomplish in Cuba, Hearst was certainly fueling one war—a circulation war among New York newspapers. And war in Cuba was good for business. The unfolding story not only attracted new readers, who followed Cuban events and U.S. policy with passion, it also added new voices to the growing rift between expansionists and anti-imperialists.[52]

Under pressure from U.S. expansionists, McKinley sought congressional support for intervention while, in a nod to the anti-imperialists, simultaneously pressured Spain to halt the reconcentrado policy. The Spanish Crown, in severe financial and political straits at home, readily complied, but McKinley then added a new ultimatum, setting as a precondition for a settlement Spain's pledge to grant Cuba "full self-government, with reasonable indemnity." In early April 1898, McKinley formally requested congress to authorize "neutral" intervention in Cuba. The vote was to take place April 6. Meanwhile, Spain declared an armistice in Cuba but declined to grant Cubans independence. Some U.S. officials, particularly those in Madrid, saw openings for diplomacy, but congressional interventionists had gained too much momentum. The debate now shifted from the question of U.S. intervention to whether or not the Uinted States should recognize the Cuban revolutionary government. McKinley, and his allies in the Sugar Trust, congress and other key sectors, opposed this. But Senator Henry Teller of Colorado and others representing beet sugar farmers, populist opposition to colonialism, and various sources of anti-imperialism, grew suspicious of expansionist motives behind U.S. policy towards Cuba.[53]

On April 11, McKinley submitted his resolution to Capitol Hill, requesting neither support for the Cuban rebels nor for their cry for independence. Instead, he requested permission "to take measures to secure a full and final termination of the hostilities" in Cuba, as well as authorization to send U.S. ground and naval forces there if necessary. A heated debate and political struggle in congress followed. The outcome was a narrow victory for the anti-imperialists in the form of the Teller Amendment, which avoided the question of recognition of revolutionary forces in Cuba altogether but achieved nearly the same ends. In short, the amendment explicitly disclaimed American "intention to exercise sovereignty, jurisdiction or control over (Cuba) except for the pacification thereof, and assert(ed) its determination when that is accomplished to leave the government and control of the island to its people." With that stroke of the pen, U.S. expansionists were forced to look elsewhere for new territory. Looking to Asia, the expansionists would use the Spanish–American War, which formally broke out in Cuba on April 22, 1898, to wrest the Philippines from Spain, ushering in a new era of colonial struggle in the Philippines while marking as well the emergence of the United States as an international colonial power.[54]

The Less "Splendid" War

Earlier in 1898, and prior to the outbreak of hostilities with Spain, Theodore Roosevelt, then Assistant Secretary of the Navy, had developed a plan to simultaneously attack Spanish forces in Cuba and Manila in order to ensure U.S. success in Cuba. Militarily, the plan did not make much sense, given that Spanish ships in Manila could not have been deployed rapidly to Cuba and, in any case, were outmoded relics of Spain's earlier grandeur. Nevertheless, the plan was put into effect while Roosevelt's less expansionist boss, Secretary of the Navy John Long, was out sick one afternoon. Aware of the plan months before its execution, Aguinaldo, from his exile in Hong Kong, met with U.S. diplomats. Through unauthorized negotiations, the substance of which has been contested by Filipino and American historians, the U.S. diplomats secured promises of an alliance with revolutionary forces in what Filipinos believed was an exchange for U.S. support for Filipino independence. Though the U.S. diplomats later claimed not to have made such an offer, Aguinaldo wrote in his memoirs that Dewey himself had assured him that the United States was "rich in territory and money, and needed no colonies." Whatever the deal was, three weeks after "the splendid little war," as fighting escalated from Manila Harbor into a battle for control of the city and outlying areas, the United States requested and received support from Aguinaldo and his forces in the war with Spain. Its meager fleet in Manila destroyed, facing growing revolutionary pressures throughout the Philippines, embattled at home, in Cuba and now with the United States, Spain nevertheless still held Manila. To help put down Spanish forces, the United States summoned Aguinaldo and his troops, who quickly rallied in support of the Americans. Numbers of Filipinos now quit the Spanish army to join the insurgency.[55]

While U.S. forces awaited reinforcements from newly assembled volunteer troops, including a batch of 2,500 shipped out on May 25 from San Francisco,

Filipino troops encircled Manila, cutting off supplies to the Spanish. By now, nearly all of the native auxiliaries had defected from the Spanish army, and the revolutionaries had amassed thousands of rifles and rounds of ammunition from defeated Spanish outposts and Chinese smugglers.[56] On June 12, Aguinaldo declared Filipino independence from his home in Cavite, near Manila, and affirmed Philippine freedom "under the protection of the mighty and humane" United States. Though Aguinaldo had invited Dewey to attend the ceremony and had hoped for an official U.S. presence, only one retired American officer, who was in the Philippines on business, attended. Still, it was not until late June, when U.S. forces began to crowd in with his near Manila, that Aguinaldo began to grow suspicious of U.S. intentions. He became even more wary when an invitation to U.S. Independence Day celebrations addressed him as General, not President.

Aguinaldo boycotted the event but continued to seek reassurances from the United States. He also moved his headquarters from Cavite to Bacoor, ten miles farther out from Manila, to reduce the chance of friction between his and U.S. forces. In addition, he continued to provide U.S. forces with supplies, though he was able to secure no more than vague promises of U.S. support for his cause. In late July, fresh U.S. detachments arrived under the command of Generals Arthur MacArthur and Francis Greene, but in order to attack Manila they would have to first cross through the Filipino encirclement. Under strict orders from McKinley to preserve peace with the Filipinos, an unofficial delegation of Americans resorted to a ruse, promising Aguinaldo artillery and a measure of official recognition if his forces would withdraw from their trenches south of Manila. Aguinaldo complied and U.S. forces quickly moved in.[57] The Filipinos realized too late that they had been duped, as U.S. forces gained control of the fight against the Spanish in Manila.

Now entering their fourth month of siege, the Spaniards in Manila faced serious food and water shortages as well as disease, as 70,000 people crammed into the walled Spanish enclave within Manila known as the Intramuros, which previously had housed just 10,000.[58] Literally walled in, the Spanish officials sought an alternative to capitulation, in part because this would have led to court-martial at home and in part because they wanted to surrender to Americans not to Filipinos. After covert negotiations between American and Spanish forces, a plan was devised. On August 13, 1898, U.S. and Spanish troops staged a mock battle, allowing Spain to call a ceasefire with honor and open diplomatic talks with the United States. Caught by surprise, the Filipinos were then blocked by U.S. forces from entering Manila. Still, the peace between the Americans and the Filipinos held. Soon, U.S. forces, approximately 75 percent of whom were civilian volunteers with diverse educational and professional backgrounds, established in Manila a legal system for addressing criminal cases; penal reforms allowing for the release of 2,000 unsentenced prisoners; public works projects to build or repair bridges and restore water supply systems; and public health policies, including the creation of improved sanitation systems, a smallpox vaccination program which reached over 80,000 of Manila's inhabitants, and the monitoring of prostitutes for venereal disease. The Americans also reopened the schools and deleted courses on religious instruction, a reform the Philippine revolutionaries had long sought under Spanish rule. Finally, the American forces introduced tax reforms, revised customs and tariff regulations, and prohibited the entry of Chinese immigrants to the Philippines, all reforms the majority of the Filipinos appreciated.[59]

While some Filipinos cooperated with the American forces in the development of new health, education, tax and immigration policies, widespread resentment persisted, particularly when the Americans prohibited popular pastimes like gambling and cockfights and sought to enforce such new sanitation codes as the cleaning of sidewalks. The tensions were exacerbated by the U.S. military's penchant for centralized bureaucracy, wherein public works projects were assigned directly to the U.S. military rather than to an agent of the private sector of the economy.[60] Hostilities really heated up, however, when Filipinos were excluded from peace negotiations between the United States and Spain in Paris, which began in September of 1898. In open protest, on September 15, Aguinaldo convened a national assembly in the city of Malolos, a market town located about twenty miles from Manila. There, he reasserted Philippine independence and the legitimacy of his revolutionary government, as he waited to see what the United States would do. Even America waited, as U.S. officials vacillated among various options, with no apparent plan. Regional elections conducted by Aguinaldo's regime late in 1898 limited suffrage to a very small, affluent elite, who sought to reclaim the power and privilege conferred upon them by the Spanish. Meanwhile, Americans and Filipinos refrained from outright conflict, but tensions heated up further after December 10, when the United States acquired the right to purchase the Philippines from Spain for $20 million under the terms of the Paris Peace Treaty. The treaty also granted Cuban independence as well as U.S. control of Guam and Puerto Rico.[61]

The expansionists still would not garner control of U.S. foreign policy without a fight from the anti-imperialists, however. The U.S. Congress now entered a contentious debate on ratification of the treaty and related issues, as U.S. troops were ordered not to fire upon Aguinaldo's. No clear plan or consensus drove U.S. policy during this period and debates raged as to whether the United States should take Manila, all of the Philippines, or apply the Teller Amendment and simply withdraw. U.S. expansionists, led by Theodore Roosevelt, Senator Henry Cabot Lodge of Massachusetts, and segments of the religious and business communities, sought Philippine annexation, reviving arguments that the economic depressions of the late 1800s could be resolved through expansion of international trade in surplus goods and capital. They pointed to the Social Darwinists as well as Mahan's writings to support their views. They argued further that if the United States did not take the Philippines, another power such as Germany, Japan or Britain was sure to, with serious implications for America's prospective China trade, as well as the global balance of power should a scramble for control of Asia result from American hesitation. The expansionists made their case forcefully in popular newspapers, religious journals and in the congressional debates.[62]

The anti-imperialists were led by a coalition of labor unions, African-Americans, and beet sugar farmers, as well as former abolitionists and intellectuals. The latter group included former president Grover Cleveland, Massachusetts Senator George Frisbie Hoar, George Santayana, Andrew Carnegie, Mark Twain, William James, and Charles Eliot, all of whom participated in the Anti-Imperialist League, which had formed at Boston's Faneuil Hall on June 15, 1898, just days after Aguinaldo's declaration of independence in Cavite. Together, the anti-imperialists argued that conquest in the Philippines would reignite and internationalize the racism of the Civil War while damaging key sectors of the U.S. economy. Republican congressman Henry Johnson of Indiana, for instance, argued that annexation would bring the Philippines within American tariff walls, precluding the possibility of "a tariff against their sugar, tobacco, hemp and other products raised by cheap tropical labor." Like others taking this line of reasoning, Johnson predicted "immense injury to the American farmer and laborer."[63] Added to the threat of competition from "tropical labor," Johnson and others cited the cost of sustaining an overseas colony, and anticipated a heavy increase in taxation to support the attendant military requirements. Addressing even the trade issue, some in Congress questioned the logic of having to possess the islands in order to successfully spread American commerce there and in Asia. Like the expansionists, the anti-imperialists made their case in the popular press, appealing to increasingly politicized immigrant, labor, and other groups with a stake in restructuring American economic and political life.[64]

The anti-imperialists also actively lobbied senators to their cause, with Senator Hoar becoming one of the most articulate of the congressional anti-imperialists. In late January 1899, however, Hoar and a group of anti-imperialist senators caved in to pressure from business interests, later accused of vote-buying, as well as from the military and from President McKinley to authorize an early vote on the Paris Peace Treaty. The vote was now scheduled for February 6, 1899. Two days prior to the vote, however, any chance of peace was lost. On February 4, a minor incident led to a general war between Americans and Filipinos, to be described in chapter two. The war was to last until 1902, and would occasion a crucial debate within the United States not just on questions of strategy but on more fundamental questions of interests and the appropriate role of foreign policy to serve these interests. Some analysts have argued that the outbreak of war was not accidental and that it was scheduled to coincide with the treaty ratification vote in Congress. Whether this allegation is true or not, the war did increase pressure on Congress to ratify the treaty. Even with passions high, however, the vote of 57 in favor of ratification versus 27 opposing was extremely narrow, with only 1 vote more than was needed to carry the required two-thirds majority. Moreover, several last minute defections from opposition to ratification occurred when William Jennings Bryan, the Democratic presidential hopeful for the 1900 elections, decided prior to the vote to support ratification. Urging his followers to do the same, Bryan argued that this would allow for the formal conclusion of hostilities with Spain while clearing the way for his free silver and anti-trust campaigns.[65]

McKinley now claimed divine guidance as the source of his decision "to educate the Filipinos, and uplift and Christianize them...," somehow overlooking the fact that roughly 90 percent of Filipinos were already Catholic. And he lobbied hard for annexation. So, too, had Senator Lodge, Theodore Roosevelt and others. In all, eleven Democrats changed sides and only two Republicans, including Hoar, remained opposed to ratification. Lodge later noted that it had been "the hardest, closest fight I have ever known, and probably we shall never see another like it in our time."[66] The outcome of the debate, one of the most pivotal in the history of U.S. foreign policy, was the painful birth of the United States as an imperial power. It authorized not only acquisition of the Philippines, but also annexation of Hawaii, said to be needed to carry out the war with Filipinos, and new possessions in Puerto Rico, Guam and the Virgin Islands, all taken during the war against Spain. Moreover, for the first time in U.S. history, U.S. soldiers would fight overseas, totaling 70,000 at the peak of the Philippine–American War.[67] This would further raise the stakes of the debate on expansion while underscoring for the U.S. public and its volunteer army the attendant costs of such ventures, a lesson Americans would learn again decades later in Indochina.

In fact, Filipino opposition would prove broader and more potent than U.S. expansionists had anticipated.[68] The Americans, like the Spanish before them, would soon create a military alliance with the Macabebes to help suppress Filipino opposition.[69] Where the Americans would prove more proficient than Spain, however, was in the exploitation of divisions within the Philippine opposition between revolutionary and reformist elements. Working with the reformists to establish the foundations for Filipino participation in a post-war colonial administration, the United States would establish the beginnings of a transnational democratic alliance, helping in the process to undermine the political strength of revolutionary opposition. The next chapter will describe the evolution of revolutionary opposition as well as the transnational "bullets and ballots" tactics deployed during the early years of the U.S. colonial experiment in the Philippines.

Notes

1. The term *transnational* encompasses here private as well as official interactions that link segments of states and/or society in one nation, albeit an emerging nation in the Philippine case, with those in another. This approach builds on the work of Robert Keohane and Joseph Nye, Jr., *Transnational Relations and World Politics* (1970) who emphasized nongovernmental interactions as well as relations among governmental actors "not controlled by the central foreign policy organs of their governments." Building further on Cox's work in Robert Keohane's edited collection on neorealism *Neorealism and its Critics* (1986), the approach here does not separate state and society but rather emphasizes the complex interactions between the two. And these interactions are characterized by "a range of private transnational activity as well as transgovernmental networks of relationships among fragments of states." It is this notion of the state as fragmented, with each fragment forming coalitions with society and across national boundaries, that is the cornerstone of the analysis here.

2. See Donald Kirk, *Looted: The Philippines after the Bases* for a compelling account of the Philippines following the removal of U.S. military bases.

3. The historical methodology, tracing the political sources of regime transitions through time, is informed by the work of Fernand Braudel, *Capitalism and Material Life, 1400–1800* (1973), who understood the interdependencies created over centuries between countries linked by colonialism, and enduring long afterwards.

4. Stanley Karnow, *In Our Image: America's Empire in the Phillipines* (1989) 34-36. See also Francis Guillemard's biography of Magellan, *Life of Magellan* (1890).

5. See Emma Helen Blair, and James Alexander Robertson, *The Philippine Islands: 1493–1898* (1973), for a comprehensive collection of original documents covering the Spanish colonial era, including papal bulls, Pigafetta's eyewitness account, etc.

6. The term *Filipino* was used throughout the Spanish colonial period to describe Spanish colonists based in the Philippines. The modern usage describes natives of the Philippines, including those with Spanish, Malayan, Chinese, American, and other ancestry. For the sake of simplicity, this book applies the term Filipino in its modern usage for all periods, referring to Philippine-born Spaniards as "criollos."

7. Karnow, *In Our Image*, 43-47. See also Blair and Robertson.

8. Karnow, *In Our Image*, 43-47.

9. The very size and power of the two indigenous American empires actually contributed to their strikingly rapid demise. The empires may have been in crisis at the moment of conquest; but the Spanish invasions undid them, as the long-standing and large-scale

brutality of the top Incan and Aztec echelons left them with very little support from their subjects. Collaboration with the Spaniards was widespread.

10. Information for this paragraph is from Renato Constantino, *The Philippines: A Past Revisited* (1975), 42-55, and Karnow, *In Our Image*, 48-57.

11. Constantino, *A Past Revisited*, 42-55 and Karnow, *In Our Image*, 48-57. See also, Rene Ofreneo, *Capitalism in Philippine Agriculture* (1980), 3-13 for an explanation of the Spanish debates on the encomienda system.

12. From the Arawak tribe now living primarily along the coast of Guyana, the term *cacique* refers to native chiefs who served as local bosses carrying out Spanish colonial rule.

13. Information on the role of the Macabebes of Pampanga is from Constantino, *A Past Revisited*, 94-99.

14. Constantino, *A Past Revisited*, 85-112.

15. Information on the conflict between the church and the encomenderos is from Constantino, *A Past Revisited*, 12-25. See also John Leddy Phelan, *The Hispanization of the Philippines: Spanish Aims and Filipino Responses, 1565–1700* (1967), 31-40.

16. These drives were carried out through several modes of acquisition, including land grants from the Spanish Crown, the official owner of all lands in the colony; purchases of land from the colonial government; donations and inheritance from religious Filipinos; purchases from natives, typically at very low rates; foreclosure of lands mortgaged by natives to the friars; and outright landgrabbing. At the moment of U.S. conquest, friars owned 185,000 ha or about 1/15 of the total land under cultivation. Of this, about 110,000 were in prime land surrounding Manila. From Constantino *A Past Revisited*, 74.

17. Ofreneo, *Capitalism in Philippine Agriculture*, 3-13.

18. Constantino, *A Past Revisited*, 75.

19. Ibid. 58, 75.

20. D. K. Fieldhouse, *The Colonial Empires: A Comparative Survey from the Eighteenth Century* (1965), 142.

21. Information for this paragraph is culled from Fieldhouse, *The Colonial Empires: A Comparative Survey from the Eighteenth Century,* from George H. Nadel and Perry Curtis, *Imperialism and Colonialism* (1964)and from Harold Livermore, *A History of Spain* (1958), 183-206.

22. Karnow, *In Our Image*, 61-63.

23. Constantino, *A Past Revisited*, 85-112, and Fieldhouse, *Colonial Empires*.

24. The description of the Maniago Revolt is from Constantino, *A Past Revisited*, 94-99.

25. Information for this paragraph is culled from Constantino, *A Past Revisited*, 113-149 on the patterns of resistance to Spanish rule; Fieldhouse on Spain's colonial policies; Karnow, *In Our Image*, 57-77 for an overview of the period, notably the evolving Chinese role as well as Charles III's economic and church reforms; Ofreneo, *Capitalism*, 1-13 on the economic role of the Chinese and on Charles III's agricultural policies; and Michael Doyle, *Empires*, 117-118 on the evolution of Spain's imperial economic policies.

26. Ofreneo, *Capitalism in Philippine Agriculture*, 10.

27. Ibid. See also Constantino, *A Past Revisited*, 55-65, 113-132, in particular.

28. See Raymond Carr, *Spain: 1800–1975* (1982) for a thorough description of the Spanish politics during the French occupation and the implications for the colonies. See Karnow, *In Our Image*, 57-77, for a concise account of the implications for the Philippines in particular.

29. See H. Butler Clarke, *Modern Spain: 1815–1898* (1969) for a detailed description of Spanish politics from 1815–1898. See also Carr, *Spain: 1800-1975*, 72-154.

30. See John N. Schumacher, *Readings in Philippine Church History* (1979), and *Revolutionary Clergy: The Filipino Clergy and the Nationalist Movement, 1850–1903* (1981), for detailed descriptions of Spanish policy toward the Filipino clergy and the Filipino reaction.

31. Carr, *Spain: 1808–1975*, 257-306; and Clarke, *Modern Spain: 1815–1898,* 251-335.

32. Karnow, *In Our Image*, 66.

33. Constantino, *A Past Revisited*, 145-154.

34. Jose Rizal's novel, *Nole Me Tangere*, a biting satire of the friars and other Spanish colonists, can be found in translation. Information for this paragraph was culled from Constantino, *A Past Revisited*, 150-172; Karnow, *In Our Image*, 66-72; and Schumacher, *Revolutionary Clergy*, on the role of the revolutionary clergy from 1850 through the uprising against first Spain and later the United States.

35. Information for this paragraph was culled from Constantino, *A Past Revisited*, 150-172 and Karnow, *In Our Image*, 67-77.

36. Constantino, *A Past Revisited*, 150-203.

37. Ibid.

38. Karnow, *In Our Image*, 78-80, and Jerald Combs, *The History of American Foreign Policy* (1986), 155-56.

39. The above information is culled from Combs, *The History of American Foreign Policy,* 1-100.

40. Combs, *The History of American Foreign Policy,* 101-129.

41. Ibid., 131.

42. Daniel Quinn Mills, *Labor-Management Relations* (1986), 29-35 provides a concise description of rising labor activism from 1794 through the particularly volatile period through the end of the nineteenth century.

43. Daniel B. Schirmer, *Repulic or Empire: American Resistance to the Philippine War* (1972), provides an excellent, detailed account of the anti-imperialist movement and its role in the U.S. campaign to take the Philippines.

44. The data is compiled from Combs, *The History of American Foreign Policy,* 132; Mills, *Labor-Management*, 34-35; and Walter LaFeber, *The New Empire: An Interpretation of American Expansion, 1860–1898* (1963), 197-203.

45. LaFeber provides a detailed account of the economic, social, moral, political and other forces contributing to the rise of imperialism. He argues that U.S. foreign policy from about 1893 through the Spanish–American War was driven by a belief in the need for expanding foreign markets as a cure for domestic depression caused by surplus production.

46. Combs, *History of American Foreign Policy*, 120-23.

47. The amount of the gift has been estimated at between $250,000 and $500,000. From Luzviminda Francisco and Jonathan Fast, *Conspiracy for Empire: Big Business, Corruption and the Politics of Imperialism in America, 1876–1907* (1985), 67.

48. For a detailed account of the role of the Sugar Trust in U.S. foreign policy debates during the late 1800s, see Francisco and Fast, *Conspiracy for Empire.*

49. Combs, *History of American Foreign Policy*, 141-44.

50. The above is from Karnow, *In Our Image*, 88-105 and Schirmer, *Republic or Empire.*

51. Ibid.

52. Michael Schudson, *Discovering the News: A Social History of American Newspapers* (1978), 88-120.

53. Information on the debates leading to the Teller Amendment is culled from Francisco and Fast, *Conspiracy for Empire*; Combs, *History of American Foreign Policy*, 148-49; and Schirmer, *Republic or Empire.*

54. Francisco and Fast, *Conspiracy for Empire*; Combs, *History of American Foreign Policy*, and Schirmer, *Republic or Empire.*

55. This paragraph is culled from Karnow, *In Our Image*, 100-138.

56. Karnow, *In Our Image,* 115.

57. See John Morgan Gates, *Schoolbooks and Kregs: The United States Army in the Philippines, 1898–1902* (1973), 3-42, for a detailed description of U.S. relations with the Filipino revolutionaries during the siege of Manila following Dewey's success in Manila Harbor on May 1, 1898.

58. Gates, *Schoolbooks and Kregs,* 55.

59. All statistics and information on the role of the U.S. forces in Manila during the period of occupation after August 1898 are from Gates, *Schoolbooks and Krags,* 3-42.

60. Ibid.

61. Karnow, *In Our Image*, 106-138; H. W. Brands, *Bound to Empire: The United States and the Philippines* (1992), 20-35; and Constantino, *A Past Revisited*, 237-41.

62. This paragraph is culled from Schirmer, *Republic or Empire*, and from Brands, *Bound to Empire*, 20-35.

63. The quotes from Johnson are from Brands, *Bound to Empire,* 29.

64. This paragraph is culled from Schirmer, *Republic or Empire*, and from Brands, *Bound to Empire*, 20-35.

65. Schirmer, *Republic or Empire*, and from Brands, *Bound to Empire.*

66. Schirmer, *Republic or Empire*, and from Brands, *Bound to Empire.*

67. Karnow, *In Our Image*, 185.

68. For a description of the evolution of the Filipino resistance, see Gates, *Schoolbooks and Kregs,* 156-178; Brands, *Bound to Empire*, 39-59; and Karnow, *In Our Image*, 139-195.

69. Brands, *Bound to Empire*, 56-59.

Chapter 2

Conquest and Coercion:
Early U.S. Colonialism, 1899–1916

This chapter provides an historical overview of the early U.S. colonial legacy in the Philippines from the outbreak of war between U.S. forces and Filipino nationalists on February 4, 1899, through the Jones Act of 1916, in which the United States pledged eventual independence for the Philippines. The chapter first describes the transnational "bullets and ballots" strategies the United States used to assert colonial control of the Philippines, and then examines the reasons behind the 1916 decision to begin relinquishing this. Although the key explanation for the Jones Act lies in the United States, the locus of decision-making on Philippine governance throughout the colonial period, Filipinos used transnational strategies to press their nationalist cause, lobbying effectively in the United States for eventual independence.

Specifically, American imperialism was hotly contested along partisan lines in the United States throughout the period, with Republicans generally supporting it and Democrats generally opposing it.[1] For most of the period from 1899 to 1916, Republicans controlled the presidency and used the authority conferred on the office by congress to appoint Republican governors to manage the

31

Philippines and to establish political, economic, military and social institutions in the service of U.S. interests there. When Democrats won the White House under Woodrow Wilson in 1912, however, Filipino nationalists and their allies in the U.S. Congress capitalized on the opportunity for change, pushing through the Jones Act in 1916. They also helped appoint a Democratic governor who would loosen U.S. control of the colonial government in the Philippines and pave the way for eventual self-rule.

Conquest by Krag:
The Transition to U.S. Colonial Rule

Prior to the U.S. Congressional vote on ratification of the Paris Peace Treaty, which accorded the United States the right to purchase the Philippines from Spain for $20 million, tensions had mounted between Filipino and U.S. forces surrounding Manila. Tensions reached a pitch in January 1899, when Major General Elwell Otis, head of the U.S. operations, moved the Nebraska regiment to an area inside territory claimed by the Filipinos. Though McKinley had directed the troops to preserve the peace, Otis authorized his troops to use force if necessary for self-defense. On the evening of February 4, 1899, while on a routine patrol, Private William Grayson of Beatrice, Nebraska stumbled upon four drunk, unarmed Filipinos. When he ordered them to halt, the Filipinos mocked him. Grayson repeated the order and again the response was mocking. Grayson fired and one man was felled. Grayson's partner, Orville Miller, shot another while Grayson reloaded and shot a third Filipino. Miller and Grayson then rushed back to camp to inform the other Nebraskans. Within minutes, war exploded along the ten-mile front separating United States and Filipino forces near Manila. "The ball has begun," yelled one Major Wilder Metcalf of Kansas.[2] Two days later, the U.S. Congress narrowly voted to ratify the Paris Treaty, as a war to subdue Filipino nationalists raged. The United States would confidently term the struggle the "Philippine Insurrection," dismissing the insurgents as *ladrones* or bandits. Ultimately, however, the war would serve as a cautionary tale to American expansionists regarding the frailty of a European treaty in the face of nationalist opposition abroad as well as anti-imperialist opposition at home.

Immediately following the Grayson incident, U.S. regiments of volunteers from Kansas, Idaho, California, Montana and Pennsylvania captured bridges, Filipino arsenals and other key strategic sites. In the process, they leveled nipa huts and churches, and slaughtered roughly 3,000 Filipinos in the first day of fighting, while U.S. troops suffered only minor losses, including 59 dead and 300 wounded. U.S military officials issued forecasts that the war could be won quickly, with little loss of American lives. Meanwhile, Aguinaldo, stunned, sent two representatives to offer a truce, the creation of a buffer zone and peace talks. Otis rebuffed these offers and turned instead to the business of war. Although President McKinley had not clearly stated whether the aim of U.S. forces was to control Manila or the entire archipelago, Otis expanded the conquest, ordering troops to seize the port in Iloilo and the nearby Visayan Islands of Cebu and Negros. An alliance was also formed between the U.S. forces and Macabebe soldiers, the long-time military aides to Spain, who acted as scouts and helped carry out the military policies of the war. Still, American military strength totaled just 24,000 men, about a third of the number mobilized by Aguinaldo.[3] To manage military strategy, administration of U.S. policy towards the Philippines now shifted from the State Department to the Department of War, as McKinley issued his "benevolent assimilation" proclamation:

> It should be the earnest wish and paramount aim of the military administra-
> tion to win the confidence, respect, and affection of the inhabitants of the
> Philippines by assuring them in every possible way that full measure of indi-
> vidual rights and liberties which is the heritage of free peoples, and by prov-
> ing to them that the mission of the United States is one of benevolent assimi-
> lation, substituting the mild sway of justice for arbitrary rule.[4]

Unfortunately, such benevolence did not extend to the battlefield. U.S. forces inflicted terrible casualties on Aguinaldo's troops, easily overcoming entrenchments that were "beautifully made and wretchedly defended,"[5] as Aguinaldo's choice of conventional rather than guerrilla tactics proved increasingly untenable. Despite heavy losses, however, Aguinaldo continued to control the main island of Luzon and maintained a favorable ratio of about two Filipino soldiers to every one American, as the U.S. forces soon learned that they could win battles but could not hold territory. The first major offensive of the war, launched by Brigadier General Lloyd Wheaton in March, was carried out with efficiency and exacted a heavy toll on the revolutionaries; but it also revealed the breadth and effectiveness of the opposition. Afterwards, Otis was forced to concede that he did not have enough troops to wage war in the interior, nor to occupy territories captured there, and still defend Manila.[6] By the end of March, U.S. troops under the command of Brigadier General Arthur MacArthur captured Malolos, seat of Aguinaldo's government, only to have Aguinaldo relocate the capital to San Fernando in Pampanga province. As one American journalist wrote, Aguinaldo simply "took up the goal-posts and carried them back," whenever U.S. forces advanced.[7] In spite of early U.S. military forecasts of a quick and easy victory, Otis now struggled to proclaim success while simultaneously, and somewhat paradoxically, requesting additional troops. Concerned that he would be replaced should officials back home learn the truth, Otis increasingly exercised the right of press censorship that the War Department had conferred upon him.[8]

Though coverage of the U.S. campaign in the Philippines was initially favorable since the early reporters[9] relied almost exclusively on U.S. military sources, it became more and more negative after the rainy season descended in the Spring, bringing with it a host of tropical diseases. The correspondents now began to hear of illness as well as atrocities of the war from the men at the front; yet the military continued to announce victories known to be fictitious, while issuing false reports on the number of U.S. casualties. Disillusioned, the journalists sought alternative sources of information, particularly from soldiers returning from the "boondocks," from the Tagalog *bundok* or mountains. By early summer, the correspondents complained of "wholly ridiculous estimates" of enemy killed and other misrepresentations of the war, while Otis criticized the press for trying to influence opinion back home and for playing into the hands of the enemy. Otis now ordered censorship of dispatches sent via the trans-Pacific cable that was controlled by the U.S. military and was at the time the only direct line of communication to the United States. With the censors allowing less and less to pass through, the correspondents, led by Robert Collins of Associated Press, drafted a statement in July protesting that Otis was feeding the American public "an ultra-optimistic view that is not shared by the general officers in the field." Though Otis threatened court-martial for "conspiracy against the government," the statement was transmitted to American journals via Hong Kong, and even pro-imperialist papers printed it.[10] McKinley publicly backed Otis but instructed Secretary of War Elihu Root to urge Otis to adopt more liberal press policies. Instead, Otis continued to withhold cable privileges to any reporter who implied, as most American soldiers now believed, that the U.S. forces in the Philippines were inadequate.

Meanwhile, back home, the Anti-Imperialist League had been narrowly defeated in its attempts to prevent ratification of the Paris Treaty. As described in chapter one, they had lobbied hard in congress, and claimed among their ranks such notables as former president Grover Cleveland, Senator George Hoar, Mark Twain, George Santayana, Andrew Carnegie and William James. Defeated but not deterred, they now launched an active anti-war campaign. Given that no military draft was then in effect, the army relied on good relations with the American public for its new recruits. Focusing on the Northwest and the South, where most of the 12,000 new volunteer soldiers had been recruited, the League published anti-war advertisements in local newspapers, held meetings and helped stir up discussion about the war. Meanwhile, letters home from soldiers at the front spoke of the brutality of the U.S. troops as well as the much higher levels of U.S. casualties than the government had been reporting, all undermining the credibility of and support for the U.S. operations in the Philippines. When U.S. officials tried to intercept mail, further outcries about freedom of speech were heard, as attention to the subject mounted in the press. By the Spring of 1899, when many of the volunteers were becoming eligible for discharge, the cry to bring home the troops had mushroomed in the Northwest and South, while disaffection spread as well among the troops. Only about 7 percent were expected to reenlist.[11]

As U.S. troops became more and more mired in the war abroad, opposition at home continued to grow. The Anti-Imperialist League now had about 40,000 members nationwide, and opposition spread even among former imperialists. Senator Frye of Maine, for example, publicly said he felt "deceived" by the military's initial claims of easy victory, while General Frederick Funston began to sense from the battlefield no benefit of the war save for "big syndicates and capitalists." Meanwhile, many African-Americans and their supporters linked war atrocities with the growing problem of lynchings and other racial violence in the United States, as former abolitionists linked suppression of Filipino national-ism to the issues for which the Civil War had been fought just a few decades earlier. By October 1899, the League was a national organization with an eye toward the upcoming 1900 elections. Democratic candidate William Jennings Bryan had earlier tried to focus primarily on the free silver issue, but now made opposition to the war in the Philippines a centerpiece of his presidential cam-paign, rallying labor, African-Americans, and others to the anti-imperialist cause.[12]

October 1899 also brought the fiercest battles of the war, as Otis launched an all-out effort to destroy Aguinaldo's army. On the main island of Luzon, Otis ordered one division to head south from Manila while another, led by General Arthur MacArthur, headed north. American soldiers then took Aguinaldo's newest capital on October 12, forcing the rebels to move once more. Days later, the United States captured that capital, only to have Aguinaldo merely skip away yet again. Though the United States prevailed in most battles, Otis conceded: "Little difficulty attends the act of taking possession of and temporarily holding any section of the country...but (the U.S. troops) would...again prey upon the inhabitants, persecuting without mercy those who had manifested any friendly feelings towards the American troops."[13] Thus, American conduct fueled oppo-sition both at home and in the Philippines, a problem that grew when the war took a new turn.

In November 1899, forced to concede that a conventional approach could only fail, Aguinaldo ordered his troops to scatter and adopt guerrilla tactics. In part, Aguinaldo was playing for time, hoping, like his U.S. anti-imperialist counterparts, that the 1900 U.S. presidential elections might usher in a new, Democratic administration open to peace and, perhaps, to an independent

Philippines. Otherwise, he hoped to simply wear down the Americans through a war of attrition. Leading one of the larger groups, a contingent of 1,200, Aguinaldo fled into the mountains. Waging a guerrilla war had the advantage of keeping the Americans on the run, as Filipino forces easily blended in with the populace, making it difficult for the U.S. forces to distinguish friend from foe, but it had disadvantages as well. The military reversals of the past months had reduced the numbers as well as the appeal of Aguinaldo's campaign; yet now more than ever Aguinaldo's troops were dependent upon the masses of Filipinos for protection and support. At first, Aguinaldo revived the Katipunan as an agency to enforce revolutionary codes and punish collaborators. Soon, however, the Katipunan dispensed with trials for suspected collaborators, declaring it the policy of the revolution to simply "exterminate all traitors."[14] Meanwhile, U.S. forces used increasingly gruesome methods such as the "water cure" to force information from potential informants, who eventually included almost everyone in the countryside. Now Filipinos risked punishment from the Americans for keeping quiet and assassination by the revolutionaries for talking. Given that choice, most apparently found greater safety as well as prospective gains in the revolutionary cause, which remained strong, as ever more U.S. troops were needed to combat it.[15]

At top levels, however, dissent among the revolution's leaders threatened the movement, as it had in the final phases of the uprising against Spain. Now, as then, the ilustrados and other Filipino elites grew concerned that their own social, political and economic interests might be threatened by the spreading rebellion in the countryside. Though Aguinaldo consistently favored the elites in the countryside, allowing them to keep estates confiscated from the Spanish while granting them exclusive political rights,[16] top ilustrados began defecting from the revolutionary movement, particularly after Aguinaldo switched from conventional to guerrilla warfare.[17]

The Schurman Commission and the Emergence of Soft-Line Strategies

American soft-liners did their best to widen the rift by working on the political, as well as the military, front. As early as January 1899, following advice from Dewey, McKinley had established an official civilian Philippine Commission to study the situation and possibly avert warfare. McKinley had appointed avowed anti-imperialist Jacob Gould Schurman, President of Cornell University, to head the commission, with conservative Democrat Charles Denby, and ornithologist Dean Worcester as members. The commission soon after traveled to Manila under

McKinley's directive to "facilitate the most humane, pacific, and effective extension of authority throughout these islands, and to secure, with the least possible delay, the benefits of a wise and generous protection of life and property to the inhabitants."[18] Arriving in March, one month after the outbreak of hostilities, the Philippine Commission was too late for diplomacy, and Otis argued that the onset of fighting annulled the commission's authority. Though nominally a member, Otis first tried to effect the commission's recall. When this failed, he boycotted the meetings, in protest of the commission's plans to eliminate the military government he had helped establish in the Philippines. And so began the split between hard-line and soft-line U.S. officials.[19]

Despite such resistance from the U.S. military authorities, the commissioners met daily with prominent Filipinos and foreigners at the *Real Audiencia* in Manila. There they discussed Filipino aspirations in order to carve out an appropriate form of government for the islands. By institutionalizing such consultations, the commission hoped to demonstrate for their Philippine and American audiences U.S. good will toward the Filipinos while allowing them a voice in their prospective governance. In fact, though, the commission never once ventured beyond Manila, and most of the sixty witnesses they heard from were American, British and other Western residents of Manila.[20] The few Filipinos they did interview were ilustrados and defectors who had abandoned the independence movement as too radical. On April 4, after just one month of research, the commission published its initial findings, offering the revolutionaries a modicum of political autonomy under U.S. colonial rule, as well as public works projects, a revitalized judicial system, universal education, economic development programs, and other reforms. At the same time, the commission threatened that American "supremacy" would be "enforced" throughout the Philippines, and that those who resisted would "accomplish no end other than their own ruin."[21] The revolutionary leadership publicly rejected the commission's offer, but quietly approached the Schurman commission to offer a ceasefire. Though Schurman urged U.S. officials to explore the peace bid, Otis, as he had at the war's outbreak, rebuffed the Filipino offer. Denby and Worcester, and subsequently McKinley, concurred. Hard-line not soft-line strategies now prevailed.[22]

Otis did realize that force alone could not subdue the revolutionaries, however, and he continued the kinds of sanitation, education, and public works projects as well as food distribution programs and judicial reforms first launched a year earlier during the occupation of Manila, as described in chapter one. He also began organizing town councils comprised of the Filipino elites Aguinaldo had helped promote in the 1898 elections. This was done through limited suffrage, with U.S. officers in charge.[23] At the same time, the Philippine Commission continued its work through the long rainy season, the worsening conditions of war, and the increasingly negative dispatches from the correspondents, which fed, in turn, debate back home. Though Schurman continued to press for diplomacy, Denby and Worcester argued for an intensification of the military campaign. Concurring with the hard-liners, McKinley ordered additional troops. By the summer of 1899, the U.S. troops numbered 60,000, straining levels set by Congress. Before leaving in September 1899, the commission issued a comprehensive report, recommending a degree of self-government under U.S. supervision. Under the plan, provinces and municipalities would be run by elected local officials with American guidance, and a national legislature would govern the islands, with a civilian U.S. governor exercising veto power over its decisions.[24] Upon returning to the United States, the commissioners continued to advise U.S. legislative and executive officials on policy towards the Philippines, urging soft-line not hard-line solutions. On January 31, 1900, the commission reported to McKinley:

> The general substitution throughout the archipelago of civil for military government (though, of course, the retention of a strong military arm) would do more than any other single occurrence to reconcile the Filipinos to American sovereignty, which would then stand revealed, not merely as an irresistible power, but as an instrument for the preservation and development of the rights and liberties of the Filipinos and the promotion of their happiness and prosperity.[25]

The Taft Commission:
U.S. Colonial Policy Takes Form

Until now, McKinley had ruled the Philippines by executive fiat, acting in his capacity as commander-in-chief of the armed forces to pass laws and regulations for the islands. With the end of hostilities nearing, however, the U.S. Congress pressured McKinley to establish a permanent government in the Philippines while providing for a congressional role in overseeing it. McKinley consulted the Schurman study for guidance, and he enlisted Republican Senator John Spooner of Wisconsin to help expand the presidential war powers in order to allow for the implementation of colonial policies and institutions. Although Spooner had not ranked among the party's ardent imperialists, he defended America's right to annex overseas territories based on such precedents as U.S. control of the Louisiana territories. After studying the statutes that had enabled Jefferson to annex and then govern the Louisiana territories, Spooner approached Congress with a bill that would have given a second Philippine commission, appointed by the president, a virtually free hand to govern the colony.

While Congress debated the bill,[26] a second Philippine commission to develop a Filipino government was established, with William Howard Taft, a federal circuit judge from Ohio and, like Schurman, an avowed anti-imperialist, designated its leader. The Taft Commission arrived in Manila in June 1900, just a month after the increasingly despised General Otis resigned, giving over his post to MacArthur. As with the earlier conflict between Otis and the Schurman Commission, MacArthur argued that the civilians had no place in a war. He had seen too many Filipinos die for their cause to believe they would easily lay down their arms for vague promises of autonomy from the likes of Taft. He also knew that his powers would be diminished with the presence of civilian authority. Thus we see the ripening of the conflict among U.S. hard-liners and soft-liners, as much for ideological reasons as for individual and institutional interests. Given the continuing uncertainty regarding U.S. leadership in the Philippines, MacArthur treated the Taft Commission with a measure of disdain. In fact, the U.S. reception upon the Taft Commission's arrival in Manila was so cold that Taft later remarked that it "banished his perspiration," sparking an enmity Taft would later use as president to block MacArthur's advancement. To further rile Taft, MacArthur maintained his residence in the well-appointed Malacanang palace, relegating Taft to Manila's suburbs.[27]

Despite the hostility from MacArthur, Taft's team spent the summer collecting information. Luke Wright, an attorney, focused on the militia, the police and criminal codes; Dean Worcester, a hold-over from the Schurman Commission, studied agriculture, mining, and health; Henry Ide, a former Samoa judge, reviewed the courts, banking and currency; Bernard Moses, an historian, examined education; leaving Taft the toughest questions centering on the civil service, the disposition of public lands, and the status of the remaining Spanish friars. Like the Schurman Commission, however, they conferred with the same affluent Filipinos who continued to press for limited suffrage and the retention of social, economic, and political structures that protected their interests, while the gross inequities inherited from centuries of Spanish rule, and the source of on-going rebellion in the countryside,[28] were overlooked. By late August, the Taft Commission cabled its findings to Secretary of War Root. Contrary to the aims of MacArthur and his military colleagues, the commission recommended the establishment under civilian direction of a local constabulary, a new tax system, public works, judicial reforms, and universal education in English. The Taft report also urged passage of the Spooner Bill in order to institutionalize a colonial government empowered to pass laws, distribute public lands, grant mining claims, and pass other measures for luring U.S. investment.[29]

The Spooner Bill was rejected on September 1, 1900; but McKinley nevertheless granted the Taft Commission the responsibilities of a legislative body, with the authority to raise taxes, appropriate funds, fix tariffs and set up law courts.[30] Taft and his colleagues could now enact laws and, by December, fifty-five acts had been passed, allotting over $3 million for public works, establishing a civil service system, courts, and a civil government.[31] Moreover, Taft now controlled $2.5 million in funds collected by the U.S. Army from customs duties and other sources. This gave Taft considerable power vis-à-vis MacArthur, who continued to chafe at the civilian challenge to his authority, particularly since no formal delineation of colonial powers beyond executive fiat had as yet been established by congress.[32] At the same time, elections in the United States brought McKinley to power again, despite the hard campaigning of Bryan, the Anti-Imperialist League and others who sought a change in administration and in U.S. foreign policy. Bryan had argued that the rise of militarism threatened those at home who challenged industry, as evidenced by the recent rise in police actions against strikers. Bryan had also argued that the funds diverted to fight the war abroad were needed to fight poverty at home. In an early transnational strategy, representatives of Aguinaldo had approached the Democrats in October of 1900, offering to announce that they would lay down their arms should Bryan be elected president. Fearing charges of treason, the Democrats rejected the offer; but already Filipinos were learning to work through U.S. political channels in order to influence policy towards their country.[33] McKinley won by a narrow margin, with much of the opposition centering on his Philippine policy. Nevertheless, McKinley accepted victory as a sign of approval for his foreign policy and, one day after the elections, vowed to continue the war.[34]

While MacArthur waged war on the military front, Taft reasoned that a credible moderate opposition would eviscerate Aguinaldo's movement. As part of his "policy of attraction," designed to entice Filipinos into accepting U.S. rule, Taft cultivated a core group of elite Filipinos who were open to some form of power-sharing under U.S. colonial rule. Reluctant to ally with any U.S. administration until after the elections, however, the Filipinos working with Taft waited until December to formally organize.[35] On December 23, 1900, with Taft's guidance, a group of ilustrados formed the Federalista Party, which they formally launched on February 22, 1901, in commemoration of George Washington's birthday. Comparing themselves with America's founding fathers, the Federalistas sought to become a state of the United States, as Rizal and earlier ilustrados had under Spain. The Federalista platform envisioned a preliminary period for the establishment of peace and the recognition of U.S. sovereignty. Throughout this period, municipal, provincial and national governments would be initiated, while local self-government, separation of church and state, freedom of worship, public education for all children, and guarantees of individual rights and liberties would be institutionalized. A constitutional period was to follow, during which institutions for Philippine representation in the United States as well as U.S. rule in the Philippines would be established. Taft distributed money to one ilustrado, Pardo de Tavera, to help revive his failing newspaper *La Democracia*, which had been launched in May 1899 to encourage Filipinos to lay down their arms.[36] Taft also granted the Federalistas a virtual monopoly on all government jobs reserved for Filipinos. With such tangible rewards to offer, the party rapidly recruited more than 200,000 supporters.[37]

While Aguinaldo had tried to balance moderate and revolutionary, elite and peasant factions of his movement; Taft and his allies understood, or at least capitalized on, what Spain had not. That is, the economic and social differences among the Filipinos created schisms, which, if exploited, could seriously weaken the revolutionary movement. By working with the ilustrados, Taft had driven a wedge in Aguinaldo's organization, isolating the moderates from the revolutionaries. And Aguinaldo now faced a growing political challenge, as many from his ranks defected.[38]

Meanwhile, the United States continued to fight hard on the military front, as well. At the end of 1900, U.S. troop levels reached 70,000, about three quarters of the entire U.S. Army.[39] By late 1900, several of Aguinaldo's best officers had either surrendered or had been captured and now swore allegiance to the United States.[40] A key goal for U.S forces was now the capture of Aguinaldo. In February 1901, the opportunity came. That month, a Filipino courier, with a coded letter from Aguinaldo requesting additional troops and describing his location, was captured. Using the information, General Funston, with MacArthur's approval, devised a plan involving eighty Macabebe soldiers. On March 24, the Macabebes posed as partisans and, together with a group of Americans posing as their prisoners, entered Aguinaldo's secret encampment. Once inside, the Macabebes and Americans easily defeated Aguinaldo's inner network of supporters. They then captured Aguinaldo and brought him to MacArthur's headquarters at the Malacanang palace. There Aguinaldo swore allegiance to the United States and urged his followers to do the same, though he would wear a black bow tie forever after until his death in 1964 as an expression of mourning for his lost republic. The resistance, though seriously weakened, nevertheless continued.[41]

The Development of U.S. Military and Democratic Institutions

In March 1901, a revised version of the Spooner Bill, now an amendment to a military appropriations bill, passed, empowering the President of the United States to continue to administer the Philippines until such time as Congress enacted legislation establishing a permanent colonial government there.[42] A few months later, on July 4, 1901, Taft, who had actively lobbied from the Philippines and in the United States for such an amendment, became governor of the Philippines, while MacArthur was replaced by Major General Adna R. Chaffee. The new division of authority granted Taft control of civil government in areas that had been pacified and Chaffee control of military government where the war still raged. Two weeks later, on July 18, the United States established the Insular Police Force to create a native organization capable of suppressing revolutionary opposition, as the existing transnational authoritarian alliance with the Macabebes became institutionalized.[43] Under the command of Captain Henry Allen, the force numbered 180 Americans reinforced by carefully recruited Filipinos, notably Macabebes.[44] The Spooner Amendment was not to apply long to McKinley, however. In September, he was shot by presumed anarchist Leon F. Czolgosz. Mckinley died eight days later, on September 14, and Theodore Roosevelt, the man who had engineered the conquest of the Philippines, ascended to the presidency.

More severe hard-line policies were now introduced. On November 4, for example, Taft passed the Sedition Law, which imposed either the death sentence or a long prison term on anyone advocating independence, even by peaceful means, while allowing for severe fines and punishment for anyone uttering "seditious words or speech" against the U.S. government. All parties except the Federalistas were also banned.[45] Even worse, on December 25, General Franklin Bell directed his commanders to set up reconcentration zones to closely monitor the comings and goings of the roughly 300,000 inhabitants of the Batangas region. All property outside the zones was confiscated, and the people were herded into the camps. It was a desperate attempt to isolate the insurgents from the general populace, but, with the hostile and unsanitary conditions that quickly resulted in the zones, the policy instead further fueled revolutionary opposition to the United States. It also fueled opposition back home since the main impetus behind the war with Spain had allegedly been to undo Spain's harsh reconcentration policy in Cuba.[46]

The war was to drag on through the early months of 1902, with U.S. tactics becoming increasingly brutal. These tactics were effective in the Philippines, seriously weakening the revolutionary opposition there; but, as word spread to the U.S. public, via newspaper correspondents and letters home from soldiers at the front, domestic U.S. opposition exploded into a political and social crisis much like that experienced generations later over U.S. policy in Indochina.[47] One massacre on the island of Samar in late 1901 had gained particular notoriety. While the U.S. press ranked it with the Alamo and Custer's last stand as one of the worst tragedies in American military history, congressional hearings were initiated in January 1902 under the direction of Senator Hoar. Confirming the worst fears of the anti-imperialists, Major Littleton Waller Tazewell Waller revealed orders he had been given by Brigadier General Jacob Smith to kill everyone over the age of ten and to make the island of Samar a "howling wilderness."[48] Smith was the only U.S. soldier to be disciplined for conduct in the Philippine war and, at that, was merely "admonished," yet the outrage expressed in the United States chastened U.S. imperialists. Resistance in the Philippines continued sporadically over the next months, and indeed would continue for the next decade before dying out then reemerging in various forms by the 1920s. Nevertheless, the war was brought to a formal conclusion on July 4, 1902, though 50,000[49] U.S. soldiers remained to suppress the ongoing, albeit diffused resistance.

In all, 126,000 Americans took part in the war,[50] with a toll of 4,234 dead, 2,818 wounded, thousands succumbing to disease once home, and some $600 million spent on the war effort.[51] For Filipinos, the toll was much greater, with the number of deaths estimated at between 200,000 and 600,000, 90 percent of all carabaos—a critical farm animal—dead, the rice harvest down to one-fourth normal levels, and vast areas of the countryside in ruin.[52] Despite the desperately fought bid for independence, the Filipinos were forced to cede control of their country to a new colonial power. Still, America's first experience with international warfare in the service of overseas colonization was sobering. Not only had U.S. expansionists had to contend with a far more potent Filipino opposition than they had anticipated; they had also been constrained by a domestic U.S. opposition that threatened political careers as well as the ability to mobilize a sizable army without the benefit of conscription. In the end, hard-line strategies, including the transnational alliance with Macabebes and eventually an Insular Police Force as well as the continued presence of U.S. troops in the Philippines, prevailed in efforts to conquer territories. But soft-line or reformist strategies, including the transnational alliance with ilustrados and eventually the Federalista Party, prevailed once territory had been won and needed to be controlled. At the formal conclusion of the war, U.S. moderates took control of Philippine politics, though the on-going challenge from persistent revolutionary opposition in the countryside required as well a strong military designed more for domestic than for international conflict.

From Bullets to Ballots: 1902–1916

While hard-line strategies, and the early transnational alliance with the Macabebes, were responsible for the transition to U.S. colonial rule of the Philippines, more moderate strategies, including the transnational alliance with the ilustrados, now Federalistas, were crucial in the establishment of nonmilitary institutions required to run the colony once it had been won. Building on the military's work during the war, the colonial regime instituted sanitation and sewage treatment facilities, hospitals, and vaccination programs to contain the spread of infectious diseases, virtually eradicating smallpox and cholera in the process.[53]

The colonial regime also mobilized cadres of young civilian Americans, men and women, to establish schools in the countryside. Known as "Thomasites" for the ship that brought an early batch of 500 to the Philippines in August 1901, the Americans spread out into rural areas to teach math, science, hygiene, vocational skills, English, and American history, while preparing native Filipinos to teach as well. As the first head of the program, Fred Atkinson promoted vocational educa-tion, despite the preference among Filipinos for broader training, and he distributed educational materials depicting snow and other things alien to rural Filipinos. In late 1902, anthropologist David Barrows replaced Atkinson and introduced more culturally appropriate materials. He also inaugurated a program in 1903 for young Filipinos to study in the United States and then return to the Philippines to serve in government or in schools. By the time of his departure in 1909, Barrows had in-creased the number of elementary schools three-fold to roughly 4,000, doubled the number of students to 400,000, and tripled the size of the native teaching corps to 8,000. These figures were misleading, however, given that truancy was high and most of the native teachers had not gone past the sixth grade. Because of this, the United States returned to Atkinson's idea of vocational training, while stressing secondary education for the select few over primary education for the masses. The new policy also reassured the Filipino oligarchy, which had grown concerned about the political implications of mass education.[54]

The economic system was also overhauled. First, currency, which still included Spanish gold coins, Mexican silver, and now U.S. dollars, was fixed to U.S. currency in order to stem wild fluctuations in exchange rates and reassure foreign bankers and merchants. Taft, followed by subsequent U.S. governors,[55] then brought American government and private investment to infrastructural development projects, while raising as well Philippine taxes to cover the costs of building networks of roads and shipping lines as well as wharves and warehouses. All of these were needed to stimulate inter-island and, by extension, foreign trade. Railway development was more problematic, though U.S. rail magnates J. P. Morgan and E. H. Harriman agreed to subscribe should Congress underwrite the expenses and grant the companies freedom from supervision in the Philippines. A bill to this effect was approved in the House but stalled under opposition from Democrats and Republican reformers in the Senate, and Morgan and Harriman backed out. Two smaller syndicates did win the franchises and, though they floundered for lack of funds, were able to expand the rail system from a hundred miles to more than six hundred during the next decade.[56] The infrastructure was needed to transport goods, notably raw materials, from the countryside to ports in exchange for imported goods, primarily manufactured products, and the United States targeted areas of the countryside where particularly important raw materials such as hemp were produced. At the same time, tobacco-growing regions were ignored, a nod to American tobacco farmers concerned about foreign competition.[57] Taft also sought to encourage private U.S. investment, particularly in agriculture, logging and mining; but he failed in 1902 to win congressional approval for various proposals to grant U.S. investors the special concessions and protection they sought.

Moreover, Taft lost out to U.S. beet lobbyists as well as tobacco and other American farmers, who feared competition from the new colony, when congress passed the Cooper, or Organic, Act in 1902. The Act formally established U.S. colonial rule in the Philippines as promised by the Spooner Amendment, with provisions for a bicameral legislature comprised of a Filipino-majority assembly of elected representatives in the lower chamber and an American-dominated commission and an American governor with veto power in the upper chamber. The commission and the governor were to be appointed by the U.S. president, subject to the approval of Congress, thus allowing the American president to retain considerable control over colonial policy though with congressional oversight. In defining American economic rights in the colony, however, the Cooper Act prevented the expropriation of church lands by prohibiting private U.S. corporations from purchasing any of the roughly 422,000 acres of prime agricultural lands owned by the Spanish friars. Taft then opened negotiations with Pope Leo XIII to transfer the lands from the Vatican to the U.S. government. After protracted bargaining, the United States completed the negotiations in 1903 for $7.5 million,[58] though the Vatican rejected Taft's demand that the friars be expelled, leaving them instead to simply die out gradually. With the Organic Act, Taft also lost in a bid to allow U.S. investors the right to buy tracts of 20,000 to 25,000 acres or more, especially needed in sugar production, where economies of scale were critical. Instead, the Cooper Act allowed individuals to purchase up to no more than forty acres while U.S. corporate landholdings were to be limited to just 2,500 acres.[59]

American economic intervention through land ownership was thus limited, as was, by extension, commercialization of Philippine agriculture. In the decade prior to 1913, Americans bought or leased only about 40,000 acres of public land, and later attempts to lift or circumvent the restrictions were deflected. Years later, when Taft was president, a scandal erupted when it was discovered that the largest of the friar estates had been transferred, illegally, to the family of American sugar magnate Henry Havemeyer.[60] For the most part, however, the Organic Act limited direct U.S. investments in Philippine land.[61] Meanwhile, Filipino elites were allowed unlimited access to the newly released church lands, further increasing the concentration of Philippine wealth and power. Far from addressing the roots of social unrest in the Philippines, which centered on the unequal land tenure patterns inherited from the Spanish colonial era, as described in chapter one, U.S. policies deepened these. Though statistics on such key indicators as the distribution of land or the amount of land devoted to cash versus food crops are unavailable for the period, a fact-finding survey years later in 1936 would find the vast majority of rural Filipinos living in dire poverty, deprived of civil and political rights as well, with no formal right to vote due to property requirements.[62] "The average tenant," the survey found, "...cannot openly join associations nor participate actively in any movement organized for his betterment without courting the displeasure of the land-owner and running the risk of being deprived of the piece of land he tills... ."[63] The land tenure question would remain an on-going source of peasant anger and revolution, as described in later chapters.

While elite Filipinos gained most from the new colonial policies in land tenure, American corporate strategy now turned to trade policy as an alternative route to profits.[64] Under the terms of the Paris Treaty, the United States had agreed to allow Spain equal access to Philippine markets for ten years, with Spain paying the same duties as Americans. Given these conditions, Taft then endorsed, with Republican and corporate support back home, a "reciprocal free trade" arrangement. Anything but "free," it gave Philippine agricultural goods unlimited access to U.S. markets, while allowing U.S. manufactured goods an unrestricted market in the Philippines, as U.S. exporters gained a virtual monopoly in the archipelago. In 1909, with Taft now president, provisions under the Paris Treaty allowing for Spain's equal right to the Philippine market were to expire, and American manufacturers now pressed for elimination of the tariff. Since one of Taft's campaign promises had been tariff reform, he now called a special congressional session on tariffs, sparking a heated debate while creating a schism in the Republican Party which would contribute to its loss in 1912 presidential elections. Nelson Aldrich, Chairman of the Senate Finance Committee and close ally of the Sugar Trust,[65] worked with Sereno Payne, head of the House Ways and Means Committee, to resolve the question of tariff reform, with its implications far beyond trade with the Philippines. In the United States, lobbyists fought hard on both sides of the debate, while the Filipino assembly passed a resolution against free trade in part to protect Filipino goods at home and abroad and in part because existing tariffs on U.S. goods entering the Philippines were an important source of revenue. The Filipino resolution was swiftly vetoed by Governor Cameron Forbes, however, and the Payne-Aldrich Act was passed on August 5, 1909.[66]

The act allowed all U.S. goods to enter the Philippines duty-free and in unlimited quantities, while Philippine products were allowed to enter the U.S. duty-free, though with some quotas on sugar and tobacco, later lifted in 1913 with the passage of the Underwood–Simmons Act.[67] The result was an expansion of Philippine land devoted to export production[68] and a concomitant drop in land devoted to food production, as hostilities in the countryside simmered. At the same time, foreign commerce in the Philippines jumped between 1908 and 1910, quadrupling in dollar terms from 1908 to 1926. Yet the economic dependence of the Philippines on the United States also increased greatly. In 1908, exports to the United States accounted for 32 percent of total Philippine exports. By 1926, the figure had increased to 73 percent. The increase in imports was even greater. In 1908, imports from America comprised 17 percent of total Philippine imports. By 1926, these comprised 60 percent.[69] What Taft had failed as governor to accomplish with the Organic Act, he now accomplished more subtly with the Payne-Aldrich Act's clarion call to American investors and business leaders.

Meanwhile, on the political front, America was also establishing its new colonial position, with important implications for the evolution of transnational U.S.–Philippine politics and the ongoing debate between "bullets" vs. "ballots" proponents. Strengthening the "ballots" position, the ban on pro-independence political parties was finally lifted in 1906 and Filipinos were allowed in 1907 to elect a legislative body. Under colonial law, the legislative body's direct influence over policy was severely restricted in that it functioned under the U.S.-appointed American governor, who held veto powers. Moreover, suffrage was restricted to landowners, taxpayers and the literate,[70] leaving just three percent of the population eligible to vote.[71] On an indirect basis, however, the political opening allowed Filipinos to more freely argue for independence both at home and abroad. Even the once powerful Federalistas, discredited by their U.S. connections and pro-statehood stance, had disbanded in 1905 and then reformulated as the Partido Progresista, which now favored independence. Under the leadership of two Filipino lawyers, Manuel Quezon and Sergio Osmena, several opposition cliques had also fused together five months before the 1907 elections into the Partido Nacionalista, which also favored independence.

Competing more as rival clans than on ideological grounds, the Nacionalistas captured 58 of the 80 seats in the 1907 elections, and were to dominate Philippine politics for decades to come. And despite the restrictions they faced in directly promoting Philippine independence, the Nacionalistas quickly devised transnational strategies for doing so indirectly. Of particular importance here was the U.S. colonial policy allowing two Philippine representatives to sit in the U.S. House of Representatives. Under colonial law, the Philippine representatives were allowed to hold seats as resident commissioners of the U.S. House, where they could speak but not vote. One was appointed by the U.S. Governor and until 1916 favored U.S. statehood. The other was appointed by the Philippine assembly. From 1909 to 1916, this appointment went to Manuel Quezon. A charismatic and gifted politician, Quezon used his time in the United States to study the workings of the American system and to establish himself as the eventual leader of an independent Philippines, the prospects for which seemed to brighten in 1912 with the election of Democrat Woodrow Wilson.[72]

Transnational Politics and the Opportunity for Change

Although Filipinos seeking independence hailed the new president, Wilson's cabinet was, in fact, split between the isolationism of Bryan, now Secretary of State, and the imperialism of William Redfield, Secretary of Commerce, a split defined by contrasting ideological, political and economic interests. Moreover, Wilson was quickly distracted from Philippine issues by on-going debates on tariff reform, revision of the banking system, and anti-trust legislation as well as the more immediate concerns raised by the Mexican revolution[73] and the growing threat of war in Europe. Meanwhile, in the Philippines, elected Filipinos increasingly resented the veto powers of the governor, which they argued made the Filipino assembly less a legislative body than a debating society. They also resented the large numbers of Americans in government posts. The problem was exacerbated after 1909, when Governor Forbes repeatedly vetoed attempts by the assembly to increase the number and authority of Filipinos in the colonial administration. Though the number of Filipino officials had actually doubled to roughly 6,000 by 1913, Wilson mediated the conflict, opting to replace Forbes as governor. Quezon, as a resident commissioner in the United States, intervened in the selection of a candidate, urging New York Congressman Francis Harrison to go for the job. Harrison, a Democrat, had opposed imperialism, had promoted lower tariffs, and had eventually championed Philippine independence, all positions Quezon appreciated. Harrison agreed to apply and Quezon then orchestrated the appointment in just four days, obtaining Bryan's endorsement, Wilson's nomination, and then support from key members of congress.

Unlike Taft, Wilson did not believe that Filipinos had to prove themselves worthy of self-government prior to being granted independence but rather that they might learn by doing, and he encouraged Harrison to promote policies toward this end.[74] Speaking for the president, Harrison announced shortly after his arrival in Manila in 1913 that the Wilson administration would immediately give Filipinos a majority in the appointive commission, which until then had been controlled by Americans. The governor would also no longer have veto powers. Moreover, because Filipinos already held a majority, by law, in the elected legislature, they now predominated in both the Upper and Lower Houses of the Philippine government. In one bold stroke, the United States had essentially given Filipinos a significant measure of self-government, though the United States retained responsibility for the security of the islands and for its foreign policy. Harrison also made clear his intentions of weeding out Americans from administrative posts and filling these with Filipinos, as McKinley had first promised but as each successive governor until Harrison had ignored. By the end of his first year in office, Harrison had trimmed the American contingent in government by nearly 20 percent while raising Filipino representation by a comparable figure.[75] In his eight years as governor, Harrison Filipinized the American establishment, shrinking the U.S. corps from about 3,000 to about 600 while increasing the number of Filipinos to more than 13,000.[76] When U.S. interests in Manila complained, Harrison threatened to audit their finances. The U.S. community soon adapted and Harrison was to become one of the most revered Americans in the Philippines of the century.[77]

In addition to influencing the gubernatorial selection, Quezon worked with Virginia Congressman William Atkinson Jones of the insular affairs committee to write what was to become known as the Jones Act, which eventually passed in 1916. Part of the impetus behind Quezon's actions had to do with politics back in the Philippines, where a new independence-oriented party was gaining popularity. Formed in 1914 by a leftist faction led by Teodoro Sandiko, a well-known veteran of the revolution with close ties to Aguinaldo, the party posed an increasing challenge to Quezon's Nacionalistas. This spurred Quezon to forge a moderate alternative to the leftist challenge on the issue of Philippine sovereignty, with a timetable allowing for at least twenty more years of colonial rule by the United States,[78] though Harrison together with various members of the U.S. Congress sought a more immediate transfer of power in the Philippines. After consulting with Quezon on this, Wilson agreed to support legislation pledging that the United States would confer independence upon the Filipinos though at an unspecified point in the future. In August 1914, just as World War I was breaking out in Europe, Congressman Jones submitted the bill he had crafted with Quezon to redefine the relationship between the United States and the Philippines. Without actually offering any provision for independence, the bill's preamble pledged a commitment to the cause and endorsed Wilson's Philippine policy.[79] The bill passed 212–60 in the House in October but languished in the Senate and then vanished in March until the new congress met several months later in December 1915.

Now the proponents of independence, almost entirely Democrats, were ambushed not by Republican retentionists but by Democratic Senator James Clarke of Arkansas, who proposed an amendment requiring a transfer to independence within four years. Quezon and his Nacionalista colleagues back home could not afford politically to oppose such an amendment, nor could they let the bill fail as they had invested too much in it. Likewise, Wilson had already gone on record as favoring independence and, distracted by the revolution in Mexico and the war in Europe, refused to openly oppose the Clarke amendment. While Wilson and his Nacionalista allies held their breaths, the U.S. Senate passed the bill with the Clarke Amendment's four-year timetable kept intact. The House, however, deleted the amendment, leaving Harrison and the Nacionalista leaders with whom he worked closely to worry that the bill might die altogether. Harrison lobbied from the Philippines for some form of the bill, preferably without a timetable but at the very least with some clear provisions, as the uncertainty had hampered progress in the Philippines. Quezon, too, discerned that any bill, even with the Clarke Amendment, was preferable to no bill, but he worried that the voices of retentionism in the United States were more powerful than those favoring independence. In a keen observation with on-going relevance, Quezon told Harrison "I have not the slightest doubt but that the American people in general are favorable to Philippine independence. The trouble is that the people at large are not interested enough to write their congressmen, and the only voice that is being heard is the voice of those who are interested in retention, who are, naturally, actively working to defeat the bill."[80]

Fortunately for Harrison, the Nacionalistas and other proponents of the original Jones bill, the Senate eventually dropped its insistence on a timetable for independence and the resolution, minus the Clarke Amendment, passed. Quezon now returned to the Philippines to parlay his success into a political career, while the Jones Act, which Wilson signed into law on August 29, 1916, acknowledged Philippine sovereignty and established provisions for a gradual transfer of power. It also allowed for continued Filipino control of both houses of the Philippine legislature.

The 1916 Jones Act:
A Transnational Explanation

In sum, the key explanation for the 1916 Jones Act lies in the United States, the locus of decision making on the issue of independence throughout the colonial period, but Filipino nationalists such as Quezon lobbied effectively at critical moments to influence policy. The U.S. debates on the Philippine question were configured largely along partisan lines, with Republicans generally supporting U.S. colonialism there and Democrats generally opposing it. Though it was beyond the scope of this work to cover the complex machinations of these debates, the conflict was rooted in the broader economic struggles between populist small farmers and their Democratic allies versus increasingly powerful industrialists and their Republican allies. While the Democrats sought to protect small farmers from their Philippine competitors by keeping the latter outside tariff walls, the Republicans sought to protect the interests of industrialists and agricultural refiners, notably the Sugar Trust, by keeping the Philippines as a colony in order to bring Philippine goods within tariff walls. Though the Republicans succeeded in their efforts by making the Philippines a colony of the United States at the turn of the century, the debates would continue in various forms throughout the colonial period, as discussed further in the next chapter. When Republicans held the White House, they used the considerable power conferred on the office by congress under the Spooner Amendment and later the Cooper Act to appoint Republican governors to manage the Philippines and to establish political, economic, military and social institutions in the service of U.S. colonial interests there.

When Democrats held the White House, however, Filipino nationalists and their allies in the U.S. Congress capitalized on the opportunity for change. During the period covered here, the only Democratic administration was that of Wilson, and anti-imperialists in the Philippines and the United States did indeed capitalize on the opportunity for change. Soon after Wilson moved into the White House, Quezon began pressing first for a new governor for the Philippines who would promote the cause of independence. With Quezon's help, anti-imperialist New York congressman Francis Harrison was appointed governor and swiftly granted Filipinos a measure of autonomy. Quezon then worked closely with Congressman Jones of the House committee on insular affairs to revise U.S. policy toward the Philippines. Quezon's efforts were, in part, a soft-line response to the growing radicalism of renegade Philippine nationalists led by Teodoro Sandiko; while the efforts of U.S. Democrats stemmed from the recent tariff debates and from their success in the election of Wilson as President. Passage of the Jones Act in 1916 formally expressed the U.S. commitment to Philippine independence, though without a specified timetable. As the next chapter will show, this question of a timetable would then be set aside through the Republican eras of Harding, Coolidge and then Hoover, resurfacing only when the onset of the Depression ushered in the Roosevelt administration, with its ties to the large numbers of small farmers and others actively seeking to push Philippine agricultural products beyond the protection of tariff walls.

While U.S. forces are primarily responsible for the Jones Act, and the eventual transition to independence in 1946, as described in Chapter 3, neither purely international factors governed by the United States nor purely domestic politics within the Philippines fully explain it. Rather, the transnational lobbying efforts of Quezon, from his perch within the U.S. House of Representatives, helped establish a vital link between Filipino nationalists and American anti-imperialists. This link proved crucial in the selection of anti-imperialist New York Congressman Francis Harrison as governor of the Philippines, who helped establish Philippine capacity for independence. The link also proved crucial in pushing the Jones Act through Congress.

The transnational politics and institutions formed during the early colonial period in response to U.S., Philippine and international pressures also hold important implications for the later transitions in 1972 and 1986, as described in later chapters. In particular, the period saw the emergence and evolution of transnational alliances of hard-liners and soft-liners, both comprised of Filipino elites and U.S. officials. While U.S. officials needed the Philippine elite to insure political stability and the production of raw materials, the Philippine elite needed the United States to protect them militarily from revolutionary opposition in the countryside and to promote capital development for trade and finance. From the outset, the main threat to both Filipino elites and U.S. colonialists was revolutionary opposition in the Philippines, which sought independence as well as structural economic and political change, particularly in land tenure. Though both the hard-line and soft-line transnational alliances sought to contain the kind of revolutionary opposition expressed so forcefully during the war of 1899–1902 and recurring thereafter, the hard-liners emphasized military repression while the soft-liners emphasized political attraction and incorporation. Working in tandem, the hard-liners allied with the Macabebes and created the Philippine Insular Police in 1901, later known as the Philippine Constabulary, while the soft-liners created public institutions to manage health, education, economic development, political change and other issues of central concern to the masses of Filipinos.

Just as Filipinos were poised for greater autonomy under the Jones Act, however, the combined lessons of the Mexican Revolution and World War I would reignite the debates in the United States between interventionists and isolationists, hard-liners and soft-liners, and in the Philippines among soft-liners, hard-liners, and revolutionaries. The Depression and World War II would then intensify these debates, as the economic, political and strategic interdependencies between the United States and the Philippines, all of which had become institutionalized during the colonial period, were reinforced by international events, with implications for the continued evolution of Philippine political, economic and military institutions as well as the prospects for independent democracy there, as described in the next chapter.

Notes

1. The reasons for the partisan division are complex, rooted in the broader economic struggles in the United States of the time, and are beyond the scope of this chapter. In brief, however, the division centered on powerful agricultural and industrial interests which

expressed themselves forcefully through their congressional and presidential allies. While the Democrats tended to ally with populist movements of small farmers, who were most threatened by imperialist efforts to bring Philippine competitors within tariff walls, the Republicans tended to ally with industrialists and agricultural refiners, notably the Sugar Trust, who sought to circumvent the restrictions the tariffs imposed on their access to cheap agricultural supplies. For an excellent account of the Sugar Trust's links with the Republican party and its influence on foreign policy, see Francisco and Fast, *Conspiracy for an Empire.*

2. Stanley Karnow, *In Our Image: America's Empire in the Philippines* (1989), 140.

3. From Karnow, *In Our Image,* 139-167.

4. Charles Farkas, "Partido Federal: The Policy of Attraction," (October–December 1978), p.33.

5. Brian McAllister Linn, *The U.S. Army and Counterinsurgency in the Philippine War, 1899–1902* (1989), 12, and Sand-30 (pseud) "Trench, Parapet, or the 'Open' " (1902).

6. For a detailed description of this and other early offensives and their effects on Otis' policy, see Linn, *U.S. Army and Counterinsurgency,* 1-13.

7. Karnow, *In Our Image,* 147.

8. The information for this paragraph is from Henry Lee, *The War Correspondent and the Insurrection: A Study of American Newspaper Correspondents in the Philippines, 1898–1900* (1968).

9. In part because so many reporters had been sent to Cuba and in part because the U.S. War Department had predicted that the war in the Philippines would end quickly, few reporters were sent to the Philippines.

10. Lee, *War Correspondent.*

11. The information for this paragraph is from Schirmer, *Republic or Empire,* a detailed account of the U.S. debates on Philippine policy and the role of the Anti-Imperialist League in these.

12. All of the above discussion on the anti-imperialist debates, the League, etc. are from Schirmer, *Republic or Empire.* Discussion of Aguinaldo's calculations are from Constantino, *A Past Revisited.*

13. The above information is from Brands, *Bound to Empire,* 52.

14. Ibid, 55.

15. Information for this paragraph is from Brands, *Bound to Empire,* 39-60; Karnow, *In Our Image,* 139-167; and Linn, *U.S. Army and Counterinsurgency,* 1-29.

16. As noted in chapter two, the Philippine constitution, written by the ilustrados, extended suffrage to a very small minority of affluent elites. When elections were held in late 1898 under Aguinaldo's newly declared administration, these elites added political power to their long-standing economic power in the countryside.

17. Information on the internal debates within the revolutionary movement is from Constantino, *A Past Revisited,* 204-237.

18. First Report of the Philippine Commission, Vol. 1, 185.

19. The description of the Commission's efforts in the Philippines, and its conflicts with the U.S. military command, is from Brands, *Bound to Empire,* 51.

20. Ibid.

21. Karnow, *In Our Image*, 151.

22. Information on the commission's work is from its reports to the President. Information on the U.S. policy-making process surrounding the commission's findings is from Karnow, *In Our Image,* 139-167, and from Brands, *Bound to Empire*, 39-60.

23. Information on the U.S. military's role in the Philippines is from Gates, *Schoolbooks and Krags*, 54-156 and from Karnow, *In Our Image*, 171.

24. Information on the number of troops sent to the Philippines and the general debates surrounding U.S. policy towards the Philippines at the time is from Karnow, *In Our Image,* 152.

25. The quote is from Brands, *Bound to Empire*, 54.

26. For descriptions of the politics surrounding the Spooner Bill, see Frank Golay, "The Search for Revenues," in Peter W. Stanley, ed., *Reappraising an Empire: New Perspectives on Philippine–American History*, 236; Brands, *Bound to Empire*, 60; and Constantino, *A Past Revisited*, 296-99.

27. Information on the formation, reception, and role of the Taft commission is from Karnow, *In Our Image*, 168-177 and from Brands, *Bound to Empire*, 60-85.

28. From Constantino, *A Past Revisited*, 256-287.

29. Information for the paragraph is from Constantino *A Past Revisited*, 297 and from the reports of the Taft Philippine Commission, 6, 34-35.

30. Karnow, *In Our Image*, 173.

31. Farkas, "Policy of Attraction," 36.

32. Ibid.; and from Brands, *Bound to Empire*, 74-76.

33. Schirmer, op. cit.

34. The description of the role of the Philippines in the elections is from Karnow, *In Our Image*, 181.

35. Farkas, "Policy of Attraction," 37.

36. Gates, *Schoolbooks and Krags*, 94.

37. Information on the emergence and role of the Federalistas is from Farkas, *"Policy of Attraction."*

38. From Constantino, *A Past Revisited*, 244-46, and Linn, *U.S. Army and Counterinsurgency*, 163-170.

39. Constantino, *A Past Revisited*, 247. See also Pomeroy, *Philippines.*

40. Constantino, *A Past Revisited*, 247.

41. The description of the capture of Aguinaldo, also fictionally recreated on film by Thomas Edison, is from Karnow, *In Our Image*, 182-88.

42. For information on the Spooner Amendment, which is surprisingly underplayed in the literature, see Brands, *Bound to Empire*, 60; Constantino, *A Past Revisited*, 296-7; Golay, "Search for Revenues," in Stanley, ed., *Reappraising an Empire*, 236-7; 56th Congress, 1st Session, S. 2355; PL 118, 3/2/1901, 31 Stat. L. 895.

43. Constantino, *A Past Revisited*, 247.

44. The Final Report of the Fact-Finding Commission, 27.

45. Constantino, *A Past Revisited*, 251.

46. For information on the reconcentrado policy and its impact in the Philippines, see

Constantino, *A Past Revisited*, 250. For its impact on U.S. debates, see Karnow, *In Our Image*, 188-195.

47. Constantino, *A Past Revisited*, 250. For its impact on U.S. debates, see Karnow, *In Our Image*, 188-195.

48. Karnow, *In Our Image*, 191-93.

49. Constantino, *A Past Revisited*, 247.

50. Ibid.

51. Karnow, *In Our Image*, 194.

52. Constantino, *A Past Revisited*, 251.

53. Karnow, *In Our Image*, 211. While this figure is somewhat misleading given the war in 1900, the Americans did improve health substantially.

54. Information on the U.S. role in Filipino education during the period is from Gates, *Schoolbooks and Krags*, especially 136-39, and Brands, *Bound to Empire*, 71.

55. For a complete description of the life and contributions of each U.S. governor in the Philippines during the colonial era, see Lewis E. Gleeck, Jr. *The American Governors-General and High Commissioners in the Philippines: Procouncils, Nation Builders, and Politicians* (1986). Taft served from 1901–1903, when he was recalled to the United States to serve as Secretary of War, after Root resigned. Taft was followed by Luke Wright (1903–1906); Henry Clay Ide (1906); James Smith (1906–1909); W. Cameron Forbes (1909–1913); Francis B. Harrison (1913–1920); Leonard Wood (1921–1926); Henry L. Stimson (1928–1929); Dwight F. Davis (1929–1931); Theodore Roosevelt Jr. (1932–1933); Frank Murphy (1933–1935); J. Weldon Jones (1936–1940) acting High Commissioner on and off through tenure of Paul McNutt (1937–1938) and Francis B. Sayre (1939–1942).

56. Karnow, *In Our Image*, 218-19.

57. Constantino, *A Past Revisited*, 302.

58. Brands, *Bound to Empire*, 99.

59. Francisco and Fast, *Conspiracy for Empire*, 262-63.

60. Ibid.

61. Note that Constantino, *A Past Revisited*, 303-305, says friar lands were not included in prohibitions against land ownership until 1914 when the Philippine assembly enacted a law that put these as public lands. Prior to that, the Sugar Trust bought San Jose Estate in 1910 by getting Forbes to amend the Friar Lands Act to allow the government to sell friar lands without acreage limitation. The Commission and the War Department cooperated and the sale pushed through. The Commission approved many other questionable deals, including approval to lease various estates to Americans.

62. Ofreneo, *Capitalism in Philippine Agriculture*, 24.

63. Ibid.

64. Karnow, *In Our Image*, 221.

65. Brands, *Bound to Empire*, 96.

66. For a detailed discussion of the processes in the United States and the Philippines leading to the Payne-Aldrich Act, see Francisco and Fast, *Conspiracy for Empire*, particularly chapters 3, 29, and 30.

67. Ofreneo, *Capitalism in Philippine Agriculture*, 15.

68. The amount of land devoted to export crops more than tripled, from 469,353 hectares, or about 1.2 million acres, in 1902 to 1.6 million hectares, about 4 million acres, by 1939. From Ibid., 16.

69. All of the economic statistics are from Brands, *Bound to Empire*, 98.

70. The Election Law, Manila Bureau of Printing, 1907. From the National Archives in Maryland.

71. Ibid. From Brands, *Bound to Empire*, 98.

72. An estimated 10,000 Filipinos marched in celebration through the streets of Manila while roughly twice that number gathered in Manila's Luneta Park for ceremonies led by Quezon, Aguinaldo and Osmena commemorating the election. From Brands, *Bound to Empire*, 106. Information on the political role of the United States during the period was culled from Brands, *Bound to Empire,* 60-84; Karnow, *In Our Image*, 227-256; and Farkas' article, "Policy of Attraction," on the emergence and role of the Federalistas.

73. When Wilson first came to power in 1912, a military coup in Mexico had recently installed Victoriano Huerta as provisional president. Reluctant to embroil the United States in Mexican politics, Taft had sidestepped the issue; but Wilson threatened to withhold recognition until Huerta called a ceasefire and scheduled elections in which he would not participate. Wilson then called for an arms embargo and encouraged Europe to do the same. Under pressure from Republicans to take military action and seeing diplomacy faltering, Wilson staged an invasion of Vera Cruz, Mexico's second city. After a bloody invasion costing 100 U.S. and 500 Mexican lives, U.S. forces took the city but then did not know what to do with it. Only mediation from Argentina, Brazil and Chile allowed for a face-saving withdrawal of troops. The experience chastened Wilson regarding foreign intervention thereafter. From Combs, *History of American Foreign Policy*, 190-92.

74. For a detailed discussion of Wilson's approach to the Philippine question, see Farkas' article on the topic, "Reviving the White Man's Burden: President Wilson and the Philippines" (January–March, 1978).

75. Brands, *Bound to Empire*, 109.

76. Karnow, *In Our Image*, 245.

77. For a full discussion of Harrison's role as governor, see Gleeck, *American Governors*, 134-161 and Brands, *Bound to Empire*, 107-112.

78. Brands, *Bound to Empire*, 113. After consulting with Frank McIntyre, chief of the Bureau of Insular Affairs, Quezon proposed an arrangement calling for a census in 1925 and every ten years thereafter until literacy rates in English among adult males reached 60 percent, or 75 percent in any language. At that time, he proposed that a referendum on independence be held. Should the vote favor independence, a constitutional convention would follow, leading to a transfer to sovereignty.

79. Brands, *Bound to Empire*, 114.

80. Brands, *Bound to Empire*, 116. From Bureau of Internal Affairs records of notes from Harrison papers.

Chapter 3

Colonialism amid Crises: The Road to Independent Democracy, 1917–1946

This chapter follows the transnational processes that shaped Philippine political, economic and military institutions during the later colonial years, from the period following ratification of the 1916 Jones Act through the international crises of World War I, the Depression, World War II and the Japanese occupation of the Philippines. The chapter will describe the effects of these crises on United States–Philippine relations and the implications for Philippine domestic politics leading up to independence in 1946.

World War I

Although the Jones Act allowed for eventual independence for the Philippines, it also allowed American military forces to remain in the Philippines for twenty more years, until 1936. By 1917, these forces included a small naval station at Subic Bay and an army fort at Clark Field, for which the U.S. Congress had authorized funding in 1904 after protracted debates on the defensibility of the islands. Concerned that military bases in the Philippines might become the "Achilles heel" of the United States, Theodore Roosevelt had warned while President in 1907 that it would be imprudent to retain the islands "without adequately fortifying them" from a rising Japanese threat, given Japan's recent successes in wars with China and Russia.[1] Other strategists, however, had argued that the islands could be defended and, in any case, they predicted a war at sea with Japan, not one on Philippine soil. Roosevelt dissented, arguing that Congress should either provide funds for military fortification or should vote to withdraw from its new colony. Instead, the issue languished, though in 1908, U.S. military strategists decided to base America's Pacific fleet at Pearl Harbor, not Subic, due largely to concerns that the fleet would be overly exposed to Japan if based in the Philippines.

In 1910, the Naval War College devised a plan, code-named the Orange Plan, for a prospective war with Japan. Envisioning only a war at sea, the plan ordered the U.S. Garrison to secure Manila Bay until the American fleet had time to arrive to defeat the Japanese and reestablish U.S. control of the islands. Despite the improbability of such a plan actually working, the U.S. forces in the Philippines were, nevertheless, to provide external security. Meanwhile the Insular Police Force, renamed the Philippine Constabulary in 1917, was to provide internal security, largely from the recurring threat posed by revolutionary opposition. What the plan did not prepare for was a full-scale land and air war by Japan in the Philippines, an oversight difficult to understand given Japan's increasingly clear hegemonic ambitions in the region. Hostilities between the United States and Japan had also risen in 1913 when the California legislature passed a measure excluding Japanese, among other immigrants, from owning land. The possibility of a two-ocean war was growing. Moreover, American involvement in the European war was becoming more and more likely. Despite Wilson's efforts to maintain American neutrality, such acts of apparent belligerence by Germany as the sinking of the Lusitania in May 1915 and the February 1917 announcement of German plans to sink all ships sailing in the war zone, including neutral ones, were pressing the United States toward war. The discovery of the Zimmerman telegram, in which Germany sought a Japanese as well as a Mexican alliance against the United States should the Americans join the war, was perhaps the final push that spurred Wilson to do just that.[2]

This time, Japan sided with the United States and a two-ocean war was averted. Nevertheless, just as passage of the Jones Act in 1916 offered the possibility of Philippine autonomy, the subsequent spectre of war with Japan exposed the vulnerability of U.S. military installations in the Philippines. The United States would have to decide whether to maintain a military presence there, in which case substantial investments would be needed, or the unfortified islands could still prove the "Achilles heel" Theodore Roosevelt had warned against. Instead, the United States would again allow the issue to languish. As a result, World War I served less as a military warning regarding the U.S. role in the Philippines than as a spur to increased Philippine dependence on the U.S. economy. Not only did the war create a huge global demand for raw materials, which enriched the islands, but also demand for coconut oil, used in explosives, skyrocketed. Forty new coconut oil factories sprung up throughout the Philippines during the war, amassing tremendous profits from the seemingly limitless demand. All collapsed after the war, however, when demand proved limited after all, though some resurfaced during the boom years of the roaring twenties. Moreover, the sharp drop in postwar prices shattered the Philippine economy, betraying the lopsided, export-dependent form it had taken in order to supply the United States. And while sugar and coconut barons had grown rich, rice farmers and other basic foodstuff growers had fallen further and further behind, presaging a resurgence of revolutionary activity among the peasantry in the 1920s. Meanwhile, events in Russia defied Marxist expectations of industrial revolution, revealing the potential power of a mobilized peasantry, establishing as well an apparently vital alternative to capitalism.

Revolutionary Resurgence: Domestic and Transnational Factors

It would be more than a decade following the Russian revolution before the Philippines would have a communist party, but a wave of religious-based revolutionary movements throughout the 1920s helped lay the foundation for this. Known collectively as Colorums, a corruption of the *et saecula saeculorum* used in Mass to end certain prayers, the movements were characterized by religious fanaticism and a common belief in messiahs as their path to redemption.[3] Embedded in these beliefs was a desire for structural economic, political and social change, with a shared dream of a messiah who would confiscate and reapportion among Colorums all land in the Philippines. Members also typically believed that *anting-anting*, or amulets, would protect them from enemy bullets, which allowed for a level of militancy not necessarily commensurate with their numbers. Recruited from the peasantry and the urban poor, the Colorums lacked connections to Filipino elites, who were content for the most part with U.S. rule, or to any intelligentsia which might have provided more ideological and strategic direction, as the ilustrados had done for the Katipunan. As a result, the Colorums were often ideologically confused and poorly organized, groping blindly for solutions to profound socioeconomic problems, and so were often dismissed by U.S. and Philippine officials as mere fanatics. Nevertheless, because of their capacity to enlist the support of the masses and their desire for structural change, however inadequately formulated, the movements warrant attention for their role in articulating and mobilizing peasant anger during the period.

The first major Colorum movement of the period formed on the island of Surigao and then spread to other islands, leading to an uprising there in 1923 in which five Constabulary soldiers were killed. Colorums in Agusan, Samar, and Leyte then rose up too, forcing the government to dispatch an American warship and hundreds of Constabulary reinforcements to suppress the rebellion, which lasted until October 1924. To avenge the deaths of Philippine forces, the Constabulary then cracked down with full force, ordering one town burned while the corpses of Colorums were allowed to rot in the open in order to prove that they would not come back to life. One hundred peasants were killed, 500 arrested, and the rest dispersed. Though the government acknowledged the economic and nationalistic aspirations of the Colorums while the campaign of suppression was underway, officials dismissed the uprising as mere fanaticism when it was over, and the Constabulary hailed the government's military approach. Undaunted, other Colorum organizations rose up elsewhere in the archipelago, including one organization with an estimated membership in 1924 of 12,000 in Nueva Ecija and another in 1927 in the Visayas with an estimated 26,000 members.

In 1929, an Ilocano named Pedro Calosa who had spent several years as a laborer in the sugar fields of Hawaii but was dismissed for trying to organize his coworkers, organized in Pangasinan the last major Colorum organization of the period. By January 1931, his movement attacked the prosperous town of Tayug with the vague notion that this would spark revolution throughout Luzon, leading to independence and an equal redistribution of land. As with the earlier uprisings, the superior weaponry of the Constabulary forced Calosa's surrender after just one day of fighting. Following this, U.S. and Philippine officials continued to ignore the roots of peasant discontent. Focusing on military not political strategies, they simply added 10,000 to the Constabulary while Quezon, now Senate President, and other leading Filipinos decried the ignorance and fanaticism behind the revolts.[4]

Yet something was happening that Filipino leaders failed to recognize. As exemplified in Calosa's story, Filipino peasants were migrating in large numbers to the United States, particularly to the sugar fields of Hawaii and the fruit farms of California, which one author has termed "factories in the field." Though Filipinos had long been recruited for such work, the levels of Filipino migration to the United States rose sharply in the 1920s, just as the Immigration Act of 1924 excluded new waves of immigrants to the United States. Concerned that the act would curtail the supply of cheap armies of farm labor, upon which Hawaiian and Californian agriculture relied, growers sought refuge in the special immigrant status conferred on Filipinos because of the colonial relationship. American growers now actively recruited Filipino peasants and, in 1923, 2,426 entered California alone.[5] Between 1920 and 1929, the net increase in the Filipino population in Hawaii and the U.S. mainland amounted to some 80,000.[6]

The situation was fraught with conflict. The structural deflation in agricultural markets from 1925 to 1929, characterized by excess supply in world primary products, created tremendous uncertainty for growers.[7] To control wages as well as the flow of labor between crop seasons, growers associations in California began using a single recruiting agency to contract laborers, significantly increasing their bargaining power vis-à-vis workers. The Mexicans, who now represented the largest ethnic group of farm workers in California and had likely had some exposure to peasant organizing during the Mexican revolution of 1910, responded in 1927 by forming the Confederation of Mexican Labor Unions. Soon after, the Mexicans staged a cantaloupe pickers strike. When this turned violent, large numbers of Mexicans were arrested or deported and the strike failed. The Filipino farm workers, composed largely of single male peasants from regions of the Philippines with rich revolutionary traditions and recent Colorum activity,[8] brought their own ideas about peasant organizing, learning as well from the Mexican experience. They formed a type of guild system wherein a single contractor developed a wage scale with employers for organized bands of workers. The Filipinos then used their enhanced bargaining power to underbid other groups, notably the Mexicans, and would then strike at critical moments to demand higher wages.

This soon undermined their attractiveness to employers, while creating friction between the Filipinos and the other farm labor groups. Though some of the friction resulted from competition, it was also used by growers as a divisive strategy. In January and February 1930, for instance, Mexican and Filipino farm workers joined forces to strike against lettuce growers in the Imperial Valley, with a total involvement of roughly 5,000.[9] The Mexican strikers were issued a warning, however, that if they associated with Filipinos, they risked deportation. Over 100 organizers and strikers were then arrested, residences and meeting halls raided, and the strike ultimately failed, as tensions between Filipinos and Mexicans resurfaced. How ironic that these two groups, once linked by the galleon trade, should now be brought together again, competing for a meager existence in the land Urdaneta had discovered so long ago.[10]

But the 1930s were to bring in a new group of competitors who would ultimately reduce the relative importance of both Filipino and Mexican farm workers between 1930 and 1935. These new competitors were the displaced whites from the dustbowls of Oklahoma and Arkansas. Racism against Filipinos now escalated in California and elsewhere, as sympathy for the whites spread amid the uncertainty and mass anxiety created by the Depression.[11] The sugar, coconut, and dairy lobbies further exploited the situation to reignite debates on Philippine independence, arguing against the special colonial relationship that allowed Philippine agricultural products to compete with American ones. Only a few large American companies with investments in the Philippines together with importers of duty-free products and exporters with monopoly privileges in the Philippines worked to maintain colonial ties there. Otherwise, momentum for Philippine independence was building in the United States in the guise of protectionism and reduced overseas expenditures.

At the same time, the American Communist Party (CPUSA) was gaining a deeper understanding of Philippine issues, in part through contact with Filipino farm workers and others in the United States. In fact, the first documented visit to the Philippines by a communist was in 1924 when CPUSA leader Harrison George invited a Philippine delegation to a conference of Pacific transport workers to be held in Canton. A delegation from the Philippines accepted the invitation and participated in the Canton conference later that year. This initial contact with the CPUSA proved influential in the development of both Philippine communism at home and the transnational campaign for independence. The CPUSA now actively lobbied on behalf of Philippine independence while helping as well to establish the Philippine Communist Party (PKP), formed in 1930 with one of its main goals being independence.[12]

On another front, the Japanese invasion of Manchuria in 1931 further fueled debate on U.S. policy in Asia.[13] President Hoover together with Secretary of State Stimson and then–Army Chief of Staff General Douglas MacArthur, Arthur's son, argued for an increased U.S. presence in the Philippines to deter the Japanese. Those U.S. policy makers who sought to avoid foreign entanglements held sway, however, when Democrat Franklin Roosevelt was elected President in 1932, upsetting the Republican party's twelve-year hold on the White House. Several independence bills proposing sovereignty for the Philippines had been defeated in Congress in the 1920s; but now the stage was set for renewed debate on the question of Philippine independence.[14]

Transnational Politics and the Transition to Commonwealth Status

Meanwhile, in 1930, Manuel Quezon sent one of his closest political rivals, Sergio Osmena, together with another contender, Manuel Roxas, to Washington to lobby on behalf of Philippine independence. In the United States, the congressional debates centered more than ever on diverse views regarding American interests. Opponents of independence cited the strategic importance of a U.S. military presence in the region, particularly vis-à-vis Japan. Supporters, on the other hand, cited the impact on American farmers of Philippine agricultural exports to the United States, though the actual impact was in fact relatively small. In the negotiations for what was to become the Hare–Hawes–Cutting Act, Osmena and Roxas submitted to a provision allowing the United States to retain military bases in the Philippines without requiring Filipino consent in exchange for a promise of independence within ten years. Osmena and Roxas also submitted to economic provisions that limited Filipino migration to the United States and curtailed Philippine access to U.S. markets, posing a serious challenge for the U.S.-dependent Philippine economy. The bill passed in the Democrat-controlled House by April 1932 but Republican Senator Arthur Vandenberg succeeded in shelving it in the Senate until late 1932, when Hoover lost in a landslide victory for Roosevelt. The Senate now approved the bill, Hoover vetoed it, but, in January 1933, congress overrode this, as the Hare–Hawes–Cutting Act now needed only Philippine approval to become law.

Surprisingly, Quezon swiftly set about to block its passage in the Philippine legislature. Though many accused him of seeking to upstage his rivals and claim credit for independence for himself, Quezon argued that the bases provision violated Philippine sovereignty while the economic provisions would seriously undercut the Philippine economy. He was also concerned about Japanese militarism and Philippine prospects for defending against this. To defeat the measure, he duplicitously assured radical nationalists that he could hasten independence from the ten-year period specified in the Hare–Hawes–Cutting Act, while promising the sugar barons that he could guarantee their U.S. market by delaying independence. Quezon's efforts prevailed, and the Philippine legislature rejected the bill.

Quezon then arrived in the United States in November 1933 to assemble a new bill. To assist him, Quezon hired Harry Hawes, one of the architects of the Hare–Hawes–Cutting Act and now out of the Senate, as a lobbyist. Together, Quezon and Hawes approached democratic Senator Millard Tydings of Maryland, who chaired the Senate committee responsible for the islands, and Representative John McDuffie of Alabama to repackage essentially the Hare–Hawes–Cutting Act and resell it to Congress. There was one major difference, though. With the new bill, Franklin Roosevelt agreed to transfer U.S. Army property to Filipinos after independence, with the disposition of naval bases to be settled through negotiations.[15] Unlike Hoover and Republican presidential predecessors who viewed the colony as a strategic and economic boon to the United States, Roosevelt, like his Democratic predecessors, viewed the colony as a drain on U.S. resources, now more needed than ever at home due to the Depression. Speaking bluntly in a confidential meeting with congressional leaders during negotiations for the act, Roosevelt said, "Let's get rid of the Philippines—that's the most important thing. Let's be frank about it."[16]

Though not for the reasons Filipinos had hoped for, the Tydings-McDuffie bill nevertheless passed in the United States in 1934 and Quezon returned to the Philippines where the bill was unanimously passed in the legislature. A Philippine convention assembled to write a constitution for the nascent government. Drawing upon the U.S. and the Malolos constitutions, the convention called for a separation of executive and legislative powers, as well as regular elections for a unicameral legislature and a Commonwealth President. The Philippine president would hold extensive veto powers far greater than his American counterpart, while a U.S.-appointed High Commissioner would help manage the transition to self-rule for the ten years prior to independence. Suffrage was also extended to men and women over the age of 21, though continued linguistic and property restrictions kept the proportion of eligible voters to less than 14 percent of the adult population. Upon his return to the Philippines, Quezon used his victory in the United States to launch his campaign for the presidency.

Almost immediately, however, domestic conflict undermined the resolve of Philippine officials to relinquish ties to the United States. Just after the new constitution was approved by Roosevelt in early 1935 and two weeks prior to a Filipino plebiscite on the Tydings–McDuffie Act, a revolutionary movement called the *Sakdalistas*, or "strikers," opposed the bill. The Sakdalistas also opposed Quezon's bid for the presidency. Formed in 1930 and comprised primarily of peasants in central Luzon, the Sakdalistas were relatively overlooked until May Day 1935, when they stormed municipal offices, constabulary barracks and police stations. A bloody battle ensued, killing about 60, with 80 more casualties, and 500 arrests. The Sakdalistas were quickly subdued and, by September, Quezon was elected commonwealth President. The Sakdalista uprising was nevertheless better organized and more ideologically grounded than the Colorum uprisings had been, and tapped a reserve of peasant anger, which deepened when the worldwide depression undermined the profitability of Filipino agricultural exports.[17]

Some U.S. and Filipino officials searched for New Deal remedies to alleviate the agrarian unrest under a well-publicized Social Justice Program, but their attempts to redistribute land failed to alter the existing social structure or property relations, though greater freedoms in collective bargaining and peasant organizing were achieved.[18] Others, however, sought a military solution. Their calls for a native Filipino army were reinforced by the growing external threat of rising Japanese militarism. In his inaugural address, Quezon stressed the urgent need to formulate an adequate defense plan for the Philippines during the ten years prior to independence. Quezon then requested the services of General Douglas MacArthur, head of the army's Philippine department since 1928, to help create a Philippine military.[19]

MacArthur sailed for Manila in the autumn of 1935, just as the Commonwealth regime was being launched with Quezon installed as the new nation's first president. MacArthur then set to work devising a military strategy for the Philippines from his plush headquarters on the top floor of the Manila Hotel. Like his father, MacArthur enjoyed the trappings of power. Working with assistant Dwight Eisenhower, MacArthur used Swiss military policy, its army of citizen-soldiers, as a model for the Philippines. Under such a scheme, the Philippines would be divided into ten military districts, each responsible for recruiting 4,000 men annually. After six months of training, these recruits would then return to civilian life. At the end of ten years, the plan envisioned a trained reserve force of 400,000. A small regular army of fulltime officers and enlisted men would provide the leadership for the reserves, with a coast guard and an air force complementing the army. Budgetary constraints, however, impeded MacArthur's plans, so he adjusted the budget down to just 16 million pesos annually, though Eisenhower projected costs of 50 million pesos annually. MacArthur prevailed and, despite misgivings, Eisenhower complied. Quezon subsequently resisted MacArthur's proposal to shift resources to the army from the Philippine Constabulary, which was still needed for internal defense, and he undercut plans for a costly military build-up. Though the Constabulary was temporarily disbanded in 1936 as part of the reorganization, it was reactivated in 1938.[20] When the Philippine assembly concurred with Quezon, control of the pace of build-up passed to Quezon, further increasing the Philippine president's hold on power while MacArthur's plans became even less tenable.[21]

Meanwhile, a joint Army–Navy board of U.S. military strategists revisited the Orange Plan in 1935, under a Roosevelt directive to reconsider American strategy in the Pacific. Constrained by tight budgets and concerned that the Philippines were too distant and too exposed for anything short of an all-out defense, the United States chose to focus on a Pacific perimeter that ran from Alaska through Hawaii to Panama, while leaving the Philippines essentially open, with just 10,000 U.S. forces assisted by Filipino forces. The revised 1936 version of the Orange Plan did not envision holding even the region of Manila Bay, and called only for a concentration of defense on Corregidor island at the bay's entrance in order to deprive the Japanese access to the harbor. The plan also required an American relief mission to fight its way through to the Philippines, which could take two to three years, with no provision for reinforcements. U.S. and Filipino troops would simply have to fight as long as they could, then surrender or be killed. In short, the Philippines had been declared expendable. Now called the "mosquito fleet," MacArthur's forces could not hope to defend against a Japanese invasion.[22] Moreover, Japanese fisherman, easily convertible to sailors, knew Philippine waters almost as well as native Filipinos did, contrary to MacArthur's claims regarding the strategic advantages afforded by the archipelago's complex coastal geography.[23]

By 1937, Japan had launched a full-scale war against China, pressing south from Manchuria.[24] When the United States chose not to "quarantine" Japan, as Britain and France had hoped, Quezon, in 1938, traveled to Japan where he allegedly sought an alliance with Japan in order to avoid conflict. When the Japanese reportedly rebuffed him, he sought immediate independence from the United States in order to claim neutrality.[25] The United States denied Quezon this, and only then did Quezon pledge support of the United States should war with Japan break out. By the summer of 1941, just as legislative elections were being held in the Philippines, the Japanese advanced in Southeast Asia, edging ever closer to the archipelago. Thus, as the 1930s drew to a close, yet another international player had entered the Philippine drama.[26]

After Pearl Harbor:
The Outbreak of War in the Philippines

On December 8, 1941, just minutes after attacking Pearl Harbor, Japan struck in the Philippines, eliminating the U.S. air fleet at Clark Air Force Base and later seriously damaging the much smaller naval yard at Subic Bay. In the years since 1904 when the bases were first installed, Clark had, in fact, become the United States' largest air armada anywhere overseas, with 36 P-40 fighters and 17 B-17 bombers. All but four of the P-40s and three of the B-17's were destroyed in the attack.[27]

The United States was now at war with Japan, and the Philippines had become central to the contest, as the Philippine army MacArthur had helped organize was now made part of the U.S. forces.[28] MacArthur pleaded for an Asia-First strategy, despite the Orange Plan, but the only convoy of troops and supplies that was sent to him was diverted to Australia when U.S. Navy commanders refused to run Japan's blockade of the archipelago. MacArthur then turned to a press strategy, as Otis had done earlier, using reporters from Associated Press and the *New York Times* to declare Japanese defeat in nonexistent battles. On December 22, however, roughly 43,000 Japanese troops landed in Lingayen Gulf in Northwest Luzon and dramatically belied MacArthur's claims. Passing through one U.S. defensive position after another, the Japanese moved steadily toward Manila. Only heavy rains and United States destruction of bridges allowed American and Filipino troops enough time to stage a difficult, even brilliant, retreat to Bataan by mid-

January 1942, while MacArthur established his base on nearby Corregidor Island. Quezon again requested independence so that he could declare neutrality and prevent what was fast becoming a brutal war. Again, the United States refused him. By March 11, MacArthur left to wage a campaign against Japan in Australia, vowing to Filipinos via American reporters in a speech crafted in part by Philippine propagandist Carlos Romulo: "I shall return."[29]

Left on their own, without adequate troops or supplies and with none likely to come due to Japanese blockades, the Americans and Filipinos defended Bataan against continual onslaughts from the Japanese, who were similarly weakened and awaiting new troops and supplies. When these came, the Japanese staged one of their most effective campaigns in the Philippines on April 3, 1942, Good Friday. Indeed, the war would prove a crucifixion of sorts. By April 9, despite orders from MacArthur to continue fighting, the Americans in Bataan surrendered. Never before had so large a U.S. military force capitulated. The Japanese then pressed on towards Corregidor, bringing with them 75,000 American and Filipino prisoners of war. In what was to become known as the Bataan Death March, roughly 10,000 died from disease, malnutrition, and brutality. Of the survivors, an additional 2,000 Americans and 25,000 Filipinos were to die within three months of arrival at the inadequate internment center.[30]

Elsewhere, Filipinos left without external assistance against the Japanese reverted to traditional tactics. Although legislative elections had been held earlier in 1941, the body had not yet met when the Japanese invasion set the Philippines on a new course. The Japanese declared martial law on January 3, 1942, one day after their invasion of Manila, and then dissolved all political parties, rallying Nacionalista Party leaders to publicly support this action and announce that their party had ceased to exist. After conferring with prominent Filipinos, including several from the now defunct Nacionalista Party, the Japanese designated Jose Laurel President of a pro-Japanese provisional regime run by Filipinos. At the same time, Nacionalista campaign manager Benigno Aquino was named director-general of a newly formed pro-Japanese consortium of organizations, to replace political parties, called the Kalibapi.[31] Even Aguinaldo, still clad in his black bow tie, allied with the Japanese, persuaded by their call for Asian nationalism. On the military front, Japanese collaborators included many in the U.S.-trained Philippine military, who, like the Spanish-trained Macabebes before them, quickly changed sides when one colonial power gave way to another. In addition, the Japanese had cultivated Sakdalista leader Benigno Ramos, who established in 1939 a militant pro-Japanese organization, composed largely of former Sakdalistas. Called the Ganaps, the group was later reorganized into the Kalibapi during the war and was to form a critical base of collaboration with the Japanese.[32] Many from the economic elite, particularly those with Spanish heritage, also defected to the Japanese, surviving the loss of

U.S. markets by capitalizing on Japan's war-time shortages and much needed trade.[33]

In yet another transnational twist, the Philippines had also developed a full-blown fascist movement in the Manila Falange, which had emerged during the Spanish Civil War and had an estimated membership of about 10,000 by 1940. Comprised primarily of Spanish and Spanish mestizo families, the Manila Falange recalled an earlier era of colonialism under Spain and had ties to Franco. The Manila Falange was most effective in its covert activities, infiltrating the Civilian Emergency Administration (CEA), which had been formed to defend against the Japanese. Working under cover, the Falange operated as an Axis fifth column within the CEA to disrupt its operations and spread demoralizing rumors, particularly after the first Japanese air raids over Manila. So effective, in fact, was the Manila Falange, that the Japanese government awarded it on January 5, 1942, in Granada, Spain for its "invaluable" assistance in the capture of Manila. Though the Falange was not active during the Japanese occupation, they enjoyed the protection and privileges accorded Axis allies, and they thrived economically through continued access to international trade. Far from being punished for their war-time activities, many families who joined the Falange—the Sorianos, Ayalas, Zobels, and Elizaldes, to name a few—continue today to rank among the wealthiest families in the Philippines.[34]

Other Filipinos, however, worked closely with the United States, maintaining a shadow commonwealth regime during the war, with Quezon still President.[35] Even some of the former Falangists split their families' allegiance between Japan and the United States to serve in Quezon's government-in-exile, forming close personal and business relations with MacArthur in the process. Still other Filipinos waged effective guerrilla campaigns against the Japanese, including loyal U.S.-trained troops, Chinese in Manila with support from Chinese nationals,[36] as well as revolutionaries. The most potent revolutionary anti-Japanese guerrilla force, however, was the Hukbong Bayan Laban sa Hapon or "National Army Against Japan," which came to be known simply as the Huks.[37] Composed largely of poor sharecroppers and landless farm workers from central Luzon, the Huks built upon the earlier Katipunan, Colorum and Sakdalista revolutionary movements as well as labor and peasant unions, all of the same region. Except for the military commander, a socialist with peasant roots named Luis Taruc,[38] however, the Huk leaders were mainly urban intellectuals with links to the PKP.

In fact, the PKP played a central role in the 1942 formation of the Huks. Heavily influenced by Soviet communism but receiving little financial or political support from the Soviet Union, the PKP actually had stronger ties with the CPUSA, which provided research, directives and even leaders to the PKP. Shortly after forming in 1930, the PKP went underground but remained active until it resurfaced in 1938 when Quezon pardoned its leaders. As it resurfaced, the PKP, under the global direction of the Soviet Union, announced that Japanese aggression was the foremost threat to the Philippines, and stressed the need for an alliance with "democratic and progressive forces in the United States" The PKP declared itself ready to cooperate with all political groups regardless of differences in order to present a unified front against the Japanese. In March 1942, the PKP and Socialist Party of the Philippines established the Huks.

In Central Luzon, the primary area of Huk activity, all U.S.-linked guerrillas were against the Huks, largely because of long-standing enmity between the U.S.-trained Philippine forces, with their ties to the landed elite, and the communist-led, militant peasants. Prior to war, the Philippine forces had frequently been called upon to help put down protest actions of peasants against landlords. When these peasants joined the Huks during the war, armed clashes, kidnappings and executions between the Huks and other guerrillas were common. After the outbreak of war, the Huks sought U.S. support, sending emissaries to MacArthur while he was still in Bataan. Though they failed to meet with MacArthur, they did meet with Major Claude Thorpe, the man in charge of organizing guerrilla activities. When the Americans wanted to integrate the Huks into their political and military program, however, the Huks demurred. They were willing to follow the Americans on military matters, but they wanted to maintain their own political course. When the Americans then decided not to give material assistance to the Huks, the Huks offered to help establish a unified guerrilla command. The reactions of other guerrilla groups, however, ranged from hostile to indifferent. Nevertheless, the Huks fought for the United States in the drive to liberate Luzon, free American prisoners of war, and, they hoped, eventually carve out a role for themselves in a post-war Philippines.

At the same time, the Huks launched a broad-based revolutionary campaign in the countryside of Central Luzon, laying the foundation for postwar peasant revolutionary activity, to be described in the next chapter. In particular, they distributed pamphlets edited by academics, trade unionists and others, with the leading publication, the *Katubusan ng Bayan*, or Redemption of the People, launched in 1942. They also held meetings to discuss pressing issues like land tenure and landlord–peasant relations. In addition, they established Barrio United Defense Corps (BUDC) in rural areas to help peasants protect themselves from the Japanese as well as from the many bandits who preyed on villages in the breakdown of law and order. Each BUDC was governed by a people's council elected by all residents over eighteen years of age. A chairman, vice-chairman, secretary-treasurer, and chief of police worked with directors of various areas such as communications and transportation. The council then collected food, supplies, money as well as intelligence, while serving as a governing body for territories controlled by the Huks. The Huks also established peasant–landlord committees to mediate conflicts and distribute harvests. Moreover, trial by jury was introduced, as peasants in Huk-controlled areas came to experience first-hand the kind of self-government and democracy which U.S. governors and Philippine officials had up to then only promised.[39] With their platform of independence, land reform, and mass-based political participation, Huk ranks swelled. By 1944, the Huks controlled large areas of the country, with 70,000 guerrillas active in four provinces.[40]

Like Aguinaldo's troops in the Spanish–American War, however, the Huks' ambitions would be thwarted. Though some strategists had argued that U.S. troops should bypass the Philippines and head straight to Formosa enroute to Japan, MacArthur had fought hard in the U.S. debates, and in private discussions with Roosevelt, for a return to the Philippines, largely to uphold the promise he had made to the Filipino people after Bataan. Under pressure from MacArthur, Roosevelt relented. On October 20, 1944, MacArthur did indeed return to the Philippines, this time to the island of Leyte. With him was Osmena, newly ap-pointed commonwealth president after Quezon's recent death from natural causes. Thus opened the U.S. campaign to recapture the Philippines. By the end of December, American forces secured Leyte and began preparing to move toward Manila. The battle for Manila opened on February 4, 1945, the same day that U.S. soldier Willie Grayson had first exchanged shots with Filipinos half a century before. Two weeks later, Manila was recaptured for the allies, and, on February 27, MacArthur turned over Malacanang Palace to President Osmena. Though the battle lasted just two weeks, it left the city all but destroyed. About 1,000 Americans and 16,000 Japanese died; but roughly 100,000 Filipinos, nearly all noncombatants, died as well. Cornered, the Japanese committed atrocities matched only by their pillage of Nanking in 1937, as Japanese fires and U.S. artillery barrages conspired to leave Manila smoldering. By the end of the siege, water, sewage, electrical, infrastructural, medical and other systems were destroyed.[41]

The Huks had been preparing for the U.S. return by setting up the provisional governments in the countryside and attempting to form an underground government in alliance with other guerrilla units. Throughout the war, the Huks had remained loyal to the commonwealth government, and expected a role in a postwar administration, with the centerpiece of their platform being reforms in land tenure and labor relations.[42] Then the shock came. Far from rewarding the Huks, the American forces ordered them disarmed and then arrested several leaders, including Taruc, in late February 1945. Mass protests and more arrests followed. The Huks, now unarmed, faced retribution at the hands of powerful warlords, many of whom had fled the countryside during the war and now began to return, much to the resentment of the peasant population who had stood alone during the war to defend the country against the Japanese. Additional Huk enemies included U.S.-backed guerrilla groups[43] and others who viewed the Huk movement as a threat to vested interests.[44] In May 1945, Senator Tydings of Maryland went to the Philippines to study the problem. Upon his return to the United States just days later, Tydings proposed to Congress a nonmilitary solution involving grants to cover war damages as well as a trade act to help revive the economy.[45]

At the same time, Huk leaders displayed an openness to nonmilitary tactics, opting to participate in the political process, while recognizing Osmena as the legitimate President of the Commonwealth. In July 1945, Communists, Socialists, peasant unions and other leftist groups joined together to form the Democratic Alliance, in preparation for legislative elections scheduled for 1946. With the country in ruin, the economy shattered, and vested interests returning to the countryside, the Huk numbers continued to grow. Though the Huks openly stated that they opposed civil war, increasing repression by the returning warlords too often forced military conflict. Still, the Huks fought for a legitimate role in the campaign for legislative seats. Meanwhile, the Philippine armed forces relayed concerns to the U.S. Army that they feared repercussions following the withdrawal of U.S. forces.[46] Later in September, however, U.S. Representative Jasper Bell, a conservative Missouri Democrat and head of the House Committee on Insular Affairs which oversaw U.S. policy toward the Philippines, introduced a companion to Tydings' plan designed to ease the prospective burden on U.S. taxpayers of rebuilding the archipelago. Bell's proposal sought to encourage private U.S. investment by granting American corporations special privileges in the Philippines. After much haggling in Washington, the Bell Trade Act, as it would eventually come to be known, was to peg the peso to the dollar in order to protect against currency fluctuations while permitting free conversion of dollars to pesos and vice versa. As in the earlier "free trade" agreement at the turn of the century, U.S. exporters were also to be granted a monopoly in the Philippines while Filipinos would receive unrestricted access to U.S. markets.

Now, however, Americans were offered "parity" rights to own mines, forests and other resources, without the same privilege granted Filipinos in the United States. This clause in the Bell Trade Act violated the Philippine constitution of 1935, which reserved majority share holdings to Filipinos and called for a nationwide referendum after ratification by the Philippine legislature on any such revisions. Because the Bell Trade Act was seen to favor Philippine agricultural products in U.S. markets, U.S. competitors, mainly from sugar- and dairy-producing states, opposed it, while consumers and prospective investors, mainly from industrial states, approved the concessions to American business. Other opponents included State Department officials who were then pressing Britain to open its former colonies to U.S. trade. To insure the success of the bill, a House committee tied it as an amendment to a relief bill proposed by Tydings. After seven months of wrangling, the bill became law in the United States in April 1946, though it still needed to pass in the Philippines, where presidential and legislative elections now focused on the question. While the leading parties in the Philippines supported the Bell Trade Act, the Huks, still hoping to participate in the electoral process, came out against the Act. Moreover, they came out against plans for a continued U.S. military presence in the Philippines. Given the continued strength of the Huks, these stands were apparently popular among their constituents; yet they fed anti-Huk pressures among U.S. and Filipino officials, due in part to local interests but also in part to emerging international ones.

Yalta and Beyond:
The Seeds of Cold War and the Impact
on the Philippines

As Filipinos managed the delicate transition from war to peace, the seeds of a new war were being planted at the small seaport town of Yalta on the Crimean Sea. There, Roosevelt, Churchill and Stalin met in February 1945 to negotiate terms of governance for occupied territories in the postwar period. Among other settlements, the so-called "Big Three" came to an agreement on the question of East Asia, though this was kept secret because the Soviets were still officially neutral in the Pacific war. Under the agreement, Stalin promised to enter the war against Japan within three months of the end of war in Europe. He also promised to recognize Chiang Kai-shek as the head of the Chinese government and to press Mao to join a coalition with the Nationalists. In return, Roosevelt promised to see that the Soviet Union would regain territories, including the southern Sakhalin Island and the Kuriles, lost in the Russo–Japanese War of 1904–1905.[47]

Despite the Yalta agreements, subsequent negotiations stalled due to various disputes over political reorganization in Poland and Romania. When Allied commanders met with representatives of the German commander in Italy to negotiate a German surrender and refused Stalin's request for a Russian observer, Stalin feared a separate peace was being made. Roosevelt, increasingly disturbed by Stalin's actions in Poland and Romania, continued nevertheless to hope for a negotiated settlement to minimize postwar conflicts with the Soviets. It is possible, as some historians have argued, that Roosevelt might have been able to reassure Stalin, to finesse Stalin's tendency to mix heavy-handed oppression with surprising moments of concession, and, perhaps ultimately, to have prevented the Cold War. However, Roosevelt died of a massive cerebral hemorrhage on April 12, 1945, in the last days of the war in Europe. Now, the burden of negotiating the peace fell to his successor, Harry S. Truman, whose motto, "The buck stops here," proved particularly apt. Because Roosevelt had long skirted the State Department, relying instead on his own counsel or that of his military advisors, Truman did not know that Roosevelt had all but ceded to the Soviets control of Eastern Europe. Nor did he yet know that the United States was close to exploding the world's first atomic bomb.[48]

As a follow-up to Yalta, Truman, Stalin and Churchill met in Potsdam to finalize the negotiations. In the midst of the conference, news of the first successful test explosion of an atomic bomb near Alamagordo, New Mexico, reached Truman, who felt that the bomb could serve as a useful bargaining tool. Instead, tensions rose and Potsdam ended with many unresolved questions as well as much mutual suspicion between the United States and the Soviet Union. Having made little progress, Truman returned to the United States to make his historic decision on the question of the atomic bomb and the war in Japan. On August 6, 1945, Hiroshima experienced the world's first war-time nuclear blast. Three days later, another blast hit Nagasaki. The face of warfare had officially entered a new era. Meanwhile, the Soviet Union launched an attack on the Japanese in Manchuria. A week later, Emperor Hirohito ordered his troops to surrender, and, on September 2, 1945, aboard the U.S. battleship *Missouri* at anchor in Tokyo Bay, General Douglas MacArthur presided over the formal surrender.

As the war in the Pacific came to an end, a debate erupted among U.S. policy makers over the continued secrecy surrounding the bomb, particularly with respect to the Soviet Union. Though Stalin had upheld his Yalta promise on China and signed a treaty with Chiang Kai-shek pledging him exclusive military aid, the competing expansionist aims of the United States and the Soviet Union in the postwar period continued to sound alarms. While Secretary of War Henry Stimson had argued at Potsdam that a U.S. monopoly on the bomb would make the Soviets more compliant, he now grew concerned that it might intensify long-standing conflicts between the United States and the Soviets. Moreover, U.S. scientists estimated that the Soviets would likely have the bomb in one to five years, affording little long-term advantage to a U.S. monopoly. Stimson urged Truman to share the technology with the Soviets for peaceful uses in order to build a postwar alliance, but Truman's new secretary of state, James F. Byrnes, rejected the scientific estimates regarding Soviet nuclear capability, estimating instead that it would take them fifteen to twenty years to build a bomb. Several members of the new Joint Commission on Atomic Energy concurred, as did U.S. public opinion, and Truman opted for continued secrecy. And the Cold War grew colder.[49]

In the Philippines, the period surrounding the end of the war met with much celebration. Still, the fighting had ravaged the countryside, the infrastructure, the populace, and the economy. Moreover, the continued conflict between Huks demanding a voice in postwar politics and officials seeking to repress them, now threatened to explode into civil war. Partly because of the postwar economic crisis and its impact on the peasantry but also because of long-standing peasant opposition to the landed elites and their American allies, the Huk ranks continued to swell in the months immediately following the war. Meanwhile, in the broader context of United States–Soviet relations, the United States was becoming increasingly alarmed about the possibility of a communist revolution in the Philippines and its implications for U.S. strategic interests in the emerging Cold War. In response, the United States supported the Philippine war against the Huks. In one incident, a rival guerrilla group, with the consent of U.S. officers, rounded up 100 Huks, had them dig their own graves, and then killed all of them. The United States then named the rival guerrilla group's leader mayor of the nearby town of Malolos, ironically the site of the republic Aguinaldo had established nearly half a century earlier. The Huks waged battle through political processes under the aegis of the Democratic Alliance, which now encompassed a diverse array of organizations running the gamut from liberal to revolutionary. If denied that avenue for reforms and for a role in national politics, the Huks were also prepared for civil war.[50]

Moreover, the U.S. military under the command of MacArthur, together with his associates in the Philippines, including many former Japanese collaborators as well as former Falangists, now gained control of Philippine politics during the period immediately preceding and following the conclusion of the war. Heir to his father's rivalry with Taft decades before, Douglas MacArthur revived the long-standing competition between U.S. military and political colonialists. Like his father, Douglas MacArthur believed military tactics were the most effective means of suppressing domestic Philippine opposition. Also like his father, he believed civilians had no place in a theater of war, and he threatened to send home any civilian high commissioner appointed by Washington to Manila. Roosevelt had acquiesced, allowing MacArthur considerable freedom to shape Philippine political and military institutions. MacArthur saw himself as the man in charge of the country, while Osmena was to help establish provincial governments. Moreover, MacArthur regarded any efforts toward civilian control by the U.S. Department of Interior as dangerously meddlesome. After April 1945, the relatively inexperienced Truman was compelled to rely on MacArthur, who now battled for control of Philippine politics with Secretary of Interior Harold Ickes, a New Deal Democrat and long-time nemesis of the arch-conservative MacArthur. Despite numerous clashes over the future course of U.S.–Philippine relations, particularly with Ickes, MacArthur prevailed. In a moment of candor, MacArthur told Professor Joseph Ralston Hayden, Civil Advisor and Consultant on Philippine Affairs, that he "intended to retain full authority and responsibility" over the commonwealth government.[51]

Raising the Flag:
The Philippines Gains Independence

In fact, MacArthur left his imprint not only on Philippine internal military policy, notably towards the Huks, but also on electoral politics. In particular, MacArthur had been a close personal friend of the flamboyant Quezon and he was now close to Quezon's long-time protege, the tense, workaholic Manuel Roxas. MacArthur did not get on well, however, with Osmena, whose serious, plodding style and physical frailty contrasted sharply with MacArthur's persona. Following the Leyte landing in October 1944, MacArthur had delayed the distribution of food, clothing, and other supplies to the destitute population, who blamed Osmena. MacArthur then administered relief in his own name in order to gain the credit for himself while eclipsing Osmena. MacArthur also forced Osmena to give Filipino army veterans the bad news that the United States would pay only eight pesos per month in back pay rather than the anticipated fifty. By the spring of 1945, Osmena traveled to Washington to register his complaints with Roosevelt. Though the two did meet, Roosevelt died soon after and Truman proved a less sympathetic ear.

At the same time that he eclipsed Osmena, MacArthur promoted his friend Roxas, swiftly exonerating him in April 1945 of all charges of assisting the Japanese, leaving a cloud of uncertainty surrounding Roxas' war-time record. In June of that year, at MacArthur's urging, Osmena summoned to Manila the commonwealth legislative body, which had been elected in 1941 but had never met because of the war. Though many of these elected officials had participated in Laurel's pro-Japanese regime, Osmena hoped to incorporate the old oligarchy into the postwar regime. In opting for such an unpopular course, Osmena spelled his own political doom. As MacArthur had hoped, Roxas was selected President of the Philippine senate[52] and chairman of the powerful appointments committee. Roxas then maneuvered to dismiss two members of Osmena's cabinet who had criticized his war-time role. In August of the same year, MacArthur freed 5,000 Japanese collaborators, despite his earlier promise to "run to earth every disloyal Filipino." As it turned out, many from the landed, business and political elite had been Japanese collaborators, in contrast to the peasant-based Huks. To purge the polity of Japanese collaborators would leave a political and economic chasm apparently too vast to bridge. Instead of trying Filipinos, MacArthur chose to prosecute as war criminals the Japanese officers who had served in the Philippines. Among these was Tomoyuki Yamashita, who was sentenced to hang in September 1945, just as the Japanese were surrendering.

That same month, Paul McNutt arrived in the Philippines as the new high commissioner. A Democrat and former governor of Indiana, McNutt had been appointed high commissioner to the Philippines ten years earlier by Roosevelt despite MacArthur's best efforts to have himself named to the post. His return now reignited yet again the MacArthur family feud with civilian authority in the Philippines. McNutt expressed concern that "enemy collaborators" dominated the legislature and he urged Truman to delay independence until the issue could be investigated. Deputy Attorney General Walter Hutchinson was appointed to study this, and concluded that since nearly all of the collaborators had been known to U.S. intelligence officers, the problem should have been averted. He predicted that Roxas, if elected president in the elections scheduled for April 1946, would declare an amnesty, and that, to avoid this outcome, the United States should press for war crimes trials presided over by Filipino judges with U.S. aid. McNutt also raised concerns about the possibility of venality in Philippine elections, to which MacArthur replied that "the Filipinos will hold as honest an election as you ever had in the state of Indiana."[53]

Instead, America's new drive to "contain" communism together with the momentum building behind Roxas, displaced the earlier pledges to punish war criminals. Roxas had a newspaper empire and, as the campaign for the presidency accelerated, he used this to publicize his links to MacArthur and his anti-Huk stance, while promoting his newly formed Liberal Party. Meanwhile, Osmena miscalculated, opting not to campaign but to rely instead on local political bosses for support. He also refused to disavow the Huks, thereby alienating the United States. Still, Roxas scored only a narrow victory against Osmena's Nacionalista Party, winning just 54 percent of the nearly three million votes cast. The Liberal Party also took over the legislature. Significant too, however, were the eleven legislative seats won by opponents of the Bell Trade Act, including all six of the Huks who ran for office. Though the Act had passed in the United States in April 1946, as described above, it still needed approval in the Philippines. Immediately following the elections, Roxas denied seats to the eleven opponents of the Act, including all of the Huk representatives. Roxas cited electoral fraud, which, even if true, would likely have disqualified many more than just the eleven. As replacements, Roxas seated his own supporters, though many were under indictment for collaborating with the Japanese.

In the countryside, the expulsion of the Huks was seen by local authorities as a signal to subdue them without mercy. Huks and their supporters were arrested or killed in droves. The Huks now returned to the "boondocks," renaming themselves the "Hukbong Magpagpalaya ng Bayan" or roughly the "People's Liberation Army." In August 1946, the Huks would move from the political to the military front, waging full-scale civil war in central Luzon by 1948, as will be discussed in the next chapter.

Even with the expulsion of the Bell Trade Act's most outspoken opponents, however, Roxas feared that the measure might not pass in the Philippine legislature.

Truman wanted to delay voting on the measure until after Philippine independence, set for July 4, in order to avoid charges that the United States was extorting favorable trade agreements as a condition of independence. Nevertheless, Roxas opted for a pre-independence vote. This way he could claim that only a senate majority was needed, not the two thirds needed should the Act be seen as a treaty between two sovereign nations. Roxas then drove his legislature into an all-night marathon to debate the issue, and, on July 2, 1946, the measure was approved. Two days later, despite World War II, the Japanese occupation, and the onset of the Cold War, the United States held true to the promises of the Tydings–McDuffie Act, granting the Philippines independence.

On July 4, 1946, after decades of debate, the United States relinquished its colony. Crowds of Filipinos convened at Luneta Park, near a statue of Rizal and the bombed-out remnants of Manila. McNutt lowered the American flag. Roxas then raised the Philippine flag—one red stripe, one blue, and a golden sun with eight rays representing the eight provinces that had first risen up against Spain. As the Philippine national anthem played, a warship fired a twenty-one gun salute and church bells pealed throughout the city. MacArthur, who had flown in from his new posting in Japan to participate in the celebrations, claimed, "America buried imperialism here today."[54] Such claims to the contrary, the festivities were to mark but a new era of U.S.–Philippine interdependence. As described in chapter four, the transition to independent democracy in 1946 was compromised from the moment of its inception by the growing Huk uprising and its Cold War context. Indeed, the nascent Philippine state would be contested not only from within but also from abroad, once again finding itself in the middle of a superpower confrontation, this time between the United States and the Soviet Union.

Notes

1. Brands, *Bound to Empire*, 84.

2. The above information on the debates surrounding the evolution of the Orange Plan, as well the various factors affecting U.S. relations with Japan is from Brands, *Bound to Empire*, 116-18. See also Combs, *History of American Foreign Policy*, 194-223, for a concise description of the effects of the Zimmerman telegram and the Lusitania on Wilson's decision to enter World War I.

3. The information below on Colorums is from Constantino, *A Past Revisited*, 355-361, 139-141.

4. Ibid.

5. Roger Daniels, *Racism in California* (1972), 15.

6. Brands, *Bound to Empire*, 150.

7. Charles P. Kindleberger, *The World in Depression, 1929–1939*, 83-107.

8. For an interesting personal account of the immigrant experience of a Filipino farmworker, see Carlos Bulosan, *America is in the Heart (1945)*.

9. Cletus Daniels, *Bitter Harvest* (1981), 117.

10. The above information on Filipino labor organizing and relations with Mexican farmworkers, growers, and others in California is culled from the works of Emory S. Bogardus, "American Attitudes Towards Filipinos," and "Filipino Labor in Central California"; Cletus Daniels, *Bitter Harvest*; Roger Daniels, *Racism in California*; and Carey McWilliams, *Factories in the Field: The Story of Migratory Farm Labor in California*, *Brothers Under the Skin*, and *Race Discrimination and the Law*.

11. See in particular Bogardus' "American Attitudes Towards Filipinos" and Roger Daniels, *Racism in California*.

12. For an excellent discussion of the CPUSA's role in the Philippines, see Charles B. McLane, *Soviet Strategies in Southeast Asia: An Exploration of Eastern Policy under Lenin and Stalin*.

13. Combs, *The History of American Foreign Policy*, 260.

14. Information on the U.S. debates on Philippine policy during the period of transition to Roosevelt and the processes leading to the Hare–Hawes–Cutting Act is culled from Combs, *The History of American Foreign Policy*, 260-293; Karnow, *In Our Image: America's Empire in the Philippines* (1989), 253-56; and Brands, *Bound to Empire*, 119-157.

15. The information on the processes behind the new bill is from Karnow, *In Our Image*, 330.

16. Brands, *Bound to Empire*, 163, from a memo of Roosevelt meeting with House leaders, 5/1/34, in Morgenthau diary, Henry Morgenthau papers, Roosevelt library.

17. Information on the Sakdalista organization and uprising is from Constantino (1975), 373-380, and Karnow, *In Our Image*, 273-74.

18. Constantino, *A Past Revisited*, 383.

19. The information on MacArthur's relations with Quezon is from Brands, *Bound to Empire*, 166, and Karnow, *In Our Image*, 258-276.

20. U.S. Department of the Army, "Intelligence Research Report: The Philippine Constabulary," (December 15, 1952), Project No. 7557, 1.

21. From Fact-Finding Commission, *The Final Report of the Fact-Finding Commission*, (October 1990), 27-29. And from Brands, *Bound to Empire*, 163-68.

22. The information on the Orange Plan and the politics surrounding it is culled from Brands, *Bound to Empire*, 174-178 and Karnow, *In Our Image*, 264-283.

23. During this author's field research for another project in a rural fishing village in Bicol Province in 1986, one fisherman recounted his memories of Japanese fishermen serving as military scouts for Japan, hiding in coves, and leading forays into coastal villages during World War II.

24. Interestingly, the Japanese, like the Spanish and Americans before them, used domestic conflict in the Philippines to their own ends when they supported the Sakdalista leader, Benigno Ramos, who later collaborated with the Japanese during World War II.

25. See Constantino, *A Past Revisited*, 24.

26. For an excellent account of the Japanese role in the Philippines prior to and during the war, see Theodore Friend, *Between Two Empires: The Ordeal of the Philippines, 1929–1946*. In particular, Japan had direct as well as broader strategic interests in the Philippines by 1941. The number of resident Japanese in the Philippines had expanded substantially from a few hundred in 1905, when Japanese laborers were brought in by the United States to help build roads, to over 16,000 by the early 1930s, reaching 30,000 by the end of the decade. Japanese investments, totaling $32 million by the late 1930s were only a fraction of Chinese but they dominated in abaca, a fibrous plant used for commercial purposes particularly in textiles. In addition, the Japanese nearly controlled resource-rich Davao Province. Luzon fishing, timber and merchandising were also strong and growing Japanese enterprises.

27. Karnow, *In Our Image*, 288.

28. Ibon Facts and Figures, #176, 1985. Also U.S. Department of the Army, General Staff, "Intelligence Research Report," 1.

29. Information for this paragraph was culled from Brands, *Bound to Empire*, 185-104, and, in particular, Friend, *Between Two Empires*.

30. The figures are from Karnow, *In Our Image*, 302-305.

31. Information on collaboration with the Japanese during the war is from Constantino and Letizia, *The Continuing Past*, particularly 52-83; Brands, *Bound to Empire*, 198-204; and Friend, *Between Two Empires*.

32. For information on the role of the Sakdalistas in the Japanese campaign, see Constantino and Letizia, *The Continuing Past*, 10-11.

33. For a detailed discussion of the Japanese role in the Philippines during World War II, see Friend, *Between Two Empires*. For a description of the patterns of both collaboration and resistance, see Constantino and Letizia, *The Continuing Past*.

34. Information on the role of Spanish and Spanish *mestizo* Filipinos in the Manila Falange, is from Constantino and Letizia, *The Continuing Past*, 9-10.

35. See Constantino and Letizia, *The Continuing Past*, 27-83, for a detailed account of the various forms of political and armed resistance by Filipinos to Japanese rule during the war.

36. Constantino and Letizia, *The Continuing Past*, 146.

37. See Benedict Kerkvliet, *The Huk Rebellion: A Study of Peasant Revolt in the Philippines* (1977), and Eduardo Lachica, *Huk: Philippine Agrarian Society*; for detailed descriptions of the Huks.

38 For an in-depth account of Luis Taruc's experiences, see his autobiographical *Born of the People* (c1953).

39. The above is culled from Kerkvliet, *The Huk Rebellion*; Lachica, *Huk: Philippine Agrarian Society*; and Constantino and Letizia, *The Continuing Past*, 138-39, 142-47.

40. See McLane, *Soviet Strategies in Southeast Asia*, for a detailed account of the CPUSA's role in the PKP and Huk movement of the Philippines. See also Kerkvliet and Lachica, *Huk Rebellion* (1971), as well as Constantino and Letizia (1978), on the Huks.

41. Brands, *Bound to Empire*, 205- 209.

42. Constantino and Letizia, *The Continuing Past*, 155.

43. Except for the Huks, all guerrilla groups were adjuncts of the U.S. armed forces, as cited in Constantino and Letizia, *The Continuing Past*, 153.

44. The above information on the Huks is from Lachica, *Huk: The Philippine Agrarian Society*, 103-117.

45. Karnow, *In Our Image*, 333.

46. Secret Intelligence Report No. 109-1357, from the United States Army Pacific Command's Military Intelligence Section, December 22, 1945, from the National Security Archive collection. The report cites arsenals in Moro regions of the South, Huk activity in Luzon, as well as ethnic conflict between Filipinos and the Chinese minority.

47. Information from this paragraph is from Combs, *History of American Foreign Policy*, 305-315, and from John Lewis Gaddis, *The United States and the Origins of the Cold War, 1941–1947* (1972).

48. Combs, *History of American Foreign Policy, 305-315*.

49. Combs, *History of American Foreign Policy,* 320-24 and Gaddis, *Origins of the Cold War*.

50. See Constantino, *A Past Revisited*; and Constantino and Letizia, *The Continuing Past*; Lachica, *Huk: Philippine Agrarian Society*; and Kerkvliet, *Huk Rebellion*.

51. Constantino and Letizia, *Continuing Past*, 157.

52. A 1940 amendment altered the Philippine political structure from a unicameral to a bicameral one. From Brands, *Bound to Empire*, 230.

53. Karnow, *In Our Image*, 329.

54. Karnow, *In Our Image*, 324.

Chapter 4

The Transition to
"One-Man Democracy," 1946–1972

his chapter traces the rise of the U.S.–Philippine military alliance from the moment of Philippine independence in 1946 through the 1972 transition under Marcos to authoritarian rule. As the chapter will show, although the impetus for martial law would come from Marcos, the military capacity for, and political survival of, the 1972 transition would grow out of global Cold War politics and the rise in power of a transnational U.S.–Philippine military alliance after 1946. Throughout the period, this alliance would seek to contain global, including domestic Philippine, communism through military repression. In the process, the alliance would greatly intensify the military interdependencies of Philippine domestic and U.S. international security, setting the stage for the 1972 transition to what some observers would call Marcos' "One-Man Democracy."

"Mr. X" and the New Foreign Policy:
Implications for the Philippines

On the eve of Philippine independence, one war had just ended, but a new colder one was beginning, and the archipelago would emerge, yet again, as a critical battleground. As in 1916 and 1935, the 1946 promise of independence was undermined from the outset by the threat of world war, which again prompted the United States to mold Philippine domestic politics to meet America's economic and strategic interests. At the same time, elite Filipinos again sought shelter from the United States. Now, it was the external threat to the United States posed by communism together with the domestic challenge posed by the communist-inspired Huks that reinforced the interdependencies between the new nation and its former colonial ruler. These interdependencies were then further reinforced by the emergence of a new U.S. foreign policy that would have global repercussion in the Philippines and beyond.

The new policy was introduced by George Kennan, until then a relatively obscure junior Foreign Service officer in Moscow, whom the State Department had asked to explain the increasingly alarming hostility of the Soviet Union toward the West. On February 22, 1946, Kennan dispatched a telegram that was to have an unprecedented impact on the entire structure of U.S. foreign policy. In the telegram, Kennan argued that the key explanation for Soviet hostility toward the West lay less in the actions, or inactions, of the West than in Stalin's domestic policies of intimidation and repression. "A hostile international environment," wrote Kennan, "is the breath of life for [the] prevailing internal system in this country." Foreign policy analysts in the United States were quickly persuaded, and U.S. policy shifted from its earlier *quid pro quo* stance toward one combining "patience with firmness."[1]

Where previously the United States might have tried to conceal disagreements with its former Soviet allies, U.S. officials now agreed to air these openly but nonprovocatively. There would also be no more concessions made toward Soviet expansionism, though no challenge would be made against Soviet control of territories already held. Moreover, U.S. military strength would have to be reconstituted, with economic and military aid to U.S. allies a key part of the new global strategy. The United States also agreed to continue its negotiations with the Soviets but only in order to register Soviet acceptance of U.S. positions or to publicize Soviet intransigence. In this way, the United States hoped to stake its claim to the new international power structure while wooing allies at home and abroad. U.S. strategists hoped the Soviets would exercise restraint in the face of American firmness, finding as well the possibility of a settlement in America's patience. The United States induced the Soviets to withdraw troops from Iran and to give up its demands for boundary concessions and base rights from Turkey. The United States also intervened in Greece to support the U.S.-allied government there from a communist insurgency, while installing the Sixth Fleet of the U.S. Navy in local waters. In Asia, U.S. officials kept the Soviets from playing any substantive role in the reconstruction of Japan, while displaying as well U.S. determination to prevent the Soviets from extending southward from their occupied zone north of the 38th parallel in Korea. Though the new foreign policy had been evolving for months, it coalesced after Truman's March 12, 1947 proclamation that: "It must be the policy of the United States to support free peoples who are resisting attempted subjugation by armed minorities or outside pressures."[2]

The doctrine said nothing about "free peoples" resisting U.S. incursions, however. Just two days after Truman's proclamation, on March 14, 1947, Philippine President Manuel Roxas signed an agreement granting the United States ninety-nine year leases on twenty-two military sites, including Clark and Subic. Since June 1946, U.S. and Filipino negotiators had tangled on the question of U.S. jurisdiction over American soldiers, sailors and civilian employees at the Philippine bases. The question was not just a theoretical one. Following the end of World War II, U.S. troops awaiting repatriation had been involved in numerous traffic incidents, barroom brawls, and other conflicts with Filipinos. Racism, still institutionalized in much of the United States through segregation and "Jim Crow" laws, was a factor as well. Trying the cases in U.S. military courts, Roxas had argued, would undermine Philippine sovereignty. U.S. agencies who were rivals of the military, including the State Department, likewise contended that such privileges for the United States might poison relations with the Filipinos while discouraging other nations from allowing U.S. bases on their soil. As the debate continued through late 1946, U.S. strategists reviewed alternative Asian sites in Guam, Korea and Okinawa. Upon such review, the Philippines was given a low priority, particularly after Eisenhower, then Army Chief of Staff, argued that U.S. troop removal from the Philippines would be preferable to chronic friction with Filipinos on the issue. By December 1946, former High Commissioner McNutt was sent to Manila to inform Roxas that U.S. forces in the Philippines would soon be reduced.[3]

Fearing a complete U.S. withdrawal, and the likely economic and strategic impact of this on the war-ravaged Philippines as well as on the capacity of his administration to suppress the emerging Huk challenge, Roxas acquiesced. On March 14, 1947, Roxas granted the United States the ninety-nine year leases as well as jurisdiction not just over American but also over Filipino base employees.[4] The decision was an unpopular one and the United States now moved to secure the Roxas government from domestic opposition, but in the process increased

Philippine military dependence on the United States. On March 21, Roxas signed another agreement with the United States, wherein the Philippines was to receive $19.7 million to rebuild, train and equip its 37,000 troops with assistance from U.S. Navy, Army and Air Force officers, all to be administered in the Philippines by the Joint U.S. Military Advisory Group (JUSMAG).[5] Note that the term "joint" does not refer to both countries but to all branches of the U.S. forces.[6] That same month, Roxas also won for the Philippines a $25 million emergency loan from the U.S. Congress. Though he had requested a long-term loan of $225 million,[7] the emergency loan nevertheless seemed a reward for Filipino compliance on the bases. The loan was also an attempt, albeit a far weaker one than Roxas intended, to complement military with economic responses to the surging unrest in the countryside. In the end, the bases would prove a key source of national revenue for the Philippines, drawing U.S. military and economic aid as well as investments, employment and their multipliers. At the same time, however, the bases would also prove, as Eisenhower had predicted, an on-going source of conflict between Filipinos and Americans over questions of sovereignty, security, and access.

Moreover, the bases would add a new dimension to domestic conflicts, as the Huks quickly added opposition to the bases to their increasingly popular campaign for agrarian reform and national sovereignty. As the Huk base expanded further, JUSMAG prepared for war.[8] The United States had been supporting anti-communist efforts worldwide, but Truman's proclamation formally declared U.S. intentions to continue such support. On the other side of the Atlantic, however, Britain abruptly announced plans to cease financial and military aid abroad to fight communism. Now the Truman administration sought congressional approval of aid to replace British supplies. In the post-war fatigue prevailing in the United States, however, military expenditures were politically untenable, even more so with the 1946 election to Congress of an economy-minded Republican majority.[9] In fact, the rush toward military demobilization reduced U.S. forces from 12 million at the end of the war to 3 million by July 1946, reaching just 1.6 million by July 1947. Meanwhile defense expenditures fell from $81.6 billion, representing 85.7 percent of total government expenditures, in 1945, to $44.7 billion, or 72.4 percent of total expenditures, in 1946, down to just $13.1 billion, or 35.5 percent of total expenditures, by 1947.[10] Still, between 1946 and 1948, U.S. economic and military assistance to the Philippines totaled $329.3 million, including $72.6 million in military aid and $256.7 million in economic aid, primarily as a tacit form of "rent" for the bases.[11] The so-called Truman Doctrine, however, required the United States to focus on core U.S. economic, political, strategic and territorial interests, forcing U.S. analysts to devise new strategies for projecting American power given the apparently global nature of the Soviet challenge.

Under the direction of George C. Marshall, the newly appointed Secretary of State, a Policy Planning Staff was organized with Kennan its first director. Having defined the Soviet problem, Kennan now set to work to find its solution, and this he proffered in his famous essay, "The Sources of Soviet Conduct," published in the Summer 1947 edition of *Foreign Affairs*, under the James Bond–like pseudonym of "Mr. X."[12] Here Kennan introduced the term "containment" to postwar foreign policy and, as Kissinger would note years later, "came as close to authoring the diplomatic doctrine of his era as any diplomat in our history."[13] Though hastily written and not intended as the official pronouncement of Cold War strategy that it became, Kennan's article outlined the core objectives of U.S. foreign policy—to protect the security of the nation from the interference or threat of interference from foreign powers and to advance the welfare of Americans by promoting a world order favorable to U.S. interests. Given limited capabilities, however, Kennan saw that priorities would have to be set. Thus, to achieve the core objectives of U.S. foreign policy, Kennan argued that the United States should not try to restructure the international system but should simply try to maintain an equilibrium or balance of power within it such that no one country or group of countries could emerge predominant. In essence, the United States would have to define its core interests and sources of power in order to allocate scarce resources efficiently.[14]

Kennan's eventual list emphasized defense of the four centers of industrial and military power—the United States, United Kingdom, central Europe and Japan—with just the Soviet center in unfriendly hands. He also defined broader interests covering Canada, Greenland, Iceland, Scandinavia, Western Europe, the Iberian peninsula, Morocco, western Africa down to the bulge, South America from the bulge north, the countries of the Mediterranean and the Middle East as far east as, and including, Iran, as well as Japan and, last but not least, the Philippines. Without any apparent irony, the U.S. aim of supporting "free peoples" in the name of American interests now encompassed a breathtaking sweep of the world's population.[15]

What remained as yet unresolved was the extent to which the United States would intervene in the domestic politics of other states in order to protect its own interests. While Kennan argued in 1948 that the United States should refrain from interfering in the domestic affairs of other countries, he added that intervention might be justifiable given a sufficiently powerful national interest as well as the means to carry it out successfully. That same year, the U.S. State Department predicted that Mao's Red Army would defeat Chiang Kai-shek's

Kuomintang,[16] and U.S. anti-communism bloomed both at home and abroad. U.S. foreign policy analysts now sought an explanation within the United States for the impending "loss" of China. To these analysts, it mattered not that Mao had rallied millions of Chinese peasants to his cause. Instead, the "blame" lay with Alger Hiss, among other American diplomats with communist sympathies, who had supposedly infiltrated the U.S. government and had then aided Mao in his bid for power by undermining the relative strength of Chiang Kai-shek's Nationalists.[17] In July 1948, just as the State Department's analyses on China were coming out, the House Committee on Un-American Activities began a series of hearings in which a number of former communists gave testimony concerning the "espionage activities" of American communists prior to and during World War II. The hearings were part of a strategy by the Republicans to re-cover from their loss to Truman in the 1948 presidential elections as well as by Chinese Americans lobbying for U.S. assistance to protect their extensive eco-nomic and political interests in China from Mao.[18]

In the witch-hunt that ensued, led by a young congressman named Richard Nixon and later picked up by Senator Joseph McCarthy, Alger Hiss would be found guilty of perjury. Countless other Americans in government, academia, journalism, the arts, etc., would subsequently be tried for communist activities, as the frontline of the Cold War now extended not just to the broad sweep of "free peoples" listed by Kennan but to the American public as well. Meanwhile, many China experts were purged from official U.S. circles, notably the State Department, and from key "think tanks." The loss of these experts soon under-mined U.S. understanding of China's role in the region, with reverberations to be felt for years to come in U.S. policy toward Asia, including Korea, Vietnam and the Philippines. For now, the "lessons of Munich"—that any threat should be met quickly and forcefully without appeasement—tightened its hold on U.S. foreign policy.

In 1949, two events would reinforce this, increasing the perceived threat of spreading communism as well as the call for intervention in the domestic politics of other countries. The first was the September 1949 detection by a U.S. plane of traces of radioactivity from a Soviet atomic explosion, just three years after the end of World War II, not the fifteen to twenty years previously forecast. Though Kennan now urged diplomacy, Truman opted for continued hard-line strategies centering on the development of a hydrogen bomb. The second event of 1949 was the "fall" of China on October 1, as Mao established the People's Republic of China, forcing Chiang Kai-shek and his Nationalist army out to the island of Taiwan. Though this had been expected for over a year, it nevertheless intensified U.S. fears of spreading communism, while buttressing the arguments of U.S. interventionists, including the powerful China lobby.[19]

From the Huks to Korea:
A U.S. Policy of Intervention Emerges

During this same period, the Huk rebellion grew substantially in Central Luzon and the government of President Manuel Roxas required ever increasing amounts of U.S. assistance to combat it. Having been ousted from their six elected congressional posts in April 1946, the Huks had returned to the countryside to plot their next course. Still enraged by the congressional ouster of the Huks, the Central Luzon peasantry was primed for rebellion. Roxas tried to placate the peasants by commissioning Huk spokesmen, including leader Luis Taruc as well as Mateo del Castillo and Juan Feleo, to intercede for them. On August 24, 1946, however, while returning to Manila from a peacekeeping mission in the countryside, Feleo and other peasant leaders were taken by uniformed men. A few weeks later, Feleo's headless body was found floating in the Pampanga River.[20] Now the Huks changed their name to the "Hukbong Mapagpalaya ng Bayan" or "People's Liberation Army," relinquished all hopes of a political solution, and dug up their World War II arms. The Huk message rapidly gained popularity, as the newly independent nation struggled to find a solution. A year and a half after Feleo's death, on March 6, 1948, Roxas chose his course. He outlawed the Huks and the Philippine Communist Party (PKP). A week later, he pardoned all Japanese collaborators. Full-scale civil war now broke out in Central Luzon. Soon after, Roxas died of a heart attack and was succeeded by ultra-hard-liner Elpidio Quirino who responded so brutally to the Huks that Taruc later claimed: "We couldn't have had a better recruiter."[21] Quirino also shifted the tax burden to the poor while siphoning U.S. aid and funds for war veterans. U.S. officials grew concerned that Congress would refuse to continue granting aid to such an administration. Amid nationalist insurgencies in Indochina and Indonesia as well as civil war in China, the United States worried that Quirino might fuel not quell revolution.[22]

Nevertheless, in 1949, Quirino won the nomination as the Liberal Party's presidential candidate while Japanese collaborator Jose Laurel won the opposition Nacionalista slot. The CIA, just recently formed in 1947, accurately described Laurel as "bitterly anti-U.S." and predicted that a Laurel victory would encourage nationalists and anti-Americans. Predicting widespread electoral fraud, the Huks, whose strength was now estimated at nearly 10,000 armed cadres with a much broader base of support,[23] boycotted the elections, partly because they had been outlawed, partly to help publicize the corruption of both the Liberal and the Nacionalista candidates. In the end, the elections proved the most corrupt on both sides to date, with the vote in two provinces exceeding the number of voters and in many others the population. As one witness recounted later, "Even the birds and the bees voted."[24] An official study later estimated that at least one fifth of the ballots cast had been fraudulent, largely in favor of Quirino.[25] Still Quirino won by just a narrow margin, and U.S. Asian experts now debated policy toward him. While some, notably Secretary of State Dean Acheson, urged a withdrawal of U.S. aid, others, including Philippine desk officer John Melby, urged the continuation of U.S. aid in order to give Quirino "breathing space." Melby won. Quirino received U.S. aid and now knew, a State Department study concluded, that the United States would support him "no matter what he does." By 1950, the Philippine government had run through over a billion dollars in U.S. aid granted in the first four years of independence; yet the economy was as weak as it had been at the end of the war.

In fact, Quirino and his cronies had enriched themselves with the aid. Meanwhile, half of Philippine dollar earnings came from the U.S. treasury, while the other half was from exports, primarily copra, the price of which was grossly inflated and likely to fall.[26] The United States began to distance itself from Quirino while searching for a moderate alternative to his increasingly corrupt and ineffectual regime. Melby urged tighter controls of U.S. aid to prevent "economic chaos,"[27] while Acheson, who had recently lost political capital for pledging support for Hiss, stated publicly in early 1950 that "much of the (aid to the Philippines) has not been used as wisely as we wish it had."[28] This argument was later substantiated by Daniel Bell, a private banker and former undersecretary of the treasury sent by Truman to study the Philippine situation. Bell reported that businessmen and landed elites had grown richer since the war, while "the standard of living of most people is lower than before the war."[29] Acheson now argued that Quirino was not part of the solution to the Huk crisis but was, rather, a core part of the problem. The CIA broadened the attack to include "an irresponsible ruling class which exercises economic and political power almost exclusively in its own interests."[30] An NSC report further cited the Chinese minority as a possible source of communist agitation.[31] Others in the United States, however, saw in the recent China debacle American failure to provide adequate support to Chiang Kai-shek and now urged greater support for Quirino, arguing as well that military intervention might be needed to prevent a communist takeover.[32] Acheson and his allies argued, on the contrary, that America's blind support for Chiang's Nationalists had *spurred* communism. He urged moderation to prevent a similar outcome in the Philippines.[33]

That same year, debates also raged on broader issues of U.S. foreign policy. In early 1950, State and Defense Department officials led by Paul Nitze, Kennan's successor as director of the Policy Planning Staff, drafted NSC-68, which urged containment not only in the four key industrial centers cited by Kennan but also along the entire perimeter, including the Philippines. Amid debates on the feasibility of this, particularly the estimated defense budget of up to $50 billion, North Korea crossed the 38th parallel into South Korea in June of 1950. This closed a chapter in U.S. debates on foreign policy, as U.S. strategists quickly approved NSC-68.[34] MacArthur had long argued that Asia, not Europe, would prove the decisive battleground in the Cold War. He had wanted troops stationed at bases in the Philippines and Japan in order to project American power from the periphery into the Asian mainland. Now, the Korean War revived these arguments, presenting as well the first serious possibility since World War II of an external threat to the Philippines and U.S. interests there. Though Truman initially sent only supplies and air cover to South Korea, he soon committed American troops to fend off the 150,000-strong North Korean forces. Soon Clark Air Base became critical to the effort, home to an F-51 squadron as well as a logistics center for military supplies and a stopover point for United Nations (UN) troops headed to Korea. And the number of U.S. personnel assigned to Clark nearly tripled, increasing from 5,445 in 1949 to 15,830 by 1953.[35] Annual U.S. defense expenditures also rose from less than $15 billion before Korea to $50 billion in 1953.[36] NSC-68 was not just theory; it was in full swing.[37]

Meanwhile, U.S. commitments to the French in Indochina, formerly restrained, grew during the war, as did American aid to Chiang's forces in Taiwan. For the Philippines, Quirino learned from his Filipino aides in Washington D.C., of American fears and growing concern regarding the Huk threat to U.S. political, economic and military interests.[38] Capitalizing on these concerns, Quirino cited a "pattern of communist aggression," not his own mismanagement as the source of Huk anger, and urged increased American support for the counter-insurgency campaign.[39] However, given the level of American troop commitment in Korea together with the sensitivity of Philippine officials to American intervention, U.S. analysts argued that aid would have to be indirect, emphasizing the development of the Philippine military as well as economic and political stabilization strategies.[40] In September 1950, General Leland Hobbes, chief of JUSMAG, urged Quirino to adopt a tougher line against the Huks and other leftist groups. By November, Truman approved an NSC paper defining U.S. policy on the Philippines, arguing that defeat of the Huks should be a top priority.[41] As the Republican-dominated U.S. Congress poised to outlaw the CPUSA while overriding Truman's veto of the ominous McCarran Internal Security Act,[42] Quirino took his cue from Washington, D.C., and escalated the war against the Huks. To help him, U.S. Air Force Lieutenant Colonel Edward Lansdale, a former advertising executive, was sent to the Philippines. Based at the super-secret Office of Policy Coordination, known for its "dirty tricks" and later absorbed into the CIA, Lansdale was later caricatured in Graham Greene's *The Quiet American* as Alden Pyle. "I never knew a man who had better motives for all the trouble he caused," explained a Greene character of Pyle.[43]

The Huk Challenge and the
Transnational Response

Lansdale's first task was to find an alternative to Quirino, and he found his man in Ramon Magsaysay. A member of a U.S.-allied guerrilla unit during World War II, Magsaysay had gained the respect of several American officers, such that the U.S. Army named him provincial military governor after the war. Magsaysay then parlayed this into a political career, as he used his access to U.S. relief supplies to gain popularity and so win a seat in the national legislature in the 1946 elections. Lansdale and Magsaysay met in early 1950, prior to the outbreak of war in Korea, when Magsaysay, as a member of the Philippine legislature, came to the United States seeking benefits for war veterans. Lansdale and his boss Frank Wisner discussed the Huk insurgency with Magsaysay and both came away impressed. Magsaysay subsequently agreed to act as America's surrogate in exchange for U.S. support for his political career. Wisner then sent Assistant Secretary of State Livingston Merchant to Quirino with an offer to increase U.S. military assistance should Magsaysay be appointed Defense Secretary. Despite the threat posed by Magsaysay to his own political career, Quirino accepted and Magsaysay became the new Secretary of National Defense in late 1950.[44]

Soon after, Lansdale established an office in Magsaysay's new headquarters and set to work on two fronts to battle the Huks. Using U.S. assistance, he supplemented military strategies with political and economic ones. During the period from fiscal years 1949 to 1952, U.S. economic aid totaled $584.2 million while U.S. military aid totaled $80.2 million. On the economic front, Lansdale sought to undercut Huk promises of land reform by helping Magsaysay establish credit banks, clinics and agrarian courts, though these were soon dominated by local landed elites. Lansdale also sought to isolate the Huks from their bases of support, offering land on public tracts on the southernmost island of Mindanao, far from Central Luzon. To ensure that the homesteaders would not spread the rebellion to Mindanao, loyal ex-soldiers and civilians were to be stationed in the re-settlement communities. The program was an economic disappointment but a political success. Six years later, the land grants had benefited about 5,000 people, though only a fourth of these were actually Huks. The majority were Magsaysay's allies.[45] Though the Huks tried to relay these facts to the peasants, the peasants nevertheless came to think of Magsaysay as their patron, a view still prevalent in the countryside of Luzon some thirty years later.[46] Magsaysay also used the military for infrastructural projects, education, medical care and legal services in rural areas, and in the process significantly broadened the role of the armed forces in the countryside.[47]

At the same time, Magsaysay worked to refurbish the Philippine military. He transferred the constabulary, a particularly ineffectual and corrupt organization, from the Department of the Interior to the Department of National Defense, under the command of the Chief of Staff of the Armed Forces. He also reduced it from 17,000 in 1950 to 7,100 by the end of 1952.[48] He then purged the army of its most corrupt officers while nearly doubling its size to 56,000 by 1952.[49] Added to traditional military campaigns, Lansdale used skills he had developed in his earlier career in advertising to launch a psychological campaign of warfare against the Huks. With "talking" graves, deaths staged to resemble the work of Filipino folk creatures such as the vampire-like *aswang*, and other bizarre techniques, Lansdale tapped into rural Filipino superstitions and effectively sapped Huk morale. While such tactics contributed to Huk losses, the Huks also erred in concentrating all of their forces in Central Luzon, which made retreat and reorganization difficult. They erred further in concentrating their urban forces, the central nervous system of the campaign, in a Manila complex. In October 1950, military forces swept through the poorly defended Huk base in Manila, comprised of twenty-two houses and apartments. Captured were reams of documents, weapons, money, as well as 105 suspected Huks including 6 Huk leaders. The raid was a devastating blow to the Huks, further shattering morale.[50]

Lansdale did not, moreover, restrict his activities to the Huk insurgency. He intervened in electoral politics as well. To shore up Magsaysay's chances in upcoming 1953 presidential elections, Lansdale worked with his CIA associate Gabriel Kaplan, who arrived in Manila in 1951 under the aegis of the Committee for Free Asia, later renamed the Asia Foundation. Kaplan soon helped establish a citizen's group, The National Committee for Free Elections (NAMFREL), to monitor 1951 legislative elections. Excluded from the elections, the Huks argued that the elections were inherently unfair and called for a boycott. On election day, NAMFREL volunteers, actually Filipinos on the CIA payroll, were mobilized to monitor vote-counting. Magsaysay, with directives from Lansdale, supported NAMFREL by preventing the military from stealing ballot boxes and by stationing troops to prevent violence. When Quirino subsequently realized that the votes were not favorable to his party, he ordered ballot boxes stuffed and loaded onto army planes for delivery to polling stations. Magsaysay swiftly countermanded the order. Planes that had already taken off agreed to turn back while the others remained grounded. Meanwhile, a record four million voters ignored Huk calls for a boycott, participating in the relatively honest balloting.[51] A Huk analysis following the elections lamented the weakness of their boycott campaign, as Huk strength dropped further. As their revolutionary successors would do again in 1986, the Huks underestimated the Filipino faith in democratic processes, a legacy of the U.S. colonial era. In the end, Magsaysay's efforts paid off. Truman lauded his achievement and Lansdale continued to cultivate him as the next Philippine president.[52]

Meanwhile, the United States and the Philippines signed the Mutual Defense Treaty in 1951, which reinforced the role of the Philippine military for internal security only, with U.S. forces bearing responsibility for external security. It also bound the two nations to defend each other in the event of an attack by a third party, as the U.S. and Philippine military became even more intertwined.[53] In 1951, Huk losses included 2,000 killed and 2,500 captured.[54] By 1952, many of the remaining Huks surrendered, and Magsaysay capitalized on this by having photos taken of himself with surrendering Huks handing him their weapons. Lansdale also brought Magsaysay to the United States and arranged for him to meet with Truman, to be awarded a U.S. Army medal as well as an honorary doctorate from Fordham University, all part of a campaign to promote Magsaysay as the next leader of the Philippines by building U.S. support. While in the United States, Lansdale introduced Magsaysay to the press, which received him favorably. *Time*, for instance, dubbed Magsaysay the "Eisenhower of the Pacific" for his military prowess in combating the Huks while *Life* devoted eight pages with seven photographs to the "Honest Man With Guts."[55]

Also in 1952, U.S. policy in Asia would prove a central question in the U.S. presidential campaign. With U.S. troops mired in Korea amid growing hysteria surrounding communism, the "fall" of China, and the related hearings in the House Committee on Un-American Activities, Republican contender Eisenhower blamed the European-centered approach of Truman and Acheson for these crises and called for a new, more Asian outlook on foreign policy. Having served under MacArthur in the Philippines during World War II, Eisenhower understood Asian politics as well as the special role of the Philippines in serving U.S. interests in the region. Campaigning on the promise to "go to Korea" and undo the mistakes of the Democrats, implying that he would end the increasingly unpopular war, Eisenhower also pledged greater vigilance and competence in guarding U.S. interests in Asia. Nixon, who had gained notoriety for his anti-communist crusade in the Hiss case, was named to the Vice Presidential slot on Eisenhower's ticket, a further indication of the direction the Republicans intended to take U.S. foreign policy. Eisenhower also brought in John Foster Dulles, the party's leading expert on international affairs, to write his foreign policy platform. While a State Department advisor during the Truman administration, Dulles had urged greater attention to Asia, citing in 1950 a "comprehensive program (on the part of Moscow and Beijing) to eliminate all western influence" from Asia, including the Philippines. He had also cited the Huks as a key part of the program to "further the objectives of world communism."[56]

American intelligence analysts concurred, though the peasant-based Huks, in fact, sought reform more than revolution and received virtually no assistance after World War II from the Soviet Union, China or the CPUSA, as Taruc and other Huk leaders repeatedly complained.[57] Some American communists, notably William J. Pomeroy, did join the Huks and, at a 1951 meeting of the CPUSA, speakers cited the "heroic liberation struggle of the Philippine people" but acknowledged far too little U.S. support. Even Pomeroy was captured in 1952 and was deported home only after serving ten years in prison.[58]

Eisenhower's "New Look" Meets the "Magsaysay Mambo"

Eisenhower won the elections and, in 1953, his "new look" took hold of U.S. foreign policy, gaining a quick boost in July 1953 when the Korean War finally ended. Eisenhower had pledged in his campaign to cut defense spending. And he believed that it was time for the United States to align Cold War goals and strategy with the practical issue of available resources, an issue Truman had not adequately addressed. Thus he saw a strong domestic economy as a requisite to strategic strength. Though Keynesian economic advisors argued that military expenditures and increased deficits could simultaneously boost the economy, Eisenhower sought to uphold his campaign promises. To guard against Third World communism, Eisenhower opted for a build-up of local forces of resistance. This helped him in his crusade to cut defense spending, while reflecting as well his conviction that "no Western power can go to Asia militarily, except as one of a concert of powers...includ[ing] local Asiatic peoples." To do otherwise, he reasoned, would raise charges of imperialism or, at the very least, "objectionable paternalism."[59] The administration now emphasized military and economic aid to reliably anti-communist governments in South Korea, Taiwan, Pakistan, Iran, Saudi Arabia and the Philippines as well as South Vietnam after the 1954 installment of Ngo Dinh Diem.[60] The administration's Asian policy faltered, however, when Dulles, now Secretary of State, caved in to pressures from McCarthyites and purged the State Department of many loyal officers including the remaining "Old China Hands."[61]

Further, Eisenhower's administration allowed the CIA more latitude for covert activities than any administration before or since.[62] To protect oil and other interests in the Middle East, for instance, the CIA helped replace Iran's Prime Minister Mohammed Mossadegh, who had nationalized the Anglo-Iranian Oil Company, with Mohammad Reza Shah Pahlavi in 1953. On the same day that Mossadegh left office, Magsaysay resigned as Defense Secretary and announced his candidacy for president. Magsaysay was the U.S. choice for the Philippine presidency and the CIA actively intervened on his behalf in elections held that year. CIA's Allen Dulles, John Foster's brother-in-law, gave Lansdale $1 million to back Magsaysay with additional funds provided by American corporations in the Philippines, including the Coca Cola franchise based there, despite Philippine laws prohibiting such intervention.[63] CIA agents then wrote speeches for Magsaysay, advised him on campaign strategies, and planted articles and editorials in the Philippine and U.S. press to promote Magsaysay and smear Quirino. In addition, the CIA funded volunteers to revive NAMFREL, the implication being that Quirino was too corrupt to be trusted in the ballot counting. Finally, the CIA helped set up the National Press Club in Manila and then encouraged the U.S. press to cover the elections in order to stimulate American interest and to ensure careful news coverage. Should Magsaysay lose, the CIA also smuggled guns into the Philippines and made contingency plans for a coup. As a further warning of U.S. intentions, a group of U.S. warships arrived off Manila just before the elections, while U.S. military advisors supervised the voting.

With his jazzy theme song, the "Magsaysay Mambo," and the backing of the United States, Magsaysay buried Quirino in a two-to-one victory in the heaviest voting since independence.[64] The magnitude of the win attests to Magsaysay's broad popularity more than just the machinations of the CIA, but it nevertheless raised questions in the Philippines and other parts of Asia about the U.S. role,[65] as Lansdale earned the new sobriquet "Landslide."[66] Magsaysay quickly earned political capital, however, when, in 1954, Luis Taruc surrendered. Amid growing contention within the Huk leadership and facing charges for his "excessive humanism," Taruc sent a secret message to Magsaysay's aide Manuel Manahan suggesting a meeting.[67] With Magsaysay's approval, Manahan was preparing to meet with the Huk leader when a *Manila Times* reporter named Benigno Aquino, Jr., then just twenty-one, sniffed out the story. Aquino, son of the World War II pro-Japanese Kalibapi leader, soon won an invitation from Manahan to attend the meeting in exchange for remaining silent on the story through the talks. In January, Manahan and Aquino eluded an army cordon and met with Taruc in a small village north of Manila. Taruc requested a complete pardon, which Magsaysay subsequently refused, calling instead for Taruc's arrest. Aquino then pursued the talks alone and, as Taruc faced both Magsaysay's forces and the communists, who now planned to assassinate him, Taruc finally ceded to Magsaysay's terms. In May, he summoned Aquino and surrendered.[68] Until then, Magsaysay had retained the defense portfolio, further merging political with military programs, including the use of the military in his socioeconomic programs.[69] Huk opposition would sputter in the countryside for years afterwards, but the rebellion effectively ended with Taruc's surrender. Taruc was to spend the next fourteen and a half years in jail. For Aquino, however, breaking the story marked the beginning of a meteoric political career.

Meanwhile, for the United States, half a billion dollars in economic and military aid had been spent on the Huk conflict between 1951 and 1955. The Philippines used much of what was left after siphoning by Quirino and others to build an arsenal of modern weapons and aircraft, all expressly targeted under the 1951 Mutual Defense Treaty at internal "threats" to security, primarily peasants who remained yoked to a grossly unequal land tenure system inherited from Spain.[70] Having stabilized the Philippine countryside and ensured the sanctity of the status quo, the United States claimed victory and used the campaign against the Huks as a prototype for counterinsurgency programs elsewhere in its sphere of containment. The CIA also honed its transnational intervention strategies, applying skills developed in the Philippines to engineer in 1954 the ouster of Guatemala's Jacobo Arbenz Guzman, who had won 60 percent of the vote in 1950 elections as well as the support of the peasantry and the wrath of U.S. investors for his sympathies with the workers' strikes plaguing the United Fruit Company. Personal interests, in addition to a militant ideology, were involved as well. John Foster Dulles and his brother-in-law Allen Dulles, head of State and CIA respectively, had been members of United Fruit's law firm and now worked with General Carlos Castillo Armas of Honduras to oust Arbenz.[71] Meanwhile, the CIA sent Lansdale to Saigon in the hopes that the Magsaysay magic might be replicated with the unlikely Ngo Dinh Diem.

America's Growing Power in Asia

After 1950, responsibility for the defense of Indochina against communism turned increasingly to the United States, which funded more and more of France's ultimately vain effort to stem the insurgency. In 1953, as the war in Korea wound to an end, Ho Chi Minh's forces overran France's in Dienbienphu, raising the spectre of a new Asian conflict involving nationalist revolutionaries with communist ties. Initially, Eisenhower sought a solution involving the support of France, Great Britain, and the U.S. Congress, but the French refused to share control, Great Britain declined to participate, and the U.S. Congress rejected the proposal. Finally, at the 1954 Geneva Conference, Russia and China pressed North Vietnam to accept a truce, involving division of the country into a northern communist state and a southern noncommunist one. The division was to last only until 1956, when elections for a unified nation were to be held. Eisenhower and Dulles now set out to replace French with U.S. influence, while building a viable noncommunist regime for the 1956 elections. Much work was needed; even Eisenhower admitted that the communists would win 80 percent of the vote were elections to be held in 1954. The United States supported Emperor Bao Dai's choice of Ngo Dinh Diem as the prime minister of the newly-created South Vietnam and, with Lansdale's help, funneled aid directly to him rather than through French channels.

To further secure the region, and to meet growing cries from the Philippines and others for a NATO-like security pact for Southeast Asia, the United States met with Britain, France, Australia, New Zealand, Thailand, Pakistan and the Philippines to form the Manila pact, later known as the Southeast Asia Treaty Organization (SEATO), in September 1954. Although a condition of the Geneva agreement had prohibited South Vietnam, Cambodia or Laos from participating in an alliance, a SEATO protocol extended protection to Indochina. Despite its name, however, SEATO was not a multilateral defense treaty like NATO; it simply pledged resistance to communism with no automatic provisions for either collective action or intervention in regional or other disputes.[72] Moreover, it included no major power in the region like India or Indonesia. In fact, it turned out to be a rather blunt instrument, as Indochina continued to simmer.

Having established a toehold in Pacific security planning through SEATO, however, Magsaysay simultaneously renegotiated the Bell Trade Act, scheduled to expire in 1954. In August, Magsaysay sent a Philippine Economic Mission to the United States to press for revisions. Former Japanese collaborator, outspoken anti-American and now Senator, Jose Laurel was named to head the mission. Once again, Laurel proved his flexibility. Working D.C. as though he had never uttered an anti-American word, Laurel wooed officials with gifts from the Philippines and hosted dinners and receptions in their honor. In a letter to Magsaysay, he explained his strategy; competing American factions, notably eastern industrialists versus the western farm bloc and southern cotton and oil interests, should be played against each other, as they had in the battle for the Jones Act and later the Tydings–McDuffie Act. Meanwhile, the Philippines should "cater to the interests which might favor our cause... ." Further, Laurel sought to limit congressional entanglements as much as possible to avoid lobbying from American businesses. With his American counterpart, James Langley, Laurel signed the Laurel–Langley Agreement in December 1954,[73] winning for Philippine producers a deceleration in the rate at which Philippine exports to the United States would face U.S. tariffs and an acceleration in the rate at which American exports to the Philippines would face Philippine restrictions.[74] Whereas the Bell Trade Act had limited parity rights mainly to natural resources, however, Laurel–Langley opened the entire economy to U.S. corporations.[75] The agreement passed quickly in the Philippines and then, though more slowly, in the U.S. Congress, and was signed in D.C. on September 6, 1955.

Though it passed quickly, the agreement received harsh criticism from nationalist corners of the Philippines, including one of its harshest critics—Philippine Senator Claro Recto. Recto, though a member of the Nacionalista Party like Magsaysay, had long criticized the Philippine president for his ties to Washington. He now openly broke with Magsaysay over the Laurel–Langley Agreement's opening to U.S. corporations, announcing in 1955 that he would not support Magsaysay's 1957 bid for the presidency. Meanwhile, the Philippine economy was in decline, following a boom in U.S. demand for Philippine products during the Korean War, which collapsed after the 1953 armistice.[76] Recto capitalized on this, building a nationalist platform that addressed U.S. aid, land tenure, the U.S. bases, foreign investment, Vietnam, as well as Laurel–Langley. Amid intensifying nationalist debates in the Philippines, the Quemoy–Matsu crisis of 1955, when Communist Chinese bombarded Chiang's island outposts off Taiwan, demonstrated once again the importance of the Philippine bases to safeguarding U.S. interests in the region.[77] And American officials grew ever more concerned about Recto's campaign. Resorting once again to dirty tricks, the CIA launched a smear campaign, labeling Recto a Chinese Communist, even going so far as to distribute pin-pricked condoms marked "Courtesy of Recto—the People's Friend."[78] Through it all, Magsaysay remained a loyal champion of U.S. policies in the region, allowing Lansdale to recruit Filipinos for a CIA front in Vietnam called the Freedom Company, later renamed the Eastern Construction Company. The Filipinos, many with experience in the war against the Huks, helped train South Vietnam's police, draft the new constitution there, and usher anti-communist refugees, mainly landed elites and French colonists, from North to South Vietnam after the partition.[79]

Nevertheless, Vietnam continued to slip. In 1955 elections in South Vietnam, Diem managed to garner 98 percent of the vote, making even Lansdale's work with Magsaysay seem credible. Then, with support from Eisenhower, Diem blocked the Vietnam-wide elections and made clear his plans to further block reunification. Open rebellion broke out in the South Vietnamese countryside in 1957, where Vietminh villagers who had stayed behind for just such a contingency dug up the armaments they had buried after the 1954 Geneva accords. As in the Philippines, grossly unequal land tenure arrangements made the peasantry ripe for rebellion. Despite Diem's efforts at land reform, he actually undid the redistribution that had been carried out in areas formerly controlled by the Vietminh, leaving 2 percent of the population with 45 percent of the land, while 72 percent of the population had to survive on just 15 percent of the land. Moreover, his response to the uprising was increased repression, routing villagers from their homes and the graves of their ancestors to concentrate them in *agrovilles* where they could be more closely watched. The result was a rise, not a fall, in peasant anger and alienation, presaging later uprisings.[80] As Cold War tensions flared in Vietnam, the United States again focused attention on Philippine presidential elections scheduled for the fall of 1957. This attention grew more intense after March 1957, when Magsaysay, still President and likely to be re-elected, died in a plane crash. Speculations persist that Magsaysay's death may have been the result of foul play linked to the elections. Nevertheless, he was succeeded by his Vice President Carlos Garcia, and a new era of Philippine politics was launched.

Garcia won the nomination of the Nacionalistas and defeated Liberal candidate Jose Yulo by 600,000 of the roughly five million votes cast; but Liberal vice presidential candidate Diosdado Macapagal, running in a separate race, defeated Nacionalista Laurel by 400,000 votes.[81] Garcia quickly set up lucrative rackets in import licensing and the distribution of Japanese reparations, misruling to such an extent that the United States became concerned about a communist revival. U.S. officials were particularly concerned in light of the 1957 uprising in Vietnam, which they worried presaged a communist sweep through Southeast Asia. Alarms sounded throughout the Pentagon regarding U.S. security in the region, with an increased value now placed on the bases in the Philippines. By 1958, an analysis produced by the office of the American Chief of Naval Operations for the joint chiefs of staff summarized the Pentagon's view that the Philippine bases had now become "an essential part of a worldwide base system designed to deter communism. Any reduction in this base system creates a point of weakness which invites communist aggression."[82] Garcia tried to ingratiate himself with the United States by underscoring his anti-communist credentials, literally embracing Diem when the latter visited Manila in 1958. Garcia also initiated legislation, which the Philippine Congress approved, making membership in the PKP illegal, going further than any of his predecessors to constrict the political space for communists.[83] Garcia then used the threat of a Huk resurgence as a pretext for increased U.S. aid. With inside information channeled from Vice President Macapagal through the CIA, however, the United States knew that Garcia's corruption exceeded even Quirino's. "Look for another Magsaysay," CIA agent Joseph Burkholder Smith was told.

The perceived threat of a communist takeover from internal not external sources in the Philippines was intensified a year later when a bearded rebel named Fidel Castro actually succeeded in his indigenously based bid for control of Cuba in 1959. That communism could touch so close to U.S. shores sounded new alarms in D.C., as Cuban and Philippine domestic politics were again held hostage to the broader geopolitics of the era as they had been in their simultaneous uprisings against Spain in 1898. While the Soviets aligned with

Castro, the United States considered various strategies, including a coup or an assassination, to oust Castro. Meanwhile in the Philippines, the United States prepared for 1959 legislative elections. Seeking "another Magsaysay," Smith assembled a "Grand Alliance" of six candidates, funneling $200,000 toward their campaigns. In the increasingly costly Philippine campaigns, such backing was quite low, though the political backing of the United States carried weight with voters. In the end, however, the "Grand Alliance" candidates lost dramatically and a relative newcomer from the House[84] who had declined offers to join the Grand Alliance finished an impressive first in a landslide victory. The newcomer's name was Ferdinand Marcos.

Two years later, in 1961 presidential elections, Marcos declined to run and the United States provided financial and strategic support to Liberal candidate Macapagal in his race against Garcia. Philippine money, however, far exceeded that provided by the United States, with candidates spending an amount equal to 13 percent of the national government's budget.[85] Macapagal won but quickly lost U.S. backing when he deported American businessman Harry Stonehill, who had amassed an estimated $50 million from his Philippine enterprises. Macapagal also lost Filipino backing when his attempts at land reform alienated first the landed elites and then, when the attempts failed, the peasantry. Worse, he alienated the country's powerful Chinese community when he expelled many, even naturalized citizens, on spurious nationalist charges. He further sealed his fate when he denounced the political role of the military and terminated its civic action programs, forcing the armed forces to return to the barracks and the less rewarding regularity of military life.[86] Prices and unemployment also rose during Macapagal's administration, and he was gradually abandoned by members of his own party, including Marcos who defected to the Nacionalistas.

U.S. Counter-Insurgency Doctrine

Meanwhile, in the United States, John F. Kennedy won a narrow victory for the Democrats against Richard Nixon. Just months after taking office, in April 1961, the Kennedy administration launched a disastrous invasion at the Bay of Pigs in Cuba. Hoping to oust Castro as they had Mossadegh and Arbenz years earlier, the CIA invaded the island but was quickly surrounded by Castro's forces. Kennedy took responsibility for the debacle but lost faith in his advisors and thereafter short-circuited official channels of foreign policy decision making, arrogating more power to the presidency in the process. A year later, Kennedy would rely on his brother, father and closest aides to finesse the brinkmanship with the Soviets that he felt the Berlin wall and later the Cuban missile crises required.

Moreover, National Security Action Memorandum 182 of 24 concluded that subversive insurgency, with techniques learned from China, Cuba and Algeria, had become the major communist threat in Third World countries, not overt Soviet aggression. To combat such a threat, similarly transnational strategies were needed, the report argued, to build indigenous forces capable of internal security, while addressing as well the economic, social and political sources of rebellion. Although the memo notes the success of insurgency movements against superior forces, it is nevertheless optimistic about U.S. prospects for helping "less developed societies... to remain free... from communism or other totalitarian domination or control." In the next paragraph, however, the memo cites U.S. political, strategic and military interests as the driving force behind the new "overseas internal defense policy." On August 24, 1962, the memo was signed as policy by McGeorge Bundy who wrote that the President had approved the "national counterinsurgency doctrine for the use of U.S. departments and agencies concerned with the internal defense of overseas areas threatened by subversive insurgency, and has directed its promulgation to serve as basic policy guidance to diplomatic missions, consular personnel, and military commands abroad; to government departments and agencies at home; and to the government educational system." The Philippine campaign against the Huks, "combining the use of force with reform" while blending "civil and military" actions, was to serve as the "model of countering insurgency and winning back the allegiance of the domestic popular base."[87]

Now Vietnam emerged as the laboratory for the new policy. By the time Kennedy took office, Diem's regime was near collapse from internal rebellion, notably among peasants and Buddhists. Nevertheless, Kennedy chose to continue to support Diem, hoping to revitalize military forces there by switching from conventional to new, anti-guerrilla tactics. He established the Green Berets toward this end and sent 16,000 "advisors" to Vietnam. Kennedy also urged Diem to reform his government, tried to bring aid directly to the villages, and then set up "strategic hamlets" in an effort to isolate the insurgents from the population. Instead, revolutionary opposition swelled. The Buddhists spearheaded this, immolating themselves on Saigon's streets in order to expose the abuses of Diem's Catholic officials. In a statement reminiscent of Marie Antoinette, Diem's wife Madame Nhu decried the "barbecues," as her brother Ngo Dinh Nhu, head of the secret police, launched massive raids on Buddhist temples throughout South Vietnam, ransacking pagodas and arresting roughly 1,400 people. Diem ignored U.S. advice to reform and, worse, publicly denounced U.S. efforts to intervene as ignorant and arrogant. By August 1963, a group of Diem's generals broached the subject of a coup with Kennedy, who did nothing either to discourage them or to inform Diem. The coup failed, but it precipitated a reexamination of U.S. policy toward Vietnam. On November 1, 1963, with Kennedy's tacit approval, a revived junta brutally murdered Diem and overthrew his regime. Three weeks later, Kennedy himself would be assassinated as the torch now passed to Lyndon Johnson.[88]

If Kennedy had entertained any thoughts of a U.S. withdrawal from Vietnam, it was too late. Johnson had seen what the "fall" of China had done to the Democrats in 1949, did not want to be the first American president to lose a war, and, moreover, did not want a foreign policy debacle to spoil his Great Society program at home. The military junta in Vietnam was, however, riddled with internal conflict, proving incapable of governing the country. As U.S. military advisors warned of a 50–50 chance the war would be lost in six months unless the regime operated more efficiently, Johnson thought he could stave off a loss and bring the crisis to the negotiating table. Without declaring a change in policy, he began to escalate the U.S. effort, throwing American backing behind General Nguyen Khanh after Khanh took power in another coup on January 19, 1964. Soon after, Johnson increased the number of U.S. advisors to 23,000 and appointed General William Westmoreland to command these. He also initiated covert raids on North Vietnam. Meanwhile, U.S. official policy now declared the outcome of the Vietnamese conflict "vital" to the prevention of revolutions elsewhere, with U.S. military facilities in the region crucial to this new policy.[89] When, in August 1964, the U.S. destroyer *Maddox* was apparently attacked in Tonkin Gulf waters off land recently vacated by South Vietnamese forces, Johnson ordered retaliatory attacks against North Vietnamese torpedo boats bases. Johnson then won congressional approval with the Tonkin Gulf Resolution to take "all necessary measures to repel any armed attacks against the forces of the United States and to prevent further aggression."[90] In October, Johnson persuaded Macapagal to send sixty-eight medical/civic action teams to Vietnam and to try as well to procure Philippine congressional approval to send a 2,000-man engineer contingent there. Macapagal's efforts in congress failed, however, largely due to strident opposition led by Marcos, then Senate President.[91]

In the U.S. presidential campaign that year, Johnson defeated Goldwater in a landslide, and now saw the Tonkin Gulf Resolution as his mandate in Vietnam. Though some U.S. analysts argued that the Vietnamese revolt was targeted more at indigenous than global communist ends, with armaments coming more from captured U.S. weapons than from either China or the Soviet Union, a government White Paper nevertheless officially cited North Vietnamese aggression as the cause of war in the South. Still Johnson hoped to continue his campaign of limited warfare in an attempt at brinkmanship; but on February 6, 1965, an attack on U.S. barracks at Pleiku provided the provocation for a bombing program called Rolling Thunder. When this had no effect, Johnson extended the bombing northward, and authorized the use of napalm to defoliate the Vietnamese jungle. In March, he sent U.S. ground troops to guard the airfields needed for the bombing raids. A month later, he sent 40,000 more troops, and by July he sent an additional 100,000.[92] Moreover, he now extended Westmoreland's fiat from simply guarding U.S. enclaves to initiating "search and destroy" missions. Johnson refused to bomb North Vietnam but authorized B-52 saturation bombing of suspected enemy territory in South Vietnam. By mid-1965, U.S. policy in Vietnam had shifted dramatically, and without substantial consultation with Congress.

For the Philippines, the policy shift entailed a massive build-up of the U.S. bases, particularly Clark air and Subic naval bases. Though actual figures of the build-up are not available,[93] in July 1965, the U.S. State Department warned the embassy in Manila to expect "greatly increased use" of the U.S. bases in the Philippines, while war strategists won the right from Macapagal to fly U.S. planes over the Philippines.[94] Meanwhile, Macapagal renegotiated the bases agreement, reducing the U.S. lease of the bases from 99 years to 25.[95] Amid growing opposition at home, combined with the spreading Civil Rights movement, Johnson's "Great Society" was fast unraveling, as the United States became fully entangled in an ultimately unwinnable Southeast Asian war.[96]

"A Mandate for Greatness": 1965–1969

Also in 1965, Philippine presidential elections would further change the face of Southeast Asia, with long-term implications for the U.S. role there. Hedging its bets, the United States allegedly supported both the Liberal incumbent Macapagal and his Nacionalista opponent Ferdinand Marcos. In the campaign, serious questions about Marcos were raised, notably his conviction for the 1935 murder of his father's opponent in local elections and his subsequent release from having to serve any of the sentence by Laurel, then a judge. Moreover, Marcos proclaimed himself the leader of an anti-Japanese guerrilla movement during World War II called the *Ang Mga Maharlika* or "Noble Ones," and brought forth numerous medals to substantiate the story; yet his father had collaborated with the Japanese and his own personal debt to Laurel, among the most notorious of the collaborators, cast serious doubt on these claims. Nevertheless, Marcos garnered support from the Chinese, whom Macapagal had alienated, as well as the large numbers of Filipinos in California and Hawaii from Marcos' home province of Ilocos Norte. Imelda Marcos also made a tearful plea to sugar baron Fernando Lopez to run for Vice President with Marcos. Lopez agreed and Imelda then secured his pledge to finance the campaign from the Lopez family's vast private wealth. Though Macapagal, the son of poor peasants, tried to paint the race as one of "good" versus "evil," a theme that would be replayed two decades later, he was no match for Marcos' energy or Imelda's beauty. Marcos won by a margin of over 600,000 votes of the eight million cast, with only about 5 percent of these estimated as having been rigged.[97] Together, the two candidates had spent an estimated $100 million on advertising, festivals, and bribes, the currency of the all-important Filipino tradition of personal debt or *utang na loob*.

On December 30, 1965, in inauguration ceremonies held in Luneta Park, Marcos declared that he had been given a "mandate for greatness" and vowed to end "every form of waste or conspicuous consumption and extravagance." Behind the scenes, however, Marcos had already begun building a personal and political network in the United States and in the Philippines that would eventually help him amass a fortune estimated at close to $100 billion.[98] Like Magsaysay, Marcos held the defense portfolio for the first thirteen months of his term, and used this to secure the military's loyalty. One of his first steps was to launch the largest reshuffling in the history of the Philippine military, replacing most of the top echelon with family or friends from Ilocos Norte. Fourteen of 25 flag officers were forced to retire, including the AFP Chief and Vice Chief of Staff, Commanding General of the Army, Chief of PC, all four Constabulary zone commanders, and about one third of the provincial commanders. Many key appointments were then given to officers from Marcos' Ilocos Norte, with Brigadier General Ernesto Mata named Chief of Staff, Brigadier General Segundo Velasco named Chief of the Constabulary, and Colonel Fabian Ver, Marcos' cousin, named commander of the Presidential Security Command.[99]

Fortuitously for Marcos, President Johnson had also, just a few days earlier, on Christmas Day 1965, ordered a halt to the bombing of North Vietnam in an attempt to achieve a negotiated peace. Johnson had then dispatched foreign advisors to world capitals with the mission of gaining support for the U.S. strategy as part of a "More Flags" crusade. The crusade was part of an ultimately vain attempt to convince the American public and the world that Vietnam was not just an American war. Philippine participation was seen as crucial in this crusade and Hubert Humphrey was sent to the Manila inauguration to persuade Marcos to join. Marcos quickly sensed that Vietnam had raised the value to the United States of its Philippine bases and he exploited this as a bargaining chip. Several U.S. visits later, after extensive negotiations, Marcos agreed to send the 2,000-man engineer battalion he had so fiercely opposed as Senate President, in exchange for an invitation for a state visit to the United States. Johnson agreed. In August 1966, the first of the Filipinos were sent to Vietnam, and a month later, Marcos headed to the United States for what turned out to be a widely publicized, highly successful state visit involving much favorable press coverage and a well-received address to Congress. In the address, Marcos effusively proclaimed Philippine support for the U.S. role in Vietnam, extolled anticommunism in the region, and gave credibility to the More Flags crusade, thus proving his worth to Johnson.[100]

During the visit, Marcos agreed to send ten additional battalions, provided the United States financed these, at a cost of $7 million,[101] *and* allowed Marcos to keep some in the Philippines for his own purposes. In addition, Marcos won a U.S. commitment of $45 million in economic assistance, $31 million to settle Philippine veterans' claims from World War II, and $3.5 million for Imelda Marcos to build a Cultural Center. Upon his return to the Philippines, Marcos received another boost. Through a top secret message sent him from Johnson via U.S. Ambassador to the Philippines William Blair, Marcos learned that the U.S. bases in the Philippines housed nuclear weapons, a fact Filipino presidents had long suspected but until then had not known for certain. Perhaps Johnson thought the information would deepen Marcos' bond to the United States; instead, Marcos realized he was in an even stronger bargaining position than he had suspected. Marcos, ever the shrewd negotiator, would use this trump card over and over again throughout his regime to secure U.S. aid and other support. For the Vietnam effort, Marcos ultimately sent no more than the token 2,000-man engineer battalion and withdrew these in 1969 under pressure from Philippine opposition as well as implications by U.S. Senator Stuart Symington that the Philippine forces were nothing more than mercenary soldiers.[102] Yet Marcos deployed most of the U.S.-financed battalions sent to the Philippines as part of the deal for infrastructural projects. This brought the military back into "civic action" projects on an unprecedented scale, particularly in the construction of feeder roads linking rural communities with towns and cities.[103] Marcos also distributed much of the U.S. money, as well as the construction contracts, to a network of cronies who, unlike the traditional elites, had primary loyalty to Marcos.

Meanwhile, the Philippine bases were becoming ever more crucial to the U.S. campaign in Vietnam, as Olongapo, site of the Subic Bay naval base, expanded rapidly from a small town of 44,000 in 1966 to 200,000 a decade later.[104] And as the bases grew, so too did U.S. concerns about the internal security of the Philippines. U.S. policy toward the Philippines now centered on the need to secure the bases and encourage the development of the Philippine armed forces military capability to defend against internal security threats to them, including a rise in anti-U.S. demonstrations protesting Philippine involvement in the Vietnam War.[105] U.S. support for the Philippine armed forces was, moreover, viewed as a bargaining chip to secure Philippine engineer battalions for the U.S. effort in Vietnam.[106]

By 1967, U.S. expenditures on Vietnam had climbed to $2 billion a month.[107] About 500,000 soldiers were fighting there and more bombs had already been dropped on Vietnam than in all of the World War II theaters. Yet the United States and South Vietnam were no closer to victory over the communists than they had been two years earlier, prior to the massive build-up. Amid rising U.S. casualties and extensive media coverage—the first of its kind for American audiences who now witnessed the horrors of war from their livingrooms, opposition to the war escalated dramatically.[108] College students held sit-ins, formed the Students for a Democratic Society (SDS), and organized protest marches throughout the United States. And Civil Rights activists such as Martin Luther King denounced the war as not only unjust but also a diversion from pressing racial and economic issues at home, recalling the abolitionists who had made similar claims about the U.S. war in the Philippines more than half a century earlier. Debate spread within the administration as well, as Secretary of Defense Robert McNamara, a chief architect of Johnson's policy who now felt the United States should scale back its intervention in Vietnam, resigned. As in 1899, news reports and letters from soldiers at the front undermined the veracity of the administration's "body counts," undermining as well Johnson's credibility.

But the situation exploded in January 1968. During the Vietnamese lunar new year, the Vietcong together with North Vietnamese regulars launched a series of surprise attacks in thirty-six of South Vietnam's forty-four provincial capitals, five of its six major cities, sixty-four district capitals, and fifty villages, laying siege as well to the U.S. embassy in Saigon. Though the communists actually suffered an estimated 40,000 casualties, while United States and South Vietnamese forces suffered just 3,500 casualties, the so-called Tet Offensive horrified the American public, who looked on as Vietnamese women and children ran screaming from villages, while U.S. soldiers explained that they "had to destroy the village in order to save it." Like the Philippines before it, Vietnam was being turned into a "howling wilderness." Johnson's credibility plummeted, and on March 31, he ordered an end to the bombing of most of North Vietnam, announced plans for a new peace initiative, and withdrew from the race for reelection. Eugene McCarthy filled the Democrat's slot; but voters registered their desire for change and elected Richard Nixon, who, like Eisenhower with respect to Korea, campaigned on the promise of a "secret plan" for "peace with honor" in Vietnam. With the new administration came an opening for a shift in policy, as the lessons of Vietnam regarding the limits of intervention now challenged those of World War II regarding the risks of diplomacy and appeasement. Though some U.S. officials still pressed for all-out war in Vietnam, Nixon began a gradual withdrawal while pledging U.S. money and materiel, but not men, to support other nonnuclear nations fighting internal or external enemies of the United States.

A New "Mandate":
The Transition to Martial Law

In this, Marcos saw yet another opportunity to increase U.S. aid to his regime, as the embers of Huk resistance reignited in the Philippine countryside. On December 26, 1968, in honor of Mao's birthday, eleven Filipinos led by Jose Marie Sison split from the PKP and met in a remote village in Pangasinan province to form the new, Chinese-inspired Communist Party of the Philippines (CPP). The following March, Benigno Aquino, Jr., now a Senator and leader of the moderate opposition's Liberal Party, encouraged the radical opposition as well when he introduced Sison to former Huk guerrilla Dante Buscayno, who became head of the CPP's military arm, the New People's Army (NPA). With just a few hundred regulars and an arsenal of seventy weapons,[109] the NPA, with the CPP's direction, turned from a Soviet focus on urban workers to a Maoist emphasis on the peasantry, who represented roughly 70 percent of the total population.[110] At the same time, another insurgency led by Muslims in the South was emerging as well.[111] By the November 1969 presidential elections, opposition to Marcos had spread among moderates as well as revolutionaries. Undeterred, Marcos mobilized his network of cronies and the military to help run what were to become the most corrupt Philippine elections to date. His subsequent 2,000,000-vote margin of victory was profoundly challenged by the Philippine electorate and Marcos soon faced a crisis of legitimacy when, in January 1970, 20,000 students, workers, and peasants staged a mass protest. Later known as the "First Quarter Storm" because it coincided with the first quarter of university classes, the protest swiftly escalated into the worst peacetime riots the Philippines had yet seen. Only when a U.S. marine detachment was sent in was order restored; but opposition to Marcos continued to spread and organize.[112]

As opposition spread, Marcos became increasingly concerned about 1971 congressional elections and the implications of these for presidential elections scheduled for 1973. Although Philippine law limited presidents to two terms, Marcos had hoped to continue his legacy either by choosing his successor, with Defense Minister Juan Ponce Enrile among his top choices, or by rewriting the constitution. In the summer of 1971, Marcos acted on both fronts, launching a constitutional convention to review its precepts[113] while selecting and supporting several Nacionalista Party candidates. He also acted covertly. As the campaign opened on August 21, 1971, a Liberal Party rally at the Plaza Miranda with more than 10,000 in attendance was disrupted when two fragmentation grenades were thrown at the dais while other explosives were detonated beneath the stage, leaving 6 dead and over 100 seriously wounded. Violence erupted in the South as well, with much-publicized massacres of Muslims by Christian gangs, which caught the attention of the Islamic world.[114] Marcos immediately suspended the writ of habeas corpus, charged the communists for the violence, and accused Benigno Aquino, Jr., who was not at the site, of aiding and abetting them. Controversy about the incident continues to shroud the truth. CIA documents, corroborated by some CPP accounts, indicate that neither the CPP nor the NPA had the capability, the urban base, or the weaponry to carry out such an assault. Recently declassified U.S. documents based on evidence provided by a CIA mole in the Philippine military indicate instead that the assault was organized by Marcos or those close to him.[115] Whatever the truth, the bombing widened the chasm between Marcos and his opponents.

Marcos now attempted to stir anticommunist fears to increase his strong-arm Nacionalista Party's chances of victory at the polls; but the strategy backfired. Public opinion in the Philippines indicted Marcos for the Plaza Miranda incident, and the candidates chosen by Marcos lost badly, while the Liberals won six senatorial seats.[116] It seemed likely now that the Liberals, led by Aquino, would win in the 1973 presidential elections. Moreover, the constitutional convention was providing a venue for Liberal delegates to press for such constitutional changes as banning U.S. military bases and restricting the activities of large U.S. corporations in the Philippines. Far from using the convention to extend either presidential terms or the Marcos legacy, as Marcos had planned, the delegates used it as an opportunity to reevaluate the Philippine relationship with the United States, including the bases and U.S. investments.[117] U.S. corporations were accused of pressuring delegates at the convention to perpetuate privileged U.S. access by opposing proposed economic reforms.[118] U.S. officials also channeled money through the CIA to bribe the delegates from voting for such changes, though the convention continued for more than a year with often rancorous debate.

In early 1972, Sergio Osmena plotted with American "guns for hire" to assassinate Marcos. The plan was uncovered by Marcos spies, forcing Osmena and the others to flee to the United States; but it was a somber warning to Marcos.[119] Then a spate of bombings rocked Manila, with one a month in March, April, May, and June, and three in July. Marcos, again, blamed the bombings on the communists. By early August, Marcos met with Enrile and a few other top advisers to plan for martial law. Marcos conferred frequently with U.S. Ambassador Henry Byroade, who sought direction from Nixon while trying to dissuade Marcos from the plan. Nixon, consumed by Vietnam, Watergate and his own reelection concerns as well as his up-coming trips to China and the Soviet Union, requested a review of policy[120] but was largely inattentive, leaving Marcos to believe that as long as an internal communist threat, or the appearance of one, loomed in the Philippines, the United States would back him. August saw seven more bombings, followed by five in early September.[121] Marcos blamed the communists but the CIA learned that Marcos had been behind at least one of the bombings. On September 12, Aquino leaked information about the coup plans to U.S. Ambassador Henry Byroade, who did not believe Aquino until a text of the martial law proclamation reached him from a high level Filipino on the CIA payroll.[122] Byroade then tried to dissuade Marcos from the plan, on the grounds that it could ignite opposition in the U.S. Congress and the Philippines, but when neither the State Department nor the CIA sent Marcos a red light signal,[123] Marcos considered implementing the plans.

And he had the military capacity and backing to carry it out. The Philippine military now numbered 62,000. Most of the senior officers, a cadre of junior officers, and the troops who reported to them were loyal to Marcos, having gained considerable power vis-à-vis civilian institutions since 1965 as well as wealth from privileged access to construction contracts, U.S. aid, government funds, and promotions that circumvented standard procedures. Marcos had also provided training in civilian management for officers, initiating the first regular course at the National Defense College of the Philippines in February 1966, from which 93 graduated by 1972.[124] In addition, 145 officers received training in the United States as part of the Military Assistance Program from 1966 to 1972.[125] A notch down was the Command and General Staff College, opened in 1969 to train military personnel for "civilian leadership roles."[126] While the military did establish health, education, legal, and other community service projects during Marcos' tenure, it also emerged as a highly politicized counter-insurgency force. In particular, a special Metropolitan Area Command launched in 1968 with just 300 police had increased to a force of 1,700, with training from the United States in crowd control techniques, a skill the United States had been honing with notorious results at places like Memphis, Chicago, and Kent State.[127]

Fearing a bloodbath as well as the loss of U.S. support, Marcos vacillated. Enrile urged Marcos to respond swiftly. The final act came on September 22, 1972, when Enrile's car was strafed with bullets, though no one was harmed. Years later, Enrile acknowledged that he had ordered the attack himself to trigger the coup, and that Marcos had used it as a pretext to declare martial law, backdating the decree to September 21 so that it would be divisible by seven, his lucky number. In what the U.S. State Department wryly termed his "one-man democracy," Marcos then arrested over six thousand, including Aquino as well as priests, nuns, students, journalists, publishers, and others from both the moderate and the revolutionary opposition. Others fled the country, many to the United States, as tanks and truckloads of troops rolled through Manila. Soon after, the Philippine congress was abolished, mass activities prohibited, political parties outlawed, civil and political rights suspended, and a curfew from midnight to

4 a.m. announced. With civilian institutions abolished and the judiciary severely weakened, the military was now the primary instrument of the national government outside of the presidency. Though Marcos announced that martial law was not a military takeover, twelve men, dubbed the "Twelve Apostles" or the "Rolex Twelve" for the watches Marcos reputedly gave them, had been in constant consultation regarding the decision.[128] They included Defense Minister Enrile, Philippine Constabulary Chief Fidel Ramos, PSC Chief Fabian Ver, eight other senior military officers and Congressman Eduardo Cojuangco, Jr. who was recalled to active duty as a colonel. From within his cell at Fort Bonifacio, invoking an earlier era of resistance, Aquino would later recount his surprise, not with Marcos, but with the relative silence of his countrymen.

Days later, the American Chamber of Commerce in the Philippines informed the U.S. business community of its support for martial law.[129] Still worried that U.S. disapproval might signal military opponents to undo martial law, however, Marcos sent a trusted aide, Alejandro Melchor, to the United States to gauge the official response. Upon arriving in D.C., Melchor met with John Holdridge of the NSC who needed only to be assured that U.S. business interests would not be threatened by martial law. Melchor then met with Joint Chiefs of Staff Chairman Admiral Thomas Moorer, who was actually enthusiastic about martial law. Melchor next elicited a promise from former Defense Secretary now World Bank Director Robert McNamara for a doubling of loans if Marcos promised to use his martial law powers to develop the Philippines. These loans would actually quadruple during the Marcos regime, though very little went to development projects. Melchor then met with Senate majority leader Mike Mansfield, with Marcos' friend Senator Daniel Inouye whose Hawaiian constituency included many Ilocano Marcos supporters, and with Senate Foreign Relations Committee Chairman William Fulbright. In none of these meetings did Melchor find opposition to what Marcos had done. Even the elite U.S. press, with the exception of the *Washington Post*, endorsed Marcos, with the *New York Times* featuring him as their "Man in the News" for his "strength in a nation of uncertainty." Melchor returned to the Philippines with all of the assurances and support Marcos needed to begin a massive restructuring of Philippine society, which was to supplant in less than a decade much of the established oligarchy while greatly expanding the power of the military and a close circle of Marcos cronies, all with U.S. backing.

Marcos would retain U.S. backing for the next fourteen years of his regime, arguing essentially, like the American soldier in Vietnam, that he had to destroy democracy in order to save it. U.S. analysts in the Bureau of Intelligence and Research at the State Department understood this.[130] And a Rand Corporation study completed in November 1972 reported "considerable evidence" that martial law was carried out through U.S. collusion in order to advance U.S. objectives in the Philippines, notably the economic and strategic interests so recently threatened by the constitutional convention as well as the deeper, recurring threat posed by revolutionary opposition.[131]

In short, from the moment that the Philippine flag replaced the American one in Manila's Rizal Park on July 4, 1946, through the September 22, 1972, transition to martial law with Marcos at the helm, global U.S. military strategy and Philippine domestic politics had become increasingly interdependent. This interdependence was outlined explicitly in the 1947 agreement between the United States and the Philippines, wherein the stated purpose of the Philippine military was internal security, while the United States was to provide external security. Toward this end, the United States had won a ninety-nine year lease on its twenty-two military bases in the Philippines, and, as Cold War policies evolved, launched a military build-up that was to place Subic as America's largest overseas naval base with Clark among the top five largest overseas air bases by the end of the period. Meanwhile, Philippine officials used the bases as leverage for U.S. economic aid, totaling $1.85 billion from 1946 to 1972, and military aid, totaling $672.5 million during the same period, or $2.52 billion in all.[132] Though U.S. officials were loathe to describe any linkage between the aid and the bases, privately, successive administrations understood the aid to be a form of "rent."[133] Moreover, despite periodic, albeit weak, calls from the United States for structural reforms such as land reform in order to curtail recurring threats from revolutionary opposition, most of the economic aid was pilfered by the landed oligarchy and presidential cronies who redirected the U.S. funds for their own gain. To silence any domestic opposition, the military aid was used to increase internal security forces from 37,000 in 1946 to 62,000 by 1972.

By that point, with a wide network of Filipino cronies and U.S. allies, Marcos saw an opportunity and he took it. Over the next fourteen years, Marcos would almost succeed in his attempt to destroy democracy in order to save it, but, miraculously, it survived. The impact of martial law on Philippine society and the resurgence of electoral democracy in 1986 will be described in the next two chapters.

Notes

1. This paragraph is from Gaddis, *Strategies of Containment*, prologue.

2. Ibid.

3. Information for this paragraph is from Constantino and Letizia, *The Continuing Past*, 189-225; Brands 227-247; and Karnow, *In Our Image*, 323-355.

4. Constantino and Letizia, *The Continuing Past,* 189-225.

5. Fact-Finding Commision, op. cit., 29.

6. Ibon Facts and Figures, Volume VIII, Issue No. 176, December 1985.

7. Constantino and Letizia, *The Continuing Past*, 197.

8. Lachica, 118-136.

9. Combs, 316-346.

10. Military budgets cited are from Gaddis, *Strategies of Containment*, which are from the U.S. Bureau of the Census.

11. From Overseas Loans and Grants and Assistance from International Organizations, 1961–1988, Special Report Prepared for the House Foreign Affairs Committee, Office of Statistics and Reports, Bureau for Program and Policy Coordination, U.S. Agency for International Development. Note that the figures include Export-Import Bank and other official loans.

12. Gaddis, *Strategies of Containment*.

13. Gaddis, *Strategies of Containment*, 26 from Kissinger, *White House Years*.

14. Kennan.

15. Gaddis, *Strategies of Containment*, 30.

16. Combs, 338.

17. The State Department urged that diplomatic channels with the communists be kept open. See Combs, 338.

18. See Koen for an excellent description of the China lobby's influence on U.S. foreign policy.

19. Combs, 338-340, and Koen.

20. Kerkvliet, *The Huk Rebellion*, 153.

21. Karnow, *In Our Image*, 345. Kerkvliet cites one resident of San Ricardo in Nueva Ecija who recalled that "civilian guards and the constabulary arrested anyone they wanted, burned houses, took food, and raped. These men," he continued, "were absolutely the worst." From Kerkvliet, *The Huk Rebellion*, 159.

22. Brands, 234.

23. Brands, 240.

24. Karnow, *In Our Image*, 344.

25. Brands, 235.

26. Brands, 234-35.

27. Brands, 236.

28. Karnow, *In Our Image*, 345. See also Appendix I for U.S. aid figures, and Brands, chapter 12, for an excellent description of the U.S. role in post-war Philippine economic and political development.

29. Karnow, *In Our Image*, 345.

30. Brands, 236.

31. National Security Council (NSC) 84/2, 5.

32. Non-Classified Policy Paper from the National Security Council (NSC) to President Truman, November 9, 1950, from the National Security Archive collection. The report asserts that U.S. policy should stress reforms and the elimination of government corruption but urges the strengthening of the Joint U.S. Military Advisory Group to defend U.S. military facilities from internal security threats posed by the Chinese minority and the Huks.

33. Brands, 241.

34. Gaddis, *Strategies of Containment*, 91.

35. Berry, 78-79.

36. The description of the U.S. role in the Korean War is from Combs, 340-45. Another classic account of the war is by Whiting. See also Rees, for a discussion of U.S. policy of the period, and Schlesinger, for the conflict between MacArthur and Truman.

37. Brands, 241.

38. Information on Quirino is from Karnow, *In Our Image*, 344-45. Information on the U.S. position regarding the Huks is from NSC 84/2.

39. Brands, 241.

40. NSC 84/2.

41. NSC 84/2.

42. Combs, 342.

43. Greene.

44. Karnow, *In Our Image*, 346-48.

45. Fact-Finding Commission, 32, and from Shalom (1981), 79-80.

46. Personal field research, 1984–1986.

47. Fact-Finding Commission.

48. U.S. Department of the Army, No. 7557, 1-2. Regarding the corruption, the report cites the use of PC forces to protect mines, property and other private economic interests of politically influential people with populated areas falling "easy prey to raiding Huks." It also cites the use of PC forces as a "political tool, especially in the intimidation of voters." Moreover, the report notes that "in many areas of the Philippines, the population lived more in fear of the Constabulary than of the Huks."

49. Karnow, *In Our Image,* 350.

50. Constantino and Letizia, *The Continuing Past*, 236-37 and from Lansdale, 61-63.

51. Karnow, *In Our Image,* 351.

52. Constantino and Letizia, *The Continuing Past*, 248-250.

53. Ibon, 176, Fact-Finding Commission, 30.

54. McLane, 417-432.

55. Constantino and Letizia, *The Continuing Past*, 256-57.

56. Karnow, *In Our Image*, 336.

57. McLane, 292-303.

58. Karnow, *In Our Image,* 351.

59. Gaddis, *Strategies of Containment*, 179.

60. Ibid.

61. Koen, 160-193.

62. Brands, 250. Some examples of CIA intervention include plans to assassinate Cuba's Castro, the Congo's Patrice Lumumba, and to launch an armed revolt against Sukarno in 1958.

63. Karnow, *In Our Image,* 352. See Brands 253 regarding Philippine laws, Lansdale's role, as well as Philippine sugar interests in backing Magsaysay.

64. CIA, OCI No. 1026, 20 November 1953.

65. Ibid.

66. Brands, 254.

67. Constantino and Letizia, and a personal interview with Manahan, October 1983.

68. From a personal interview with Manahan, October 1983.

69. Fact-Finding Commission, 32.

70. Karnow, *In Our Image,* 350.

71. Combs, 362 on Iran and 365-66 on Guatemala.

72. Brands, 257-59 and Combs 366-69.

73. Constantino and Letizia, 291.

74. Brands, 264.

75. Constantino and Letizia, 291.

76. Brands, 267.

77. Combs, 369.

78. Smith, James Burkholder, 279-80.

79. Personal interviews conducted from 1984–1986 with Filipino volunteers to Vietnam.

80. Combs, 390-91.

81. Brands, 267.

82. Brands, 270. From CNO to JCS, 11/4/58 (JCS 1519/120) JCS Records.

83. Brands, 268.

84. Marcos had a held a seat in the lower chamber as a representative of Ilocos Norte since 1949, having won in one of the dirtiest elections to date. Subsequently, as chairman of the committee supervising import controls, he took bribes for licenses from the tobacco kings of his region and from American entrepreneur Harry Stonehill, who had tobacco, real estate and other interests in the Philippines. From Karnow, *In Our Image*, 370.

85. Brands, 277.

86. Fact-Finding Commission, 33.

87. Interdepartmental Committee report, August 1962, and White House memo signed by McGeorge Bundy, August 24, 1962, from the National Security Archive collection. A year later, a symposium would be held at Rand to discuss lessons of the Huk insurgency and its applications for Vietnam. Top U.S.-trained Filipinos from the Philippine campaign shared their recollections with senior U.S. strategists. Report from a symposium on the role of airpower in counterinsurgency and unconventional warfare at the Rand Corporation, July 1963, also from the National Security Archive collection.

88. Combs, 390-93.

89. In Confidential Airgram A-305 sent July 9, 1964 from the State Department to U.S. embassies worldwide, U.S. policy was defined as requiring a strong military capability in Asia and the western Pacific to deter communism. From the National Security Archive collection.

90. Combs, 395.

91. Berry, 132.

92. Combs, 395-96.

93. Several books on the bases, including Paez, Berry, Bonner, etc., cite the build-up but without figures. Defense budget analysts interviewed for this project note that overseas

base build-up figures are often buried in budgets which may specify total overseas expenditures without citing figures for specific bases. This is done for international and domestic political reasons, since U.S. bases, and so any build-up of these, is often an explosive issue within the United States and in the host country.

94. Brands, 281-82.

95. Brands, 307.

96. Combs, 395-96.

97. The above information is from Karnow, *In Our Image,* 356-388.

98. Karnow, *In Our Image,* 365, 422.

99. Fact-Finding Commission, 42.

100. Berry, 133.

101. Fact-Finding Commission, 37.

102. Berry, 144.

103. Fact-Finding Commission, 40-41. Note that the 51st Engineer Battalion alone completed 13 major construction projects in 1966, more than 50% of Corps of Engineers in 12.5 years under previous administrations. AFP's contribution to feeder roads accounted for 30% of the total from 1966–1973.

104. Bonner, 205.

105. Secret Action Memorandum, February 23, 1966. U.S. concerns regarding the anti-U.S. demonstrations are described in various airgrams from the embassy to the State Department, including Confidential Airgram A-707 sent March 2, 1966 and Confidential Airgram A-726 sent five days later, from the National Security Archive collection.

106. A Secret Cable from the U.S. Pacific Command's Commander-in-Chief to the Department of Defense proposes that the U.S. request additional Philippine civic action group deployment in the Vietnamese conflict in exchange for aid to the Philippine armed forces, sent March 1, 1966. In a Secret Cable sent July 24, 1966, the decision was made to give Marcos military supplies in exchange for battalions. From the National Security Archive collection.

107. Combs, 397.

108. See Gitlin's excellent account of the role of the U.S. media in covering U.S. opposition to the Vietnam War.

109. Karnow, *In Our Image,* 378.

110. An econometric study by the Rand Corporation cited military repression as the primary source of revolutionary activity in Luzon, not rural dissatisfaction with social conditions. Memorandum RM-5757-ARPA, January 1969, from the National Security Archive collection.

111. See Noble's account of the Muslim insurgency in the Philippines in Schirmer and Shalom, eds., *Philippines Reader,* 193-99.

112. The United States also sent riot control munitions, as noted in a secret cable sent February 10, 1970, from the U.S. Pacific Command to the Joint U.S. Military Advisory Group. Note also that a review of U.S. assistance to Marcos now reported that U.S. officials had not controlled the use of payments provided for the Philippine civic action groups and so had likely contributed to the Marcos administration's widespread corruption, as reported in Secret Report B-168501, from the National Security Archive collection.

113. A secret report completed May 7, 1971, by the Bureau of Intelligence and Research at the State Department asserted that Marcos sought to use the constitutional convention to retain power. From the National Security Archive collection.

114. Noble, in Schirmer and Shalom, eds., *Philippines Reader*, 194.

115. Confidential Memorandum from Theodore Eliot Jr. at the State Department to Henry Kissinger at the National Security Council, August 23, 1971, from the National Security Archive collection cites Marcos as the instigator.

116. Limited Official Use Cable #11770 from the U.S. embassy in the Philippines to the State Department, sent December 28, 1971, from the National Security Archive.

117. On the debate regarding the bases, see Confidential Airgram A-191, sent from the U.S. embassy to the State Department July 1, 1970, from the National Security Archive collection.

118. On the debate regarding U.S. investments and alleged U.S. corporate interference, see Limited Official Use Cable #01701 sent from the U.S. embassy in the Philippines to the State Department, February 24, 1972. From the National Security Archive.

119. Karnow, *In Our Image*, 380-81.

120. Nixon's request for the policy review is cited in a Secret National Security Study Memorandum from the National Security Council to the Defense Department, June 28, 1972. From the National Security Archive collection.

121. Information for this paragraph was taken from Bonner, , and from Confidential Cable #08372 from Ambassador Henry Byroade to the U.S. State Department, September 6, 1972, and Secret Cable #08787 also from Byroade to the U.S. State Department, September 18, 1972, from the National Security Archive collection. In the latter cable, Byroade acknowledges that the Marcos administration was exploiting the bombings for his own advantage.

122. Karnow, *In Our Image*, 359. See also Confidential Cable #08620 from Byroade to the State Department sent September 13, 1972, describing the discussion with Aquino, Byroade's reactions, and his analysis of the Filipino opposition to Marcos. From the National Security Archive collection.

123. Karnow, *In Our Image*, 356. See also Secret Cable #168484 sent September 14, 1972 from the State Department to the U.S. embassy, requesting an assessment of Marcos' assertions regarding the security threat; Limited Official Use Cable #08738 sent a day later from Byroade to the State Department, wherein Aquino reveals Marcos' plans for martial law, which Marcos confirms; and, most significantly, Secret Cable #08787 sent September 18, 1972, from Byroade to the State Department, reporting that the Marcos administration was exploiting the communist threat for his own ends, that it was not in fact an immediate threat to Philippine security. In all of these documents, U.S. officials discuss Marcos' intentions but do not establish a formal policy to dissuade him from declaring martial law.

124. Fact-Finding Commission, 35.

125. Ibid., 34.

126. Fact-Finding Commission, 35. The report notes that it was not an expressed but merely an implicit function of the college to prepare military men for such roles.

127. See Fact-Finding Commission, and Caspar, "Civil–Military Relations in the Philippines."

128. Fact-Finding Commission, 44, from a Marcos speech on "Loyalty Day" to the Armed Forces of the Philippines.

129. Telegram from the American Chamber of Commerce in the Philippines sent September 27, 1972, reprinted in the National Security Archive collection.

130. A Secret Report from INR titled "The Philippines Tries One-Man Democracy," distributed November 1, 1972.

131. Rand Corporation Report to the U.S. Army Reserve 301st Civil Affairs Group, distributed November 1972, reprinted in the National Security Archive collection. The report cites grants from Marcos to U.S. corporations for oil exploration rights following martial law, as well as safeguards to U.S. investments and property, including the military bases, and other concessions overturning Philippine Supreme Court decisions made prior to martial law which threatened $2-3 billion worth of U.S. investments.

132. Overseas Loans and Grants and Assistance from International Organizations, 1961–1988, Special Report Prepared for the House Foreign Affairs Committee, Office of Statistics and Reports, Bureau for Program and Policy Coordination, U.S. Agency for International Development. Note that the figures include Export-Import Bank and other official loans.

133. See Brands, and Berry, in particular, for descriptions of the history of U.S. negotiations on the bases with successive Philippine administrations.

Chapter 5

"Salvaging" Democracy:
The Impact of Authoritarian Rule,
1972–1983

Human rights violations and political assassinations, known in the peculiar lexicon of war as "salvagings," would become rampant in the Philippines after 1972. This chapter examines the effect of these and other aspects of martial law on Philippine society, focusing on the gradual defection from Marcos by key members of the church, the military, and the business community, and the transnational strategies they used to challenge Marcos.[1] The chapter then traces the simultaneous rise of an opposition movement in the United States after 1972, challenging a foreign policy that, since 1946, had helped create the military capacity for authoritarian rule in several allied countries, including the Philippines. Central to the growing debate over U.S. foreign policy was whether hard-line tactics fueled or quelled revolutionary opposition abroad. Intensifying the debate was first the war in Indochina, then Watergate, followed by revolutions in Iran and Nicaragua and the threat of revolution in El Salvador. In 1981, as the Republicans regained control of the White House under President Reagan, the ultra-hard-liners would hold sway. For the Philippines, however, this would soon unravel. On August 21, 1983, the assassination of moderate opposition leader Benigno Aquino Jr. would create a political and economic crisis in the Philippines, spurring Aquino's U.S. and Filipino allies, in and out of government, to mobilize against Marcos.

"One-Man Democracy" and its Effects

The Philippine constitution and system of government were imported from the United States but with one crucial difference. While both the United States and the Philippine presidents headed the armed forces, the Philippine president had the additional power to declare martial law. On September 22, 1972, Marcos had exercised this power. Proclamation 1081, signed that day and announced to the Philippine public a day later, placed America's experiment in colonial democracy under authoritarian rule. In his address to the nation, Marcos justified the act, claiming that the nation was "imperiled by the danger of a violent overthrow, insurrection and rebellion." He cited the New People's Army (NPA) and other communist organizations,[2] though these were, in fact, in their infancy. The U.S. State Department's Bureau of Intelligence and Research (INR) noted in a secret study underway in the summer of 1972 that the revolutionary movement's "military operations were at a low level and confined to remote areas." Contrary to Marcos' estimates of at least 8,000 NPA guerrillas, 10,000 active cadres and 100,000 supporters, INR put the total sum of these at fewer than 9,000.[3] A study by the Rand Corporation in November 1972 presented much lower estimates placing NPA strength at just 1,000 regulars with perhaps an additional 5,000 to 6,000 armed supporters. In its own history, prepared years later, the NPA claimed just 350 armed guerrillas at the time of martial law. Whatever the actual figure, a U.S. intelligence official involved in Philippine policy in 1972 says Marcos' claims about the NPA were "a joke."[4] Instead, the real reason for martial law was quickly apparent: Marcos was not ready to leave office. As a secret cable sent September 18, 1972, from the U.S. embassy in Manila to the State Department concluded, Marcos was exploiting the threat of Communism for his own ends. Though the cable urged the United States to press for economic and political reform, hardline tactics claimed the day.[5]

Marcos immediately arrested much of the opposition, including Benigno "Ninoy" Aquino Jr. as well as journalists, students, and members of the church, most of whom belonged to a moderate opposition seeking a democratic transition from Marcos, not a communist revolution. A confidential cable from the U.S. embassy in Manila to the State Department revealed, for instance, that of 126

Philippine citizens named on an arrest list, members of Aquino's Liberal Party formed the majority, further indicating the real aims of martial law.[6] U.S. officials were then told that martial law would serve U.S. economic and strategic interests by securing them from nationalist opposition.[7] By treating moderates as revolutionaries as the Spaniards had done at the end of their colonial rule, Marcos actually helped recruit many to the revolutionary movement, which grew from the few hundred in 1972 to roughly 20 percent of the population by the end of the Marcos regime in 1986, as described in the next chapter. Other Marcos opponents fled to exile, notably to the United States, where they launched active lobbying campaigns to expose the human rights abuses of the Marcos regime and to press for a withdrawal of U.S. support from Marcos. Among these was Raul Manglapus, Secretary of Foreign Affairs in 1957 and from 1961 to 1972 an opposition senator. In his exile in the United States,[8] Manglapus cultivated a network of well-placed American friends, wrote opinion pieces for the *New York Times* and other media outlets, frequently gave testimony before Congress urging the United States to cut aid to Marcos, and spearheaded a mass-based campaign to undo martial law, founding in 1973 the Movement for a Free Philippines.[9] He also publicized his campaign in the U.S.-based *Philippine News*, a newspaper widely read by the Filipino community in the United States. Manglapus soon gained a broad base of support among the estimated one million Filipinos living in the United States in the 1970s.[10]

The transnational influence of the church also played a crucial role, linking the anti-Marcos lobby with a growing international human rights lobby. The growth of the human rights lobby in the United States is exemplified by the increase in membership in the U.S. section of Amnesty International from 3,000 to 50,000 between 1974 and 1976.[11] Membership continued to expand thereafter, fostering as well the development of human rights organizations in countries under authoritarian rule.[12] As one participant explained: "The human rights lobby was essentially a church lobby."[13] In Latin America, Eastern Europe, the Philippines, etc., church leaders, particularly Catholics schooled in the liberation theology of Latin America as well as the new teachings of Vatican II, were being targeted by authoritarian regimes for their work with the poor. In the Philippines, opposition from an emerging cadre of politically active Catholics intensified when, immediately following martial law, four American priests were arrested. A month later, two more American priests were deported. This generated political activism among U.S. Catholic and other church groups who worked through the U.S. media and Congress, with critical support from Congressman Father Robert Drinan (D-MA). Their goal was to inform the American public and redirect U.S. support away from authoritarian regimes toward reform and democratization.[14] Meanwhile, given that roughly 85 percent of the Philippine population belonged to the Roman

Catholic Church at the time, such actions by Marcos sparked widespread indignation. Moreover, with the elimination of most other forms of institutionalized opposition under martial law, the Catholic Church in the Philippines emerged after 1972 as one of the few organizations able to challenge Marcos and articulate the growing anger against his regime, led by moderates in the Catholic Bishops Conference of the Philippines (CBCP), including the unfortunately-named Cardinal Sin of Manila.[15]

The Church was, however, not united. One of the leading voices of the Philippine Catholic Church, the CBCP, for instance, was comprised of 76 Bishops. About 15 of these advocated continued support for Marcos, between 13 and 24 advocated protest of martial law and exposure of the regime's abuses, while the remaining majority of between 37 and 48 bishops sought only moderate reforms. Led by Cardinal Sin, the moderates advocated "critical collaboration" with Marcos, although they would become increasingly radicalized against Marcos as repression, much of it targeted against the Church, continued.[16]

After attempting to silence his critics, Marcos next spent a fortune bribing the constitutional convention, which had been unable to agree on a new charter for over a year and now saw its most outspoken opposition leaders, including Manglapus, either exiled or jailed. At Marcos' behest, the convention replaced the presidential with a parliamentary system, naming Marcos Prime Minister. They also established a unicameral Batasang Pambansa, or National Assembly. Moreover, Marcos was granted the right to rule for as long as he wanted, by decree if he chose, and with the authority to decide when the nation's first parliamentary elections would be held. Meanwhile, the U.S. embassy in Manila reported that the new constitution favored foreign investments in general and American investments in particular, unlike the premartial law drafts.[17] All opposition newspapers, radio, and television stations were overtaken, and restrictions on assembly, speech, and debate imposed. To preserve the appearance of constitutionality, Marcos organized 36,000 Citizens' Assemblies throughout the country to register their views. For six days in January 1973, the assemblies responded to questions without the benefit of secrecy, as soldiers, mayors, district captains and others, all owing their positions to Marcos, tallied the results. Not surprisingly, the assemblies overwhelmingly approved the new constitution, rejected plans for 1973 elections, and endorsed martial law. INR, however, saw through the charade, reporting to Nixon that "It seems almost inevitable that [Marcos] will have to devote an increasing proportion of his time and energy to putting down opponents." The report warned that this would polarize Philippine politics, jeopardizing U.S. interests there. It concluded: "Only the United States can provide the financial aid and appearance of political backing [Marcos] badly needs."[18]

Far from heeding the warning, the United States nearly tripled military aid to Marcos from $18.4 million in 1972 to $50.4 million in 1973, while economic aid rose as well from $111.8 million in 1972 to $124 million in 1973. In fact, U.S. economic and military aid would greatly increase following the declaration of martial law, totaling close to $2 billion for the period from 1972 to the end of the Marcos era in 1986.[19] After 1972, Marcos began a massive military build-up, as the Philippines amassed by 1977 a sophisticated arsenal of "Tiger II Fighters," "Huey" helicopters, armored personnel carriers, and C-47 transport planes. Moreover, the United States supplied special forces units to conduct counterinsurgency throughout the Philippines,[20] while the U.S. State Department, under the Munitions Control Board, endorsed increases in commercial sales of weapons as well. From just 1972 to 1977, such sales totaled $8.5 million, a figure small by world standards but quite high for a small state like the Philippines. In fact, the figure was four times the value of all commercial sales from 1950 to 1972. Marcos also more than tripled the size of the Philippine military, still explicitly designed for internal security, from 62,000 in 1972 to 200,000 by the end of his regime,[21] while increasing the military's annual budget from $82 million in 1972 to $1 billion by 1980.[22] Marcos then further restructured the military to strengthen the power of his cadre of loyal officers. In exchange, he tolerated their smuggling and granted them illegal logging and mining concessions, while authorizing promotions on the basis of loyalty not competence, particularly to those from his province of Ilocos Norte. Finally, he expanded the political role of military leaders as some, notably Juan Ponce Enrile and Fidel Ramos, emerged as powers in their own right.[23] Corruption was rampant,[24] however, and those in the military who were excluded from such privileges would provide another potent source of opposition to Marcos, as described in the next chapter.

While using a portion of the U.S. aid to finance the military build-up, Marcos also used it as a personal source of power, diverting money from government banks to take over private banks, hotels, factories, shopping centers, and other enterprises.[25] In the process, Marcos disowned families to give his brother insurance, banking and real estate firms; his sister shipping concerns; and even his elderly mother tobacco, timber and food processing companies. He also drove a wedge in Aquino's family by building an alliance with wife Corazon Aquino's cousin Eduardo Cojuangco, helping him acquire a virtual monopoly on the Philippine coconut industry. At the time, the industry employed more people and earned more in exports than any other industry in the country, save perhaps for the martial law industry of "mining," as in, "That's mine, and that's mine." Cojuangco would further expand into real estate and banking, and would gain control of the country's largest corporation, San Miguel, which brewed beer and held both the Coca Cola and Pepsi bottling plants. By 1985, Cojuangco's private wealth was estimated at $4 billion. Meanwhile other "cronies" such as Herminio Disini, husband of one of Imelda's cousins, cornered the cigarette filter market when Marcos exempted him from a levy on raw materials, enabling him to eradicate his competitors. And Americans profited as well. In one striking example, Marcos took more than $600 million in loans and guarantees from Export–Import Bank Chairman, later CIA Director, William Casey to build a nuclear power plant in an area of intense volcanic activity. The contract was first awarded to General Electric but was then given to Westinghouse, after the latter gave Disini about $80 million as a fee for "construction."[26] To date, the plant remains inoperative,[27] though Filipino taxpayers have paid heavily for the project.

Not only did Marcos alienate taxpayers, by confiscating property from the traditional oligarchy, he created yet another potent, increasingly activist opposition. In one case, he imprisoned Eugenio Lopez Jr. for allegedly plotting against the Marcos regime, though his uncle Fernando had once been Marcos' Vice Presidential running mate, tearfully recruited by Imelda in 1965. The imprisonment was likely motivated by nonpolitical factors as well. By 1972, the Lopez family wealth from sugar, electric and other enterprises was estimated at $400 million. Two months after Eugenio Jr.'s arrest, Imelda's brother Benjamin "Kokoy" Romualdez spoke with the senior Eugenio, who was dying of cancer in California and was desperate to see his son. Romualdez's purpose was to discuss a transfer of the Lopez family's electric company assets to the Marcoses. Led to believe that he would thus see his son, the senior Eugenio signed over the assets. While his son still languished in prison, Eugenio Sr. was to die in San Francisco soon after, though not before providing support to the U.S.-based Manglapus campaign against Marcos, offering as well publicity in his widely read, U.S.-based *Philippine News*.[28] Still, the Marcoses would have one final encounter with the senior Lopez. At Eugenio Sr.'s funeral, held in Quezon City in the Philippines, heavily armed men made their way to the front of the church carrying an ornate black chair, and placed it among the chief mourners. Following behind was Imelda Marcos, in all black, who seated herself in the chair, amid gasps from American diplomats and others present.[29] Eugenio Lopez Jr. would eventually escape in 1977 to the United States, where he was to play a significant role in the U.S. anti-Marcos campaign. Meanwhile, the Marcoses continued to amass a fortune estimated in the billions, a fortune made all the more suspect since neither Imelda nor Ferdinand came from wealth. While Imelda went on her now infamous shopping sprees, the traditional oligarchy watched their economic base crumble.[30]

In the end, the Marcos regime's crackdown on dissidents and displacement of traditional sectors of elite society was so ruthless, expansive, and sustained that it ultimately created activist opposition from within the church, the military, the oligarchy, as well as the broader population. Gradually, this activism would extend to the U.S. foreign policy establishment, as some argued for continued support of Marcos' hard-line tactics to suppress the increasingly widespread opposition while others argued that military abuses were encouraging moderate Filipinos to ally with the revolutionaries.

Another Man's Democracy:
The Last Years of the Nixon Era

Just months before Marcos declared martial law, the scandal that would come to be known as Watergate broke in June 1972. Nixon tried to contain the subsequent investigations, but by September 15, just one week before Marcos declared martial law, a federal grand jury indicted seven men in Nixon's circle. Five days later, two principal members of Nixon's reelection committee were added to the list of defendants in the Democrats' civil suit.[31] Still, Nixon won a landslide victory in November, with help from Philippine sugar interests.[32] As the scandal unfolded, however, the Nixon administration became implicated at the highest levels in a campaign of domestic spying, involving wiretaps, black lists, break-ins, and a sweeping conspiracy against presumed opponents of Nixon in academia, the media, business, entertainment, and government. Given Nixon's growing sense of isolation for not ending the war in Indochina as he had promised in 1968, the scandal must be understood as a manifestation of the crisis in U.S. foreign policy. And this crisis, centering initially on policy toward Indochina, was fast spreading, undermining U.S. support for authoritarian allies worldwide, including the Marcos regime. In response, the Nixon administration not only spied on its own enemies, but also spied on anti-Marcos Filipinos in the United States.[33] As H.R. Haldeman, Nixon's chief of staff, later wrote, "without the Vietnam war there would have been no Watergate."[34] In fact, Nixon's spying campaign started as early as May 1969, after *New York Times* correspondent William Beecher revealed secret U.S. bombings of suspected communist sanctuaries in Cambodia, a country whose neutrality the Nixon administration had professed to respect.[35]

Enraged by the "leak," Nixon and Kissinger with FBI Director J. Edgar Hoover placed wiretaps on the phones of four journalists and thirteen officials, including members of Kissinger's own staff.[36] In March 1970, as U.S. and Vietnamese troops swept through Cambodia, antiwar protests exploded.[37] And domestic spying spread, particularly after a June 13, 1971, edition of the *New York Times* printed lengthy excerpts from a study of U.S. policy toward Vietnam. Directed by Leslie Gelb of the State Department, later of the *New York Times*, the study was leaked to the press by Daniel Ellsberg. Nixon quickly sought an injunction against the *Times* to force it to cease coverage of the so-called "Pentagon Papers;" but the Supreme Court voted against the president, and the coverage continued.[38] Stymied, Nixon established a special unit to prevent other such leaks. Known as "the plumbers," the unit named some two hundred to an "enemies list" and otherwise sought to discredit Nixon's opponents. Nixon won the 1972 elections, and Kissinger signed peace accords with North Vietnam soon after, on January 23, 1973; but the administration's credibility came under fire when congressional hearings on Watergate and the secret bombings in Cambodia began in the spring.[39]

Congress had deferred to presidents on foreign policy throughout most of the period since World War II, but now became more activist. Human rights lay at the center of the renewed congressional concern for foreign policy, as opposition to the secret bombings spread to other areas of U.S. intervention overseas.[40] Adding fuel to congressional anger, the U.S. General Accounting Office submitted reports to Congress in April 1973 detailing U.S. commitments of security assistance and military equipment to the armed forces of the Philippines as well as Korea and Thailand. In exchange, the United States was granted access to U.S. military facilities and logistical support for troop deployments to Vietnam. The reports concluded that such commitments had been made without either State Department or congressional oversight, and pressed the view that U.S. interests might be better protected through economic assistance rather than militarization.[41] And the implications for human rights were clear. In May, Congress cut funds for further bombing of Cambodia, and forced Nixon a month later to cease military activities in all of Indochina by August. Donald Fraser (D-MN), as chair of the formerly obscure Subcommittee on International Organizations and Movements of the House Committee on Foreign Affairs, later renamed the Subcommittee on Human Rights and International Organizations, also held a series of hearings in 1973 on human rights. Undaunted, Nixon and Kissinger were hard at work in Chile, where a U.S.-backed military coup on September 11, 1973, ousted democratically-elected Salvador Allende Gossens. A congressional resolution subsequently requested the executive branch to pursue the subject of human rights with Chile's Pinochet regime; but this was ignored.[42]

Another transnational tale illustrative of the tactics many anti-Marcos Filipinos used after 1972 is the story of Walden Bello.[43] A Filipino who had been in Chile writing a doctoral dissertation and returned to the United States in 1973 after the Chilean coup, Bello was impressed by the similarity of events there with those under Marcos. And he now established with other Filipinos a lobbying group in D.C. to educate the U.S. Congress on human rights abuses in the Philippines under Marcos. Chile, in fact, awakened human rights activists in Congress and in nongovernmental organizations like Amnesty International, sparking new, more heated debate on the issue.[44] Bello, with his Philippine background and Chilean experience, was well-positioned to link the debates on human rights in Chile with similar concerns in the Philippines. Working with a Philippine umbrella organization dealing with human rights under martial law, called the National Committee for the Restoration of Civil Liberties, Bello and his colleagues wrote a report on Marcos' abuses and distributed this to Fraser's committee.[45] Congressional activism on foreign policy increased further in November 1973, when Congress overrode a presidential veto to pass the War Powers Act, requiring the president to notify Congress within forty-eight hours of committing troops abroad and to withdraw those troops in sixty days unless Congress authorized a longer stay.[46] By December, Congress enacted legislation stating that it was the "sense of Congress" that the president "should" deny military assistance to any government that imprisoned people for political reasons.[47] It also amended the Foreign Assistance Act, mandating a termination of U.S. aid through the Agency for International Development's Office of Public Safety to overseas police forces and prisons.[48]

Meanwhile, Nixon's control slipped, as most of his inner circle resigned. In August 1973, Kissinger replaced Secretary of State William Rogers, while retaining the portfolio as National Security Advisor, which further concentrated his powers. OPEC's impact on world oil prices further fed political discontent, as charges against Nixon multiplied. By May 9, 1974, the House Judiciary Committee formally opened impeachment hearings. On July 30, the House Judiciary Committee voted to recommend impeachment. By August 9, his family at his side, Nixon announced his resignation. As Marcos would years later leave Malacanang, President Nixon and an entourage of his last remaining loyalists boarded a helicopter on August 10, 1974, and left the White House to Gerald Ford.

November legislative elections would usher in the so-called "New Democrats," as a new, more activist and liberal Congress, elected by a more activist public, increased its efforts to influence foreign policy. In human rights, following the Fraser hearings, Congress linked security assistance to human rights. Though it did not legally bind the president to maintain any human rights standards with allied regimes, it sent a political signal that more attention should be given to the issue in countries receiving U.S. security assistance. Moreover, Congress established a legally binding provision, introduced by Tom Harkin (D-Iowa) in 1975 and endorsed by human rights activists as well as those who sought to reduce foreign aid, that development assistance, as distinct from security assistance, be conditioned upon respect for human rights.[49] In response to congressional concern for human rights, the State Department established a Coordinator for Humanitarian Affairs in April 1975. In June, an office for human rights was established; but resistance within the State Department to anything other than "quiet diplomacy" relegated the office to a weak position within the department. The primary role of the office came to be the management of refugee and migration affairs, with its human rights purpose less clearly defined. In addition, staffing of the office was carried out by a reallocation of existing staff, rather than the hiring of new staff knowledgeable about human rights.[50]

Throughout his regime, Nixon had steadily withdrawn U.S. troops from Vietnam and had launched a program of "Vietnamization" to build South Vietnam's capacity to fight alone. Nevertheless, by 1975, after all U.S. troops had been withdrawn, Vietnam fell to the Communists and Cambodia to the Khmer Rouge, as the last Americans evacuated Saigon in April 1975. The war was over and Nixon was gone but America's faith in government had been dramatically altered. As Munich had taught a generation of Americans about the risks of appeasement, Vietnam taught a new generation about the risks of intervention. Two main, and competing, interpretations, however, formed. Some argued that the war could have been won had the military not been constrained, that, as General MacArthur once noted, there was "no substitute for victory." Others argued, on the contrary, that the United States should not have intervened militarily, that the roots of the war were political, centered on domestic Vietnamese politics; thus an appropriate response would have been diplomacy combined with economic, political, and social reforms. It was essentially a debate on strategy. What, U.S. officials debated, was the best U.S. response to revolutionary threats to allied regimes? Though the Cold War consensus to contain communism held, the means of achieving this end were under examination, and one critical aspect of the debate centered on human rights. In addition to the moral questions raised by military intervention, analysts questioned whether such intervention, in short, weakened mass-based internally-generated insurgencies or fed them.[51]

"Ninoy" and the Transnational
Human Rights Lobby

As the U.S. debate on foreign policy intensified, an anti-Marcos lobby, composed primarily of ex-patriot Filipinos like Bello as well as Marcos opponents displaced by martial law, grew and mobilized. Forming ties with the "New Democrats" and others in the United States sympathetic to their cause, the anti-Marcos lobby sought to undermine U.S. support for the Marcos regime. A key person in this was Corazon Aquino, who maintained her imprisoned husband's contacts with foreign correspondents in the Philippines, inviting them to dinners where she would relay the views of her husband and others in the opposition. Given the tight controls Marcos exercised over the Philippine media as well as the suppression of dissident voices, the journalists came to appreciate Corazon Aquino's efforts and in return they kept Benigno informed, feeding him reports from the wire services and other sources.[52]

Aquino's American friends also mobilized. Robert Trent Jones Jr., son of the golf course designer and a family friend of the Aquinos, began a U.S. campaign to free his friend from prison. In 1974, Jones wrote to James McLane, a class-mate from Yale, then the deputy director of the Cost of Living Council. McLane forwarded Jones' letter to Winston Lord, another Yale classmate, at the State Department. Lord had worked at the National Security Council under Kissinger, had supported the secret bombing of Cambodia, and had been one of five to accompany Kissinger on his historic, secret trip to China. When Kissinger took over as Secretary of State in 1973, he appointed Lord director of the Policy Plan-ning Staff. Lord was thus in a position to help Aquino and McLane knew this. Lord contacted the U.S. embassy in Manila for a status report on the Aquino case and reviewed the charges. They included illegal possession of firearms; four counts of subversion; providing weapons, supplies, shelter and medical assistance to the NPA; and providing money to the NPA for 1969 rallies and a 1970 raid on the Philippine Military Academy.[53] Lord concluded that the conditions of Aquino's detention appeared "reasonably humane," adding that "the interests of the United States would best be served if we did not attempt to comment on or characterize internal developments in the Philippines."[54] Lord overlooked the fact that the charges, allegedly trumped up, had not been filed until August 23, 1973, a full eleven months after Aquino's arrest. Moreover, carrying firearms was common-place in the Philippines, another indication that Aquino's real crime was the po-litical threat he posed Marcos.

Scheduled for a court martial in March 1975, Aquino launched a hunger strike and rapidly lost forty pounds.[55] Although Marcos released over 700 politi-cal detainees that same month, he remained as intransigent as ever on the Aquino case.[56] By April, a U.S. congressional delegation led by human rights activist Fraser visited Aquino in prison. Aquino's sister Lupita wrote to President Ford begging for help. Philippine attorneys questioned the legality of Marcos' moves. And Corazon Aquino held a press conference pleading with Marcos for her husband's release.[57] Although Marcos was still unmoved, Aquino's closest allies were beginning to understand the political strategies they would need to use to help free him while cultivating as well a transnational network of supporters, mainly in the United States and the Philippines.

After her press conference failed to yield any results, Corazon sent out appeals to American journalists, officials, and others who might help, including Paul Kattenberg.[58] A Foreign Service officer who had been critical of U.S. policy toward Vietnam as early as 1963, Kattenberg retired from the foreign service in 1972.

Concerned about Aquino, Kattenberg first wrote Muhammad Ali, who was scheduled to fight the "Thriller in Manila" in October 1975. Kattenberg described the Marcos regime's abuses against Muslims in the South,[59] where opposition under the direction of the Moro National Liberation Front (MNLF) had erupted in open warfare after martial law, leaving thousands dead, hundreds of thousands forced into exile, and more than a million displaced through the 1970s, as MNLF forces reached a peak of roughly 30,000 by 1975. In yet another piece of the transnational story, both Malaysia's Sabah territory and Libya provided arms, supplies, and money for the Philippine Muslims. Qaddafi also allowed the MNLF to use Libya as a base from which to lobby other Muslim countries, separately and through the Islamic Conference of Foreign Ministers.[60] Kattenberg argued that Aquino, if free, would help the Muslim cause. Nevertheless, the man who could "float like a butterfly and sting like a bee" went ahead with the fight, defeated his opponent Frazier and publicly praised Marcos as "decent and simple." Ali then walked away with $4.5 million, leaving a legacy that survives today, a celebration of shopping American-style called the Ali Mall.[61]

With Aquino still in jail, Kattenberg next wrote to the special assistant in the Bureau of East Asian and Pacific Affairs and to Philip Habib, who was then assistant secretary of state for East Asia. He also joined forces with Jones, who learned from Corazon Aquino that the jailed opposition leader would accept exile. Via the embassy in Manila, Kattenberg asked for a letter to this effect from Aquino, then took the letter to the Australian National University to try to procure a position for his friend. Meanwhile, Habib spoke with Ambassador William Sullivan, who had helped conduct the secret war in Laos from 1965 to 1969 and now believed Aquino to be a communist. Together, Habib and Sullivan concluded that it was "not...the time to involve ourselves as intermediaries in this case."[62] Perhaps the real reason for such intransigence was Kissinger's concurrent desire to secure U.S. bases in the Philippines with a new agreement, a policy concern made urgent in 1975 by the "fall" of Vietnam and Cambodia, the loss of American military facilities at Cam Ranh Bay in Vietnam, and the normalization of Philippine relations with China.[63] Since 1965, Marcos had threatened that he might abrogate the bases agreement signed by Macapagal, which allowed the United States a 25-year lease set to expire in 1991, unless the United States provided adequate compensation. Marcos had then pressed successive U.S. administrations for a new bases agreement, an issue which became more pressing for Marcos in mid-1975 when U.S. congressional hearings on his human rights record came under review, with implications for U.S. aid.[64] U.S. debate on the issue deepened after a December visit by Amnesty International exposed widespread detention and torture of political prisoners.[65]

By 1976, a National Security memorandum acknowledged that what Marcos wanted was more aid.[66] That year, Kissinger and Carlos Romulo opened negotiations but these stalled after Marcos rejected an offer of $1 billion over five years.[67] Apparently, Marcos thought he might do better with the newly elected Carter administration. Meanwhile, Aquino abandoned his hunger strike in May 1975 and returned to political activism from his jail cell, until he was put into solitary confinement at the end of 1976.[68] Corazon Aquino later remarked that Marcos must have studied her gregarious husband well, for he chose "exactly the right punishment for him."[69] Although United States and Philippine hard-liners retained control during the first years of martial law, splits were beginning to surface on both sides of the Pacific. In the Philippines, Marcos openly split with General Fidel Ramos in October 1976, when the latter resisted Marcos' plan to lift martial law. In the United States, losses in Indochina were fueling debates on foreign policy, as those favoring economic and political solutions over military ones gained adherents. Those favoring this approach had also had a few key successes. One such success was the congressionally mandated order in 1973 to terminate U.S. assistance to overseas police forces and prisons, to take effect by 1976. At the same time, Philippine supporters of Aquino and other Marcos opponents exploited the widening debate in the United States, building alliances with those seeking nonmilitary solutions to their problems.

Carter's Human Rights Agenda

In 1976, the United States was primed for change, and Jimmy Carter, whose foreign policy platform emphasized human rights, won the November presidential elections. Though Carter was elected by a narrow margin, his views seemed in harmony with those on Capitol Hill. By the time Carter arrived in D.C., Congress had revised the Foreign Assistance Act, defining as a "principal goal" human rights. The act also created a provision requiring the State Department to submit a report each year on the human rights conditions in countries receiving aid from the United States, though this was later changed to include all countries, so as not to single out U.S. allies. In addition, Congress elevated the position of coordinator for human rights and humanitarian affairs within the State Department established in 1975 to an assistant secretary rank with a full, independent bureau in 1977. President Carter signed the legislation in August and the bureau was created in November. Moreover, Congress widened the bureau's responsibilities, which now included preparing human rights reports required by congress, making recommendations to the Secretary of State and the AID Administrator regarding compliance with the Foreign Assistance Act, and performing other responsibilities to promote human rights worldwide. The State Department had fought against the proposal but congressional pressure forced the department to give the human rights function sufficient staff and prestige to perform the new, more clearly defined functions. The institutionalization of human rights as an element of foreign policy was intended by Congress to give human rights a bureaucratic advocate in Washington turf wars, and, though it has faced substantial opposition from older, more established sectors of the bureaucracy, it has nevertheless integrated concern for human rights into foreign policy debates.[70]

To fill the assistant secretary post, Carter named Patricia Derian, a white woman raised in Mississippi whose human rights training had been in the civil rights movement. Many of Carter's political appointees at the State Department were initially on board with the human rights policy, but defected when the policy soon began to come under public as well as bureaucratic attack as naive and idealistic. The bureau's mission also ran counter to the regional bureaus' traditional policies of nonintervention in the internal affairs of foreign states.[71] In the Philippine case, Richard Holbrooke, assistant secretary of state for East Asian and Pacific Affairs, began as an ally[72] but became a particularly strident force of opposition. What the United States should focus on, the critics claimed, was *realpolitik*, centering on U.S. interests and balance of power, not human rights and the internal politics of allied countries. Resistance grew within the State Department, as career Foreign Service officers and others chafed at the scope of conflict they would have to face worldwide if human rights were truly to become central to U.S. foreign policy. Tenacious and outspoken, Derian brought in new staff, including some traditional foreign service and civil service personnel but also some non-traditional human rights advocates from private groups and congressional staffs. Under Derian's leadership, the bureau served as an independent monitor of human rights, challenging other State Department bureaus as well as other departments notably Commerce, Defense and Treasury.[73] Moreover, representatives from the bureau participated in the newly created interagency Arms Export Control Board, which prepared military aid budgets for Congress.[74] It also raised the level of the annual human rights reports from the perfunctory, superficial ones submitted by Kissinger in the last days of his tenure to widely respected reference sources on human rights.[75]

Despite substantial opposition, Derian succeeded in energizing her department, with one noteworthy success at the beginning of her term. In May 1977, Trinidad Herrera, a thirty-five year old organizer in one of Manila's largest slums, was arrested without charges. Herrera's work on behalf of the poor had made her well known in the Philippines and among U.S. human rights activists, including Congressman Fraser, who had met Herrera during a visit to the Philippines. A mid-level U.S. embassy official in Manila was informed of the arrest by a Philippine priest. The official then transmitted the information to D.C., which instructed him to follow up on the case. Soon after, he and another embassy official went to Bicutan Rehabilitation Center and found Herrera in a state of near shock, as she described the torture she had endured. When word of Herrera's detention reached Fraser's office, he began to make inquiries about her at the State Department. A few days after the embassy officials visited her, Herrera was released. The success was widely heralded in the U.S. press and in subsequent analyses of the Carter administration, becoming a symbol of his human rights policy; but Derian's efforts were soon undermined. In early 1978, Derian attended a chiefs of missions meeting in Hong Kong, which was chaired by her nemesis, Richard Holbrooke. It proved a bitter and revealing session, with Derian urging human rights while the ambassadors urged "smooth bi-lateral relations." Only when the venerable Mike Mansfield, then ambassador to Japan, stepped in to support her was a truce called at the meeting, though resistance to her views continued to spread in the diplomatic community.

From Hong Kong, Derian went to Manila. There she threatened Marcos, to the chagrin of Ambassador David Newsom, that the United States might register disapproval of human rights abuses by voting against loans from the international development banks. Marcos, usually self-controlled, lost his composure, responding angrily that he would not submit to "dollar diplomacy." Newsom, who had thirty years of experience in the Foreign Service, later claimed he had never witnessed such a heated exchange between an American official and a head of state. Derian next confronted Enrile, who had prepared a flashy presentation complete with slides and charts to be given by polished Philippine military officers. Derian quickly interrupted, posing questions about the thousands imprisoned without having been charged as well as the reports of torture. Enrile dissembled, commenting years later to a Reagan official that the Derian visit had been the only irritant the Marcos regime had ever encountered on the question of human rights. Still, Derian pressed the issue. At a formal embassy party for her, Derian left late in the evening with CIA station chief Herbert Natzke to visit Aquino in jail. Though Natzke railed against Aquino during the ride over, Derian was impressed by Aquino during the meeting, later citing him as "somebody of monumental stature." Derian also met with Carlos Romulo, who had coined MacArthur's "I shall return" proclamation and was now involved in the bases negotiations. After the meeting, Romulo told reporters she reminded him of the durian, a Southeast Asian fruit with an odor so foul that it is actually banned from some public places. Now Patt Derian became Patt "Durian," as both U.S. and World Bank aid to Marcos remained high despite her threats.[76]

In fact, World Bank and International Development Association (IDA) loans rose from $268 million in 1976 to $317.5 million a year later and then leaped to

$526 million for 1978.[77] Secretary of State Cyrus Vance formally registered concern over the human rights violations, but nevertheless approved U.S. support for the World Bank loans.[78] An interagency committee on human rights and foreign assistance continued to press the issue, leading various U.S. officials including Newsom to suggest strategies for improving human rights in the Philippines.[79] Nevertheless, the loans spoke louder than words, signaling continued U.S. support as well as Derian's weakness, particularly given U.S. influence over World Bank decisions.[80]

In an attempt to repair his image and appear to be conforming to the human rights challenges, Marcos declared legislative elections to be held April 7, 1978, the first since martial law.[81] At stake were 165 seats. Under new constitutional provisions, however, Marcos had absolute veto powers over the legislature as well as the authority to dissolve it at any moment, for any reason.[82] Having been sentenced to death after a military, rather than civilian, trial in November 1977,[83] Aquino was becoming a focal point of the human rights debate in the United States regarding the Marcos regime.[84] Vance and other U.S. officials urged Marcos via Newsom to release Aquino for the elections.[85] The Philippine Security Council deliberated but quickly declined to release Aquino, citing his alleged ties to *both* the CIA and the NPA as risks to national security.[86] Undaunted, Aquino campaigned via his wife Corazon and his young daughter Kris, as the leader of the Lakas ng Bayan Party, Tagalog for "People Power." Laban, as the party came to be known, means "fight" in Tagalog and that was what the opponents of martial law did. They also forged an alliance with the Manila–Rizal branch of the Communist Party, though the party's Central Committee later overruled this, opting instead to hibernate, hoping for greater power in the future.[87] Despite Marcos' control of the media, not to mention the military, government and economy, the opposition established such a broad base of support that the U.S. embassy reported prior to the vote that the elections would be decided "in the counting and not in the casting of votes."[88]

Anticipating fraud, Manila residents staged a "noise barrage" the night before the elections. Church bells pealed, motorists honked horns, families banged pots and pans, and thousands clogged the streets to make as much noise as possible in a symbolic end to their years of silence. As expected, however, Marcos' Kilusang Bagong Lipunan, or "New Society" Party, swept the elections amid widespread allegations from the opposition and foreign media of fraud. Two days later, several hundred people marched from St. Theresa College to mass at the nearby Manila Cathedral. Led by priests carrying a coffin symbolizing the death of democracy, the march was disbanded by government troops, and over 500 Laban followers were arrested.[89] The Marcos regime did not, moreover, restrict its response to Filipinos. While the U.S. Congress expressed concern that alleged election "irregularities" might damage U.S.–Philippine relations,[90] Marcos used government-controlled Philippine newspapers to attack "foreign meddling" in human rights and in the elections. He also complained to U.S. embassy staff about "partisan" coverage from the U.S. media, which Marcos believed had favored his opponents.[91] One journalist from the *New York Times* was even threatened with deportation for his reports of electoral fraud.[92] U.S. embassy officials concurred, however, with assessments that Marcos had manipulated the vote-counting in order to secure his victory, and they now worried that he might strengthen martial law in response to the apparent groundswell of support for the opposition.[93]

Meanwhile, a handful of businessmen disadvantageously affected by cronyism together with Jesuit priests with some support from Cardinal Sin, social democrats and opposition politicians, all key supporters of the still-imprisoned Aquino, had been meeting regularly since 1977 to devise an anti-Marcos strategy. They now began organizing a "third force"—an alternative to both the communist forces and those of the Marcos regime. An emissary from the group, Eduardo Olaguer, traveled to the United States to raise funds from political exiles, including exiled opposition senator Manglapus, who supported the plan. Out of this emerged a small, elite organization dubbed the "Light A Fire Movement" for its campaign of non-lethal letter bombs, fires and other primarily symbolic acts of sabotage staged in the Philippines but designed to worry the U.S. government. According to one member, "We were trying to create enough stench here to waft to Washington." Throughout 1979, the group lit a series of fires but received little attention from the censored press. By December 1979, the campaign ended when the Philippine military arrested Olaguer and sixteen others.[94]

Carter's Unmet Promises

While Carter espoused a new, more moralistic approach to foreign policy, realpolitik proponents retained control, as the Carter administration proved no more willing than Nixon's had been to press Marcos on human rights. What mattered was the security of the U.S. bases, a question left open when Ford left office.[95] After negotiations with Kissinger stalled in the final months of the Ford administration, the negotiations resumed in 1977. Rhetoric aside, Holbrooke and others at the State Department worked to minimize congressional cuts in security assistance to the Philippines and reassure Marcos that the United States continued to back him.[96] Further, despite Derian's findings, as well as the intense opposition displayed during the Philippine legislative elections, Vice President Walter Mondale agreed to meet with Marcos in Manila in May 1978, just one month after the legislative elections, as the bases issue dangled. While there, Mondale refused to meet with Benigno Aquino Jr., then signed four aid agreements totaling some $41 million.[97] Two months later, Imelda arrived in Washington, following a multimillion dollar shopping spree in New York,[98] to lobby for more aid as part of the bases agreement. Grilled by liberal congressmen such as Father Drinan who asked about persecution of the church, Yvonne Burke (D-CA) who had been concerned by the Herrera case,[99] Fortney Stark and Leo Ryan both from California districts with sizable Philippine populations including exiled opposition leaders, and others, Imelda was appalled, later calling the congressmen "barbarians." In an effort to restore relations, Mondale with Holbrooke received Imelda at the White House, treating her as they might a head of state, though debate in D.C. continued to grow.[100]

In fact, the State Department's 1977 human rights report had placed the Marcos regime near the bottom in East Asia, which created much media attention in the United States and made Marcos difficult to deal with.[101] Now, as base negotiations heated up, extensive political wrangling within the State Department, notably between Derian and Holbrooke,[102] attended the preparation of the 1978 report. The realpolitik contingent led by Holbrooke urged that the report "commend Marcos" for the progress he was ostensibly making in human rights reform, such as the elections, in spite of the fraud, as well as attempts by Ramos and Enrile to tame the armed forces.[103] Marcos raised the stakes by signing a non-aggression pact with Vietnam, encouraging, as well, members of his government to criticize the bases. This served both to appease Filipino nationalists and to enhance Marcos' negotiating position. Marcos also cut tax-free exemptions for U.S. businesses.[104] Further, the F.B.I. received a tip that General Ver and two other "Liquidator Generals" were plotting to carry out assassinations of Marcos opponents in the United States, in flagrant violation not only of human rights but also of U.S. efforts to stem such abuses.[105] In November 1978, Ambassador Richard Murphy warned that the bases talks were at a "particularly critical or delicate stage" such that a human rights report like the one prepared in 1977 could have "a serious impact on bases agreement prospects in both the United States and the Philippines."[106] Not only might a bad report prompt Marcos to cut off talks, Murphy argued, but it might also dissolve U.S. support for the large aid package any deal would include.

Shortly before the deadline for the human rights report, and with the assistance of Senator Inouye, whose Hawaiian constituency included many Ilocano Filipinos, Marcos accepted $500 million in U.S. military aid over the next five years in exchange for U.S. rights to the bases until 1991.[107] Though it was half what Kissinger had offered, it was the best Carter would offer and Marcos finally agreed. On Christmas Day, 1978, forty-two leaders of the Philippine opposition wrote and signed an open letter condemning Carter's handling of Marcos and the bases agreement. The group included seven former senators, former President Macapagal, four nuns, two bishops, and others willing to risk imprisonment to voice their opposition. Carter also faced substantial opposition at home, led by Tony Hall (D-OH) who, as a member of the subcommittee on Asian and Pacific Affairs, was approached by priests and anti-Marcos Filipinos forced into exile. At their request, he introduced legislation in 1979 to cut $7.9 million in military assistance to Marcos.[108] Despite the relatively minor cut, Carter and his senior foreign policy team lobbied hard, and successfully, to secure the full aid package.[109]

Realpolitik gained more ground when Secretary of State Cyrus Vance notified Carter in February 1979 that the human rights bureau had mismanaged funds. To remedy the situation, the bureau was reorganized, with the sizable refugee programs consolidated under a separate office. The human rights bureau fought hard against this but lost in June when the new refugee office was created. This precipitated extensive bureaucratic infighting between the bureau and other segments of the State Department, notably the Bureau of Management, which now rejected staffing requests and prepared to shrink the human rights function.[110]

Though realpolitik had won out against the human rights advocates, two international events in 1979 were to reopen the debate on the "lessons" of Vietnam and the best strategies for addressing internal opposition against U.S. allies. The first was the overthrow of the shah in Iran by Muslim fundamentalists led by the Ayatollah Khomeini, despite massive aid to the regime from the United States since 1953. An oil crisis now rocked the U.S. economy, reawakening fears from the previous oil crisis in 1973. Further, in November 1979, the U.S. embassy was captured and 53 Americans held hostage by followers of Khomeini.[111] The second event was the overthrow of the U.S.-backed Somoza regime in Nicaragua by the Sandinistas, composed of moderates and leftists allied since the 1978 assassination of moderate oppositionist and newspaper publisher Pedro Joaquin Chamorro. Carter quickly recognized the Sandinistas, but cut ties in 1980, when the Sandinistas supported guerrillas in El Salvador. The Sandinistas then did exactly as Carter feared, allying with the Soviet Union and Cuba. Meanwhile, the U.S.-backed military regime in El Salvador, in power since a 1977 military coup, was in jeopardy. Carter had cut aid after the coup but by 1979, as the Sandinistas took over Nicaragua and, as the Soviets invaded Afghanistan, El Salvador was in crisis. Catholic clergy inspired by liberation theology had long encouraged resistance against the regime, and a revolutionary movement was, by early 1980, burgeoning. Still Carter sought a centrist solution. All hopes of this ceased, however, on March 24, 1980, when a death squad killed Archbishop Oscar Romero at the altar of his own cathedral. Now, the revolutionary opposition gained adherents from an outraged populace.[112]

Another event in 1979 would, at the same time, intensify U.S. concerns regarding the military bases in the Philippines. When the People's Republic of China invaded Vietnam in February and March 1979, the Soviet Union sent assistance to the Vietnamese. In return, Hanoi allowed the Soviets to use the formerly American naval facilities at Cam Ranh Bay. This provided the Soviets with a critical link in their chain of support facilities and replenishment anchorages. By the early 1980s, Cam Ranh Bay was the Soviet Union's largest onshore facility beyond its borders, a major staging complex for Soviet Pacific fleet vessels, submarines and aircraft outside Soviet Northeast Asia. The crucial counterweight to the Soviet presence were the U.S. facilities in the Philippines, particularly Clark Air and Subic Naval bases.[113]

1980 U.S. Presidential Elections:
A Return to Hard-Line Tactics

As Truman had been blamed for the "loss" of China, Carter was now blamed for the revolutions in Iran and Nicaragua, the growing threat of revolution in El Salvador, as well as the Soviet invasion of Afghanistan and the Iranian hostage crisis. In more liberal times, Carter and Congress might have interpreted the overthrow of the shah and Somoza as cautionary tales regarding support of dictators. Instead, 1980 presidential elections saw the Republicans rally hard-liners to back Reagan, amid the continuing embarrassment to Carter of the hostage crisis. Reagan's foreign policy platform was built on the odd logic of Jeane Kirkpatrick, an arch conservative anticommunist, former Democrat, and Georgetown professor who argued that "authoritarian" regimes such as Somoza's and the shah's should be supported by the United States because they were pro-American and could eventually democratize. "Totalitarian" regimes such as Castro's and the Sandinistas,' however, were anti-American, would never yield to democracy, and so should be overthrown.[114] She scolded Carter's human rights policies, as limited as they were, for leading to revolution in Iran and Nicaragua. This view found supporters in Congress, journalism and academia, while others such as Senator Howard Metzenbaum (D-OH) countered that "deals with the juntas and dictators and fascists throughout the world in the last thirty years" had failed.[115] And the debate on the "lessons" of Vietnam reopened. Meanwhile, human rights activism accelerated. This included a growing transnational effort by church organizations to draw international attention to the abuses of authoritarian regimes worldwide, abuses their own members were experiencing. Nevertheless, the hard-liners would soon score a major victory with the election of Reagan as President.

Carter would have one last success for human rights before leaving office, however. In May 1980, he helped secure the release of Ninoy Aquino from prison for heart bypass surgery in the United States. The decision also came at the initiative of Marcos, who feared charges of human rights violations should Aquino die under his care. In an odd footnote to history, Imelda visited Aquino, whom she had once dated, and talked with him for two hours in the Philippine hospital where he was being treated. During the visit, Aquino gave Imelda a gold cross from around his neck, which he had worn throughout the more than seven years of his imprisonment. Subsequently, the cross would hang from the wrist of a statue of the Santo Niño at the Malacanang Palace.[116] Aquino arrived in the United States soon after and underwent successful bypass surgery. Although he had promised to return to the Philippines after recovering, the growing prospects of a Reagan victory caused him to reconsider, afraid he would again languish in prison or worse. Aquino's many American friends lobbied to secure a fellowship for him at Harvard, anticipating, correctly, that Marcos would yield under such pressure. Professor Samuel Huntington, once ostracized by Harvard students during the Vietnam War for his positions on "forced urbanization" and other hard-line policies, intervened. Now, as Director of Harvard's Center for International Affairs, he offered Aquino a fellowship, and the Aquinos soon after established residence in Newton, Massachusetts.[117]

For the next three years, as a fellow at Harvard and later at M.I.T.'s Center for International Studies, Aquino would broaden his base of support throughout the United States, particularly in academia, Congress and journalism, as well as in the Filipino-American community. It was a time Corazon Aquino would remember as "three of our happiest years."[118] Though Imelda warned him against political activism while in the United States, Aquino spoke at the Asia Society in New York on August 4, 1980, and began his U.S. campaign against Marcos when he asked "Is the Filipino worth dying for?" Aquino answered in the affirmative. "Mr. Marcos," he said, "I will face death in the struggle for freedom if you do not heed the voice of conscience and moderation." Inevitably invoking MacArthur, he added, "I shall return."[119] M.I.T. professor Lucian Pye remembers Aquino using his office to call Marcos. "I'd leave the office and come back to find Aquino shouting into the phone," Pye recalls, "but they seemed almost like friends other times."[120] Aquino also strengthened his ties to Manglapus, other Filipinos and the broader-based lobby seeking a redirection in U.S. policy. As part of this, Aquino, together with Manglapus and other exiles helped an American named Steve Psinakis, who was married to a daughter of Eugenio Lopez, Sr., organized a successor to the Light A Fire Movement. Called the April 6 Movement, for the noise barrages that had preceded the 1978 elections, the new movement launched a Manila bombing campaign to destabilize the Marcos government in August

1980, just months before the U.S. presidential elections.[121] If the bombings had any effect at all, however, it was to raise concern among U.S. officials that the moderate opposition was indeed radical and militant, as Marcos had long alleged. Moreover, the bombings provided Marcos with a new excuse for prolonging martial law and widening his arrests of moderate opposition figures.[122]

After the bombings, Marcos asked the Carter administration to introduce an extradition treaty so that he could have his opponents abroad extradited.[123] Carter refused. Soon after, however, the 1980 U.S. presidential elections would usher in one of the most hard-line administrations of the entire Cold War era, more ideological than purely strategic in its opposition to communism. In fact, just one month after the U.S. elections, in December 1980, three American nuns and a missionary were killed in El Salvador. Upon taking office, the Reagan administration quickly dismissed the event, alleging that the nuns had been aiding the communists, a charge known to be false.[124] It was, indeed, a new day for dictators.

From Carter to Reagan:
Human Rights Cedes to the Kirkpatrick Doctrine

On January 17, 1981, after much hype from the American press, Marcos officially lifted martial law, although eight years of martial law had institutionalized his control of the economy, the press, the military and the political system. As one Filipino politician quipped, "Marcos has lifted everything else around here, so why not lift martial law." In fact, the announcement, which came just three days before Reagan's inauguration and one month before a visit from Pope John Paul II, did little for Philippine democracy. A few months prior to the announcement, Marcos had enacted legislation granting himself martial law powers even after lifting the decree. A U.S. embassy report acknowledged that "Marcos is tired of the martial law label and wants to rid himself of it—but not to the extent of giving up essential powers." After lifting martial law, Marcos introduced new constitutional amendments providing for a six-year presidential term with the right of unlimited succession and presidential power to name a successor as well as to dissolve the legislature. He then held a constitutional plebiscite on April 7, for which he controlled all media coverage and electoral monitoring systems. Not surprisingly, his constitution achieved voter approval levels as high as 99 percent in some regions, 80 percent overall.[125]

He then announced presidential elections for June, but the moderate opposition, anticipating fraud, refused to put up a candidate and allied with the leftist National Democratic Front in a nationwide boycott campaign.[126] Due to extensive government manipulation of the elections, it is difficult to know how effective the boycott campaign was. One estimate, however, is that as many as 50 percent of Manila voters declined to cast ballots.[127] For the first time since martial law, politicians active in the opposition had abandoned electoral struggle and had allied with the left. It was a striking indication of the moderate opposition's growing radicalism and disillusionment both with Marcos and with the prospects for a democratic transition under his regime since the 1978 election sham. Even former Senator Salvador Laurel, son of Japanese collaborator Jose Laurel, had abandoned his hopes of working with Marcos after running for a parliamentary seat in 1978 on Marcos' Kilusang Bagong Lipunan (KBL) ticket, only to be nudged out by Marcos cronies running in the same region, also on the KBL ticket. In preparation for the 1981 presidential elections, Laurel had helped forge in August 1980 an alliance between the Nacionalista and Liberal Parties, with support from the exiled Aquino, called the United Nationalist Democratic Organization (UNIDO); but when Marcos refused to accredit the party, Laurel too boycotted.[128] Marcos nevertheless claimed voter turnout of 90 to 95 percent, and declared himself the victor. Despite the sham, Vice President Bush attended the inauguration ceremonies, which included a rendition of Handel's Messiah. "And He shall reign forever and ever." Bush even toasted Marcos for his "adherence...to the democratic processes," as the Reagan administration fully embraced Marcos.[129] Again, concern for the bases was paramount, with a new round of negotiations scheduled for 1983 approaching.[130]

The fissures within the U.S. policy establishment were, however, widening. Amid wholesale firings in State, Defense and elsewhere, Reagan hoped to rid the bureaucracy of the so-called "Carterites." He also named Ernest Lefever as his nominee to head the human rights bureau, though Lefever had publicly advocated erasing human rights legislation from the books and was seen by many as wanting, like Kirkpatrick, to subsume all concerns for human rights under a simple anticommunist formula, arguing that to do otherwise was to "trivialize" human rights. Moreover, evidence surfaced indicating that Lefever had accepted money from the Republic of South Africa to circulate views favorable to that government. Under serious attack from human rights advocates in the State Department and outside of government, as well as from the Senate Foreign Relations Committee, which voted 13 to 4 against Lefever, the nomination was withdrawn. George Lister, a long-time human rights advocate within the State Department, described the Reagan administration's early attempts to undo the State Department's human rights operations; but, he concludes, "We won!"[131]

Elliott Abrams, also from the far right, was named instead. Abrams helped to reinvigorate the bureau, which was "in the doldrums" when he arrived. Reaffirming human rights as an "essential" component of foreign policy, Abrams outlined a two-track implementation strategy involving a positive track to herald achievements by "friendly democratic" regimes and a negative track to respond to abuses by such regimes but only in the broader context of U.S. interests. In short, where human rights violations were a problem, U.S. interests would take priority. Under Abrams, the human rights bureau became less independent, more integrated into the broader Reagan–Kirkpatrick foreign policy. Abrams also endorsed the administration's support for the governments of El Salvador, South Africa and others under attack from independent human rights organizations such as Amnesty International and the Lawyers Committee for International Human Rights. Congressional human rights activist Donald Bonker complained that Abrams served less as a spokesman for human rights than as a spokesman for Reagan's militant anticommunist foreign policy.[132] Meanwhile, many "Carterites" and human rights activists brought to the bureau not as political appointees but as civil servants during the Carter administration remained during the Reagan years.[133] Together with human rights advocates and others throughout the bureaucracy, they rejected the Manichaean simplicity of Reagan's policies and posed an ongoing challenge centered on concern for human rights.

Human Rights under Marcos
and Reagan's Foreign Policy

As fissures widened in the United States, Marcos too faced growing dissent from within his administration, particularly the military. There, Marcos had appointed his close ally and former chauffeur, now General, Fabian Ver, to serve as Armed Forces Chief of Staff in 1981, bypassing Philippine Constabulary head Fidel Ramos. Suspecting disloyalty, Marcos had also removed Defense Minister Enrile from the chain of command. Fearing assassination, Enrile then created a 200-man security force, essentially an army within the army, to defend himself against Ver, providing his troops with heavy artillery and extensive training by foreign mercenaries.[134] Enrile's forces would later form the core of a movement within the military seeking to professionalize the increasingly corrupt and ineffectual institution, one manifestation of which was a rise in human rights violations by undisciplined, "trigger happy" soldiers. Though Enrile had helped lead the country into martial law, had been a key force in maintaining it, and had profited personally, probably more than any other cabinet member, a fissure between Marcos and Enrile now formed.[135]

When Pope John Paul II visited the Philippines in February 1981, he met with Muslim guerrilla leaders[136] and decried human rights violations but advised the clergy and religious leaders to avoid involvement in political and social issues.[137] Despite the pope's caution, the entourage of reporters following him on his travels throughout the Philippines spotlighted the poverty and human rights abuses in the countryside, leading Marcos to publicly denounce the Western media's attention to such issues.[138] When confronted with human rights reports from the U.S. State Department and Amnesty International, Marcos simply claimed that the reports were not verifiable.[139] On July 7, Cardinal Sin, until then circumspect about Marcos, publicly condemned the political violence and government corruption in an interview with UPI and the *Agence France Presse*. Meanwhile, the Philippine left cited the church as being in the forefront of its campaigns.[140] When a massacre on the island of Samar gained international attention from the media by October, the U.S. embassy acknowledged that the event lowered the credibility of the military while lending credence to the U.S. human rights reports Marcos had persistently challenged. The Philippine government alleged that the massacre was the work of defectors from the military. By the end of October, however, Secretary of State Alexander Haig notified the U.S. embassy in Manila that media coverage of the massacre had damaged U.S. public opinion, and that Marcos should be advised to expect congressional hearings on the issue.[141]

Haig was right. In November 1981, Congressman Stephen Solarz (D-NY) held hearings on the human rights abuses in the Philippines, and the implications for security assistance to the Philippine Constabulary. By the end of November, others in Congress were urging that the United States deny law enforcement aid to the Philippines.[142] Meanwhile, ex-patriot Filipino opponents of Marcos throughout the United States were banding together to raise American public awareness of Philippine issues, to continue to challenge the Marcos regime despite the lifting of martial law, and to lobby for a change in U.S. policy toward Marcos. Moderates like Aquino and Manglapus now formed a tentative alliance with leftist groups such as the Philippine Solidarity Network and the Anti-Martial Law Coalition (Philippines). Moreover, the anti-Marcos Filipino lobby in the United States worked with disillusioned World Bank staffers who systematically leaked reams of documents on World Bank loans to the Philippines, exposing the corruption and ties to Marcos.[143] When Aquino and the others held a press conference to release the information and discuss the lifting of martial law, Haig found the moderate-left alliance "bizarre."[144] In an unclassified cable sent a week later, however, the Philippine News Agency reported that Aquino had been discomfited by issues raised by the leftists at the press conference. Still, the continued repression by Marcos of both moderates and leftists encouraged their continued alliance.[145] In fact, even exiled opponents of Marcos based in the United States were not safe from abuse, as new FBI reports disclosed in August and September 1981 that Marcos agents were scattered throughout the United States, notably in San Francisco, Los Angeles, and New York City, where Filipino opposition was greatest.[146]

An indication that tensions within the U.S. government were spreading came in April 1982 when a report written by Gilbert Sheinbaum, the political counselor at the Cebu consulate in the Philippine Visayan islands, was leaked to the press. Sent just one month prior to a scheduled state visit to the United States by the Marcoses, Sheinbaum painted a much darker portrait of Philippine conditions than either Marcos or Reagan admitted. Sheinbaum described one city where the mayor was allowing gambling to "flourish" while the Philippine Constabulary was "benefiting financially." Elsewhere, a governor complained about the "crime and corruption" of the military. Even more damaging, Sheinbaum described how Marcos cronies forced sales to purchase vast tracts of land for their sugar and other enterprises. Sheinbaum also described a church leader threatened with deportation because of a confrontation over human rights abuses with Constabulary officers in the Mindanao province of Davao. Further, he described the link between the deteriorating economic, political, and human rights conditions with the growth of the New People's Army, and explicitly named the Constabulary and the military as key contributors to the human rights crisis. When the report leaked, the only major paper to cover it was the *Washington Post*, and the State Department reacted less to the corruption in the Philippines than to the leak of the information to the media. That it leaked at all, however, especially just one month prior to the Marcos visit, indicates that someone, probably in the State Department, broke ranks to get the story about the Marcos regime's venality out via the U.S. press, much to the ire of Marcos and Reagan.[147]

Creeping State Cronyism

By September 1982, the Marcoses arrived in the United States for their highly coveted state visit, the first since 1965. Though they initially complained about the Sheinbaum report to new Secretary of State George Shultz, after Haig resigned over conflicts with Philip Habib on Israeli policy toward Lebanon,[148] U.S. officials encouraged the Marcoses to focus instead on the clear support from Reagan that the visit signaled.[149] Three months prior to the visit, Imelda's brother, Kokoy Romualdez, was named Ambassador to the United States to make all preparations. He hired public relations firms to cultivate U.S. journalists. He bought a restaurant in Georgetown and he bribed and bused in Filipinos to wave Philippine flags at Andrews Air Force Base and on the mall as the Marcoses arrived. The visit, carefully scripted, was designed in part to strengthen ties with the Reagan administration and in part to show Filipinos how loved their leader was in the United States. Even the Reagan administration took special precautions to ensure the visit's success, including the dispatch of officials to Aquino in Boston to warn him not to do anything that might embarrass Reagan or Marcos.[150] Following the visit, Reagan nearly doubled Carter's aid package, granting Marcos $900 million over a five-year period, though Reagan, like his predecessors, would need to secure congressional support each year during the annual budget debates.[151]

Still, opposition expanded in the Philippines. While Reagan remained a Marcos ally, U.S. analysts began to warn of "creeping state capitalism," the title of a 1983 U.S. embassy report written by Ambassador Michael Armacost during a visit by Assistant Secretary of State for East Asian Affairs Paul Wolfowitz. The report outlined Marcos' control of the steel, mining, and banking industries as well as the growing political opposition from the private sector. It detailed how the government owned or controlled over 300 companies, many formerly private, built with government funds, then taken over when they began to fail. For instance, Rodolfo Cuenca had built highways with the engineering equipment provided back in 1966 ostensibly for troops to Vietnam; but he was on the verge of bankruptcy by the early 1980s. Marcos ordered government banks to convert Cuenca's loans and loan guarantees, worth over $1 billion, into equity. Cuenca thereafter thrived. In another case, a Chinese banker named Dewey Dee fled the Philippines in 1981, leaving a crumbling empire and an estimated $100 million in debts. Manila banks, in a panic, refused to roll over short-term loans and several Marcos cronies, including Disini and others, faced bankruptcy. To bail them out, Marcos spent some $3 billion by 1983 to sustain his cronies, while the general economy reeled.[152] Moreover, the report noted, the government controlled 75 to 80 percent of all of the country's financial assets, through government banks and banks run by such cronies as sugar baron Roberto Benedicto and Defense Minister Enrile.[153] Meanwhile, the Export–Import Bank supplied an additional $204.5 million for Westinghouse's nuclear power project, now projected to cost $1.89 billion at the taxpayer's expense.[154]

Moreover, reports from the embassy in Manila increasingly cited human rights violations, the break-down of democratic institutions, corruption in the military, and the growing strength of the revolutionary opposition, which was now drawing support from traditionally moderate sectors of society, including segments of the church, the traditional oligarchy and even the military. The primary response remained, however, repression, as even foreign nationals, notably clergy from the United States as well as Australia and Europe, were targeted by the military.[155] Though the U.S. embassy in Manila began urging economic and other reforms as an alternative response to revolutionary pressures, noting the link between human rights violations by the military and the growing militancy of the opposition,[156] hard-liners still held sway. Of central concern, once again, was yet another round of bases negotiations scheduled for 1983.[157] Within the United States, Reagan's hard-line policies still prevailed, but the human rights lobby, focused mainly on

Nicaragua, El Salvador and Guatemala with primarily ex-patriot Filipinos focusing on the Marcos regime's abuses,[158] helped draw attention to the moral concerns raised by Reagan's foreign policies. The recent revolutions in Iran and Nicaragua further strengthened their arguments that such policies were also strategically flawed. Aquino apparently sensed the growing U.S. concern for human rights, understanding as well the damage his involvement in the April 6 Movement's bombing campaigns had done to his image in the United States. Influenced by the movie *Ghandi*,[159] Aquino now proclaimed his faith in nonviolence, expressed his hopes that Marcos would step down voluntarily, and made preparations for a return from his three years in exile in the United States, despite repeated attempts by the Marcoses to persuade him not to return.

Was Marcos, with U.S. assistance, going to make the same mistake that Spain had made in the 1890s when, by punishing moderates like Rizal as harshly as revolutionaries, the two movements allied? The answer to this question was swift and brutal. On August 21, 1983, Ninoy Aquino arrived at the Manila airport.[160] Aquino had shrewdly invited several foreign correspondents to accompany him. These included Ken Kashiwahara, who was married to Aquino's sister Lupita and worked for ABC in San Francisco; Jim Laurie, ABC correspondent in Tokyo; Max Vanzi of UPI; Sandra Burton, *Time* magazine correspondent in Hong Kong; Katsuo Ueda of Japan's Kyodo news agency; Togo Tajika of Tokyo Broadcasting System; and Kiyoshi Wakamiya, a freelance journalist. Upon landing, low-ranking military officials rushed onto the plane to escort Aquino off, barring all others from exiting. A tape recorder captured the confusion that followed, as the escorts shouted, in rapid Visayan, "Here he comes, I'll do it...let me shoot."[161] Clad in white, Aquino had not yet stepped onto the tarmac, when he was shot in the head from behind, his body sprawling in a heap of white cloth and red blood. Just outside the airport, some 30,000 fans awaited his arrival. Borrowing from the American song "Tie a Yellow Ribbon Round the Old Oak Tree," Aquino's legions of fans waved yellow ribbons to cheer his return from the United States after "three long years."[162] And they were among the first to hear the news. Though reports of Marcos' human rights abuses had been reaching the United States for years, the Aquino assassination was widely covered in the United States and alerted his well-placed friends to the extent, and perhaps the reality, of the problem. It also threatened to bond the moderate with the revolutionary opposition, as Chamorro's death had in Nicaragua.

Now, the political winds shifted. From the 1972 declaration of martial law through the 1983 assassination of Aquino, hard-liners in the United States had retained control of policy towards the Philippines. This was due primarily to U.S. dependence upon Marcos for access to the U.S. military bases, a dependence which rose during the Vietnam war and, again, after the 1975 loss of Cam Ranh Bay and the subsequent transfer of these facilities in 1979 to the Soviets.

Throughout his regime, Marcos used the bases to secure high levels of economic and military aid, and then used the aid to gain control of the economy and the political system, while expanding the capacity of the military as an instrument for containing opposition. Nevertheless, the human rights violations, "crony capitalism," and other manifestations of the Marcos regime's corruption created deep pockets of opposition within the military, church, oligarchy, and other traditional sources of Philippine power, as well as in the countryside. In response, both moderate and revolutionary opposition grew. Silenced at home, exiled opposition leaders such as Manglapus and Aquino also mobilized U.S. opposition to Marcos, particularly among the roughly one million Filipinos in the United States and the even larger Filipino-American community. Following Watergate and the revolutions in Indochina, Iran and Nicaragua despite massive U.S. military intervention, segments of the U.S. foreign policy establishment had become receptive to such opposition, as a growing human rights lobby gained a toehold, notably in Congress and in the State Department.

All of these opponents of the Marcos regime gradually began to work together after 1972, using transnational strategies to undermine Marcos both at home and in the United States. They operated transnationally because U.S. support was crucial to Marcos' ability to sustain his regime. And such strategies would greatly intensify after the 1983 assassination of Aquino, as moderate anti-Marcos activists in the United States and in the Philippines increasingly understood that a moderate, nonrevolutionary solution to the Philippine crisis would come neither from purely domestic Philippine forces nor from purely U.S. forces. Rather, they would have to be transnational. As the next chapter will show, the 1983 assassination of Benigno Aquino Jr. would prove a turning point in the growing struggle to unseat Marcos.

Notes

1. Although there was a vast Muslim separatist revolutionary opposition in the southern Philippines, with an estimated membership of 30,000 in the early 1970s, it did not play a key role in the 1986 transition, as the NPA/NDF did. Hence, it will be described but will not be the focus of the analysis of this period. Much has been written on the Muslims, however, including a number of articles by Lela Garner Noble (1980) as well as a more recent account by W.K. Che Man (1990).

2. Staff Report prepared for the U.S. Senate Committee on Foreign Relations, *Korea and the Philippines: November 1972*, Committee Print, 93rd Congress, 1st Session, February 18, 1973.

3. Bonner, 119. The final report was distributed December 11, 1973, with slightly higher figures, reprinted in the National Security Archive collection.

4. The above is from the Rand Corporation Report to the U.S. Army Reserve 301st Civil Affairs Group, distributed November 1972, reprinted in the National Security Archive collection, and cited in chapter five.

5. Secret Cable #08787, September 18, 1972, from the National Security Archive collection. Another secret cable, #171335, sent September 20, 1972 from the State Department to the U.S. Embassy echoes the concern that Marcos might declare martial law to protect his political power, also reprinted in the National Security Archive collection.

6. Confidential Cable #09010, September 23, 1972, from the National Security Archive collection.

7. Confidential Cable #09089, September 25, 1972, reprinted in the National Security Archive collection.

8. Note that Manglapus had initially tried to secure a fellowship during his exile at the Woodrow Wilson International Center for Scholars in Washington, D.C., but was blocked when the State Department wrote to the center's board of directors urging them against the plan in order to avoid "ruffled feathers, surprises and publicity." From Confidential Cable #100074, May 14, 1974, reprinted in the National Security Archive collection. A week later, the Wilson Center denied Manglapus the fellowship. The State Department's concern with such a matter indicates the kind of "clientitis" State Department officials now acknowledge, in interviews conducted December 1994, to be problematic in dealing with foreign leaders. This is just one small example of the foreign policy implications of U.S. government influence in nongovernmental organizations.

9. Manglapus, collection of letters, essays, congressional testimony, and speeches during his exile in the United States.

10. Thompson, 91.

11. "The Growing Lobby for Human Rights," *Washington Post*, December 12, 1976, B1, p.1. See also Hoeffel and Kornbluh (1983).

12. Ibid. See also Keck and Sikkink (1994), Sikkink (1993), Schoultz (1981), Forsyth (1989), and Donnelly (1989) for descriptions of the impact of human rights organizations on U.S. foreign policy and international relations. See the *Yearbook of International Organizations* in 1980 and 1990 for information on the growth in staffs, budgets, and memberships of non-government human rights organizations.

13. Personal interview with Bello, November 1993.

14. Personal interview with Father Tom O'Brien of the Maryknoll Mission in the Philippines, December 1985.

15. From Robert Youngblood, "Church Opposition to Martial Law," in Schirmer and Shalom, eds., *The Philippines Reader*. See also Youngblood (1990) and Yu and Bolasco (1981) for more on the relationship between the Catholic Church and the Marcos regime.

16. Ibid.

17. Confidential Cables #11157, #11160, and #11639 sent November 17, 18, and December 1, 1972, respectively. From the National Security Archive collection.

18. Information from this paragraph is from Bonner, 137. The text of the INR secret report distributed January 15, 1973, is from the National Security Archive collection.

19. From "Overseas Loans and Grants, 1961–1988," Special Report Prepared for the House Foreign Affairs Committee, Office of Statistics and Reports, Bureau for Program and Policy Coordination, Agency for International Development. Note that the economic aid figures are on an obligation and loan authorization basis only and not on an expediture basis, while the military aid figures represent the actual value of goods and services delivered.

20. Bello and Rivera (1977), reprinted in Schirmer and Shalom, eds., *The Philippines Reader*.

21. Fact-Finding Commission Report (1990).

22. Bonner, 364.

23. See "Comments of the Military and Succession," Confidential Cable #14660, June 15, 1992 from the National Security Archive collection, wherein confidential Philippine military sources reveal crony capitalism within the military.

24. See for example Secret Airgram A-117, April 11, 1975 titled "The Day of the Generals," from the National Security Archive collection.

25. As early as March 2, 1973, the U.S. General Accounting Office cited misappropriations of U.S. aid by the Marcos regime and recommended closer supervision. From an unclassified report reprinted in the National Security Archive collection.

26. The above is from Karnow, *In Our Image*, 383-84.

27. After the Three-Mile Island accident in March 1979, Marcos suspended work on the Philippine project, despite on-going pressure from Westinghouse and U.S. officials. From Bonner, 270-71.

28. From *A Pen for Democracy*, a collection of writings by Manglapus, reprinted by the Washington, D.C. Office of the Movement for a Free Philippines.

29. Bonner, 146-47.

30. For a detailed account of the economic crisis, see Gerald Sussman, David O'Connor, and Charles W. Lindsey (1984) in Schirmer and Shalom, eds., *The Philippines Reader*. See also Ibon Facts and Figures from 1984 and 1985 for data on the economic decline following the Aquino assassination. For a detailed account of what became known as the Marcos regime's "crony capitalism," see Belinda Aquino (1987). Note that she is no relation to Benigno Aquino Jr.

31. Bonner, 116.

32. Note that Filipino sugar interests contributed $25,000 to the Richard Nixon Campaign Fund. Though Ramon Nolan, who collected and disbursed the funds, denied trying to influence U.S. policy toward the Philippines, it is likely that such funds were given to improve U.S. quotas on Philippine sugar. See the nonclassified report from the Federal Bureau of Investigation, December 7, 1973, reprinted in the National Security Archive collection. In April 1974, the Watergate Special Prosecution Force would find the contributions illegal. See the nonclassified memorandum filed April 4, 1974, also from the National Security Archive collection.

33. Confidential Report from the Federal Bureau of Investigation, New York, NY printed July 5, 1974, from the National Security Archive collection.

34. Karnow, *Vietnam*, 577.

35. General Westmoreland's successor, General Creighton Abrams, had contended that no Cambodian civilians inhabited the sanctuaries, though classified documents published later disclosed that Abrams and other top U.S. officials knew otherwise, conceding that "some Cambodian casualties would be sustained in the operation." From Karnow, *Vietnam*, 591.

36. Ibid.

37. Combs, 412.

38. From a personal interview with Leslie Gelb, March 1989, and from a 1989 lecture given at Harvard Law School by Floyd Abrams, attorney for the *New York Times* in the case.

39. Karnow, *Vietnam*, 634.

40. Forsythe, 2, from Cecil V. Crabb, Jr. and Pat M. Holt, *Invitation to Struggle: Congress, the President and Foreign Policy.*

41. Unclassified reports from the U.S. General Accounting Office sent to the U.S. Congress on April 24 and 27, 1973. From the National Security Archive collection.

42. Forsythe, 102.

43 Note that many Filipinos, Americans, international church leaders, and others too numerous to name here worked long and hard, often at personal risk, to unseat Marcos and undo his regime's abuses from 1972 through 1986. Bello is used here as an example in part because of his connection to Chile, which played a crucial role in human rights debates of the time, and in part because of his direct role, as will be described, in influencing U.S. policy toward the Philippines.

44. From interviews with Bello in November 1993 and with George Lister, the first Human Rights Officer appointed to the State Department's Bureau of Inter-American Affairs and currently Senior Policy Advisor for the Bureau of Democratization, Human Rights and Labor, in December 1994.

45. Personal interview with Bello, November 1993.

46. Combs, 414.

47. Bonner, 165.

48. Limited Official Use Cable #005682, January 10, 1974, from the National Security Archive collection.

49. Forsythe, pp.9-10., and 180-82.

50. Background statement of the evolution of human rights operations within the State Department provided by the State Department, and a personal interview with George Lister, December 1994.

51. For an excellent account of this debate, see Joseph's *Cracks in the Empire.*

52. Simons, 31.

53. In fact, Aquino had allowed former Huk now NPA leader Bernabe "Commander Dante" Buscayno, to use Hacienda Luisita, the vast sugar plantation which Aquino ran for his wife's family, as a training ground and a base of organization. Aquino also supplied food and medicine to the guerrillas, who had murdered six mayors of one town in quick succession and were a tacit threat to Aquino. "Political hypocrisy aside," he told a friend, "can you name one Central Luzon politician who has not dealt with the NPA whether for

sympathy or merely as an act of survival?" From Komisar, 35-36.

54. Bonner, 149.

55. Cofidential Cable #04240, April 5, 1975, from the National Security Archive collection.

56. Unclassified Airgram A-81, March 11, 1975, from the National Security Archive collection.

57. Confidential Cable #04275, April 7, 1975, describes the Fraser visit; the non-classified letter to Ford sent April 12, 1975 reveals Lupita's concern; Limited Official Use Cable #04736 describes the lawyers' efforts; and Confidential Cable #04812, April 16, 1975 describes Corazon's press conference. All from the National Security Archive collection.

58. Karnow, *In Our Image*, 397.

59. Bonner, 151.

60. Lela Noble, in Schirmer and Shalom, eds., *The Philippines Reader*, 193-99. Formed in 1970, the Moro National Liberation Front (MNLF), whose name recalled Spain's colonization and its own struggle against the "Moros," reached a height of about 30,000 in 1973, 1974, and probably the first half of 1975, with external arms and supplies from Sabah and money from Libya's Qaddafi. Far from Manila and often beyond the eye of journalists, it became a frontier war, with thousands killed, hundreds of thousands forced into exile, notably to nearby Sabah, and more than a million displaced from martial law through the 1970s. In March 1975, the MNLF and Marcos administration met in Jidda to negotiate an end to the conflict, see Confidential Airgram A-74, March 3, 1975, and eventually signed a peace treaty in Libya with Qaddafi's help in 1976, though fighting continued sporadically thereafter. See Confidential Cable #19908 sent December 12, 1976, both reprinted in the National Security Archive collection. By the late 1970s, the MNLF was greatly reduced, though it continued to operate in the southernmost island of Mindanao. The MNLF and the NPA never united; but would have been formidable if they had.

61. Bonner, 152.

62. Bonner, 152-53.

63. Apparently seeking alternative allies while demonstrating independence from the United States, Marcos was anxious to establish diplomatic relations with China before the United States did and so sent Imelda there to meet with Zhou Enlai in September 1974. China was equally anxious to secure official recognition from its neighbor, and wooed Imelda toward this end, as an unlikely friendship formed between Mao's wife, Chiang Ching, and the Philippines' First Lady. For information on Imelda's China visit, see Bonner, 156-160, as well as Limited Official Use Cable #10486, September 21, 1974, and Confidential Airgram A-363, November 7, 2974, both from the National Security Archive collection.

64. Note that U.S. State Department officials recommended that congressional testimony defend U.S. silence on martial law as a gesture of respect for Philippine sovereignty, somehow overlooking the U.S. role in sustaining the military machinery required to sustain martial law. Note also that Philippine citizens in the United States documented attempts by Marcos to prevent congressional testimony regarding his regime. See, in particular, Limited Official Use Cable #08332, June 18, 1975 and an affidavit of

Philippine government attempts to bribe congressional witnesses, printed July 10, 1975, both from the National Security Archive collection.

65. Confidential Cable #17441, December 12, 1975, from the National Security Archive collection.

66. Brands 307, from Salinger notes on Marcos interview, December 7, 1975.

67. Karnow, *In Our Image*, 398.

68. Confidential Cable #06497, May 14, 1975, from the National Security Archive collection.

69. Karnow, *In Our Image*, 397.

70. Personal interviews with Lister and Butcher, both of the State Department; Bonner, 183; background paper on the history and evolution of the human rights operations from the State Department; and Forsythe, 119-125.

71. Ibid.

72. In Confidential Memorandum #00938, January 20, 1977, from the National Security Archive collection, Holbrooke wrote Warren Christopher, Deputy Assistant Secretary of State and head of the Interagency Committee on Human Rights and Foreign Assistance, that the time was opportune for the U.S. State Department to pursue human rights reform in the Philippines. Later in the year, however, Holbrooke went to South Korea and chastised John Salzberg, a Quaker staffmember of a congressional delegation, for meeting with opponents of martial law there. In 1979, Salzberg was hired by Derian, but Holbrooke successfully lobbied to transfer him to the African section of the human rights bureau. (from Bonner, 188-89)

73. The above is from Forsythe, 120.

74. Background paper from the State Department on its human rights operations.

75. Forsythe, 125.

76. Derian's itinerary and Philippine reactions to her visit are detailed in Confidential Cable #00719 and Limited Official Use Cable #00720, both sent January 13, 1978, reprinted in the National Security Archive collection. See also Bonner, 227-231.

77. For an intensive survey of the World Bank role in the Philippines, see Bello, Kinley and Elinson's work based on over 6,000 pages of secret documents leaked by disenchanted staff within the Bank. The loan figures are from World Bank documents the authors compiled, 207-208.

78. Confidential Cable #027678, February 2, 1978, from the National Security Archive collection.

79. See, for example, Confidential Summary of a January 20, 1978 meeting of the interagency committee, followed by Confidential Cable #01301, January 25, 1978, from Newsom to the State Department, suggesting measures to improve human rights and reverse unfavorable U.S. votes on aid. Both are reprinted in the National Security Archive collection.

80. For a comprehensive discussion of World Bank operations, see Payer. In brief, the United States is the largest shareholder with a voting power commensurate with its shares, roughly 30-35 percent of the IDA and over 20 percent of the IBRD in 1978. Moreover, as of 1978, although the World Bank was formally ruled by its Board of Governors representing each member nation, that body met only once a year. The day-to-day decisions

were made by twenty executive directors, from a cross section of member nations, and the president, who was typically a U.S. citizen, a factor deemed necessary for retaining the confidence of the capital markets and the U.S. government. From 1968 to 1980, the World Bank President was Robert McNamara, who had served as Secretary of Defense under Kennedy and Johnson and emerged from his role in the Vietnam War a committed softliner, as described in Karnow, *Vietnam*.

81. The U.S. embassy urged an amendment to the State Department's human rights reports, citing increased political participation as well as "martial law respect for human rights and fair treatment of political prisoners" in Diplomatic Note, February 14, 1978, from the National Security Archive collection.

82. From Bonner, 231-35.

83. On November 25, 1977, a military court sentenced Aquino to death by firing squad. Two days later, his mother filed a petition protesting that her son had not had the opportunity to present evidence. Marcos ordered that the trial be reopened. Though the death sentence still stood, the trial dragged on, granting Aquino, in the process, a stay of execution. From Simons, 23.

84. Many cables between the State Department and the U.S. Embassy in Manila throughout the period of Aquino's imprisonment follow the case closely, expressing concern over the issue, its implications for continued U.S. military aid to the Philippines, as well as Marcos' credibility as a leader. See, for example, a spate of cables transmitted during Aquino's trial in November 1977. Members of Congress urged Carter to express "shock and outrage" at the decision, see nonclassified letter December 1, 1977, but the administration remained quiet on the issue, continuing to work with Marcos to secure the U.S. bases, see Secret Cable #295479 December 10, 1977, all reprinted in the National Security Archive collection.

85. Secret Cable #042011, February 17, 1978, from the National Security Archive collection.

86. Confidential Cable #03127, February 27, 1987 describes the Philippine NSC decision, reprinted in the National Security Archive collection.

87. Thompson, 136.

88. Confidential Cable #05500, April 6, 1978, requests diplomatic instructions for handling the U.S. response to the elections, in which massive fraud and manipulation on behalf of Marcos were anticipated, reprinted in the National Security Archive collection.

89. Confidential Cable # 05513, April 8, 1978, and Limited Official Use Cable #05515, April 10, 1978, describe the Philippine reaction to the elections and the subsequent crackdown by the Marcos regime. Both are reprinted in the National Security Archive collection. See also Bonner, 237-39.

90. Nonclassified letter, April 21, 1978, from the National Security Archive collection.

91. Confidential Cable #05723, April 12, 1978, from the National Security Archive collection.

92. Confidential Cable #05513, April 8, 1978, from the National Security Archive collection.

93. Secret Cable #05994, April 14, 1978, from the National Security Archive collection.

94. The information for this paragraph is from Thompson, 108-130, which includes personal interviews with several participants of the Light A Fire Movement.

95. Secret Memorandum of a Policy Review Committee meeting at the National Security Council, February 22, 1978, discusses the importance of the U.S. bases in the Philippines, the status of the negotiations, and strategies for working with Congress to secure the bases despite the on-going human rights concerns, reprinted in the National Security Archive collection.

96. For State Department efforts to stem congressional pressures, see Secret Cable #225624, September 20, 1977. For Holbrooke's meetings with Marcos, see Secret Cables #230439 and #230521, both sent September 24, 1977. All reprinted in the National Security Archive collection.

97. Limited Official Use Briefing Book for the Mondale Visit, printed April 27, 1978, and Secret Briefing Paper, May 1978, both in the National Security Archive collection.

98. Bonner, 244-250.

99. In Secret Cable #08040, May 25, 1977, reprinted in the National Security Archive collection, the U.S. Embassy advised the State Department that Burke had received reports that Philippine intelligence and military officers were involved in torturing political prisoners. This information was provided to her by the Association of Major Religious Superiors of the Philippines and by Friends of the Filipino People, a leftist American organization lobbying against the Marcos regime in the United States.

100. Limited Official Use Cable #190511, July 27, 1978, and Secret Cable #192106, July 29, 1978, describe Mrs. Marcos' visit with congressional leaders, and U.S. concerns that this might hinder bases negotiations. Both are from the National Security Archive collection.

101. Brands, 309.

102. See, for example, Confidential Action Memorandum, June 5, 1978, written by both Derian and Holbrooke describing their failure to agree on military exports to the Philippines as well as munitions control policies. Note that corporations such as Gulf and Western weighed in against Derian, defending their plans to provide armaments to "friendly governments' armed forces." See, for example, Nonclassified letter, June 8, 1978. Both are reprinted in the National Security Archive collection.

103. See Confidential Cables #001392, January 4, 1978 and #001745, January 5, 1978, detailing Ambassador Newson's suggested changes, and the subsequent debate with the State Department's Human Rights Bureau. See also Limited Official Use Cable #115030, May 5, 1978, describing a visit to the United States by Philippine military officers in which plans to improve human rights are discussed, and Limited Official Use Cable #07691, May 19, 1978, citing measures taken by Ramos and Enrile to enforce new armed forces gun control policies and other attempts to curb human rights violations. All are reprinted in the National Security Archive collection.

104. Limited Official Use Cable #07771, May 11, 1978, from the National Security Archive collection.

105. Secret Cable, July 14, 1978, from the F.B.I., Wisconsin to other F.B.I. stations nationwide, reprinted in the National Security Archive collection.

106. Confidential Cable #19542, November 2, 1978, from Murphy to the State Department, which expresses concern that the State Department's upcoming human rights assessment might "jeopardize military facilities negotiations," reprinted in the National Security Archive collection. See also Brands, 309.

107. See Confidential Briefing Memorandum, January 18, 1979, in the National Security Archive collection for an overview of the agreement. See also Bonner, 253.

108. The above is from Bonner, 253-54, and 283-84.

109. Brands, 311.

110. Background paper from the State Department on its human rights operations.

111. The above information on Iran is from Combs, 450-53.

112. The above information on Nicaragua is from Combs, 473-75.

113. Gregor and Aganon, 10-32.

114. See in particular her "Dictatorships and Double Standards," *Commentary*, November 1979.

115. Bonner, 296.

116. Confidential Cable #09460, May 15, 1980, describes the Marcos–Aquino negotiations for Aquino's departure as well as the symbolic gift. The cable is reprinted in the National Security Archive collection. See also Bonner, 291.

117. Personal interview with Huntington, October 1991.

118. Personal interviews with Aquino, October 1992.

119. Text of the speech is reprinted in Limited Official Use Cable #03061, August 6, 1980, from the National Security Archive collection. See also Karnow, *In Our Image*, 400.

120. Personal interview with Pye, August 1992.

121. Information on the April 6 Movement is from Thompson, 108-130.

122. Confidential Cables #20592, October 21, 1980, and #20813, October 22, 1980, from the National Security Archive collection.

123. Ibid.

124. Bonner. Note that Bonner was fired from the *New York Times* for his reporting from El Salvador, deemed too biased for its depiction of El Salvadoran government human rights violations in the countryside. The conflict between Bonner and the *New York Times* remains unresolved, and his byline once again graces the paper periodically from far-flung locales.

125. The text of the proclamation lifting martial law is in Unclassified Cable #01479, January 19, 1981, while the embassy assessment is in Confidential Cable #01316, January 16, 1981, both from the National Security Archive collection. See also Bonner, 295-315.

126. Thompson, 137. Horacio Morales, leader of the National Democratic Front, was less Maoist than CPP founder Jose Marie Sison, and sought a coalition, or united front, with the moderates. The 1981 boycott campaign was the culmination of several months of united front organizing, according to Thompson, from David Rosenberg, "Communism in the Philippines."

127. Wurfel, 252.

128. The original name was the United Democratic Organization (UDO) but was changed in 1982 to the United Nationalist Democratic Organization (UNIDO). From Thompson, 143-44.

129. Bonner, 309-311.

130. A Confidential Memorandum, May 26, 1981, from the State Department recommends high level U.S. participation at the inauguration in order to help prepare "the atmosphere" for the up-coming bases negotiations. This position is reiterated in a Secret Memorandum to Bush from the State Department, June 18, 1981, both reprinted in the National Security Archive collection.

131. Personal interview with Lister, December 1994. Note that Butcher and others in regional bureaus refer derisively to the bureau by a rough acronym—"drivel," exposing the ongoing conflicts between the human rights bureau and the regional ones.

132. Information for this paragraph is from Forsythe, 119-136, while the quote from Bonker is from Christopher Madison, "Foreign Policy: Human Rights—Again," *National Journal* 18, May 1, 1982, 763-66.

133. Although civil servants are ostensibly apolitical, those brought in under one administration and remain when that adminisration changes, may still have an ideological, professional, personal or other loyalty to the initial administration. This is a topic for future research; but it is hypothesized that such loyalty would be particularly true in emotionally-charged issues like human rights.

134. Thompson, 149.

135. Simons, 29.

136. Confidential Cable #03687, February 13, 1981, from the National Security Archive collection.

137. Limited Official Use Cable #03753, February 18, 1981, from the National Security Archive collection.

138. Limited Official Use Cable #04124, February 23, 1981, from the National Security Archive collection.

139. Personal interview with Lister, December 1994.

140. Guerrero, 114.

141. Confidential Cable #290942 sent October 31, 1981, reprinted in the National Security Archive collection.

142. Limited Official Use Cable #27704, November 23, 1981 describe State Department concerns regarding the Bonker/Solarz hearings and spreading congressional opposition to law enforcement aid to the Marcos regime, reprinted in the National Security Archive collection.

143. Bello, Kinley and Elinson (1982), and personal interview with Bello, November 1993.

144. Confidential Cable #019298, January 24, 1981, from the National Security Archive collection.

145. Unclassified Cable #02528, January 30, 1981, from the National Security Archive collection.

146. See for example Confidential Cable from the F.B.I. in Philadelphia to other branches nationwide, sent August 17, 1981, describing Philippine intelligence officers in the United States and their diplomatic covers, reprinted in the National Security Archive collection.

147. Confidential Airgram A-3, April 13, 1982, from the National Security Archive collection. See also Bonner, 323-24.

148. The conflict centered on hard-line versus soft-line approaches to the growing crisis generated by the Palestine Liberation Organization's sanctuary in Beirut. While Habib urged the United States to support diplomatic and other soft-line efforts, Haig dissented, arguing that continued hard-line pressure was needed to encourage the PLO to negotiate. Haig's departure was a blow for the hard-liners. (From Shultz, 14-15)

149. Bonner, 323.

150. Simons, 22.

151. Karnow, *In Our Image*, 401.

152. From Karnow, *In Our Image*, 385-86, and Bonner, 328.

153. Limited Official Use Cable, #09092, April 14, 1983, from the National Security Archive collection.

154. Bonner, 328.

155. "Action Against Clergy Suspected of Radical Activities," Confidential Cable #2570, October 15, 1982, from the National Security Archive collection.

156. See, for example, Confidential Cable #17127, July 14, 1982, reprinted in the National Security Archive collection.

157. Kline and Worthen.

158. Personal interview with Bello, November 1993.

159. Thompson.

160. Aquino managed to obtain a passport in early August then traveled to the Philippines, stopping enroute to meet with the sultan of Johore who was soon to become king of Malaysia. Aquino had become friends at Harvard with the sultan and now hoped to enlist his aid in settling the on-going Muslim secessionist movement in Mindanao. Because the Marcos regime disputed Malaysia's claim to the island of Sabah, Aquino's visit was seen by Marcos as a Malaysian bid to undermine his regime. From Simons, 30.

161. Simons, 31-34.

162. From the song "Tie a Yellow Ribbon." The idea for the ribbons is thought to have come from the American yellow ribbon campaign to bring home the American hostages held in Iran, from Simons, 44. The figure of 30,000 is from Komisar, 5.

Chapter 6

People Power:
The Transition from Marcos
to Aquino, 1983–1986

T hough only a few undid democracy in 1972, it took the ingenuity, courage and commitment of many, working in the Philippines and in the United States for years, to reestablish it. This chapter examines the transnational processes after 1983 that brought the Marcos regime to its dramatic conclusion on February 25, 1986. Why, the chapter asks, did the United States withdraw support from Marcos? What implications did this hold for Philippine prospects for a transition from authoritarian to democratic rule? Why, moreover, was the transition democratic, not authoritarian from the right or revolutionary from the left? The chapter first describes the Filipino response to the Aquino assassination, its political and economic impact, and the growth of both revolutionary and moderate opposition to Marcos. The chapter then describes the U.S. debates on policy toward the Philippines, and the growing concern among U.S. officials that Filipino moderates, if denied a democratic alternative to Marcos, might ally with the revolutionaries, with the increasingly real possibility of a Sandinista-like revolution. Using transnational strategies to tilt the domestic balance of power within the Philippines away from both leftist revolutionary and rightist authoritarian forces toward moderate democrats, key U.S. and Filipino opponents of Marcos undermined Marcos' viability at home as well as his crucial network of support within the United States. In this way, they forced the withdrawal of U.S. support from Marcos, which had long sustained him, and thus heralded the restoration of Philippine democracy.

Fallen Hero:
Public Response to the Aquino Assassination

Aquino, like Rizal before him, achieved instant martyrdom as thousands lined up daily to pay their last respects at his wake. His mother chose not to clean the blood from his face, so that all who saw him would understand the brutality of the murder. This proved effective. In the streets of Manila and throughout the Philippine countryside, the three colors of the Philippine flag—blue, yellow and red—exploded. While the Marcoses retained their retinue of "blue ladies," sycophants dressed in blue butterfly-sleeve dresses, Corazon Aquino returned from the United States on August 24 and adopted yellow, for the yellow ribbons that had greeted her husband at the airport, as the color of her mourning and a symbol of moderate opposition. Meanwhile, revolutionary slogans scrawled in red paint proliferated in the countryside and in the cities. On the day of the funeral, even the business community expressed their indignation, unfurling a yellow and black banner from a Manila office building which read: Ninoy Aquino—Once a Name, Now a Legend. Massive crowds chanting "Ninoy, Ninoy" and "Hindi ka nagiisa," Tagalog for "You are not alone," accompanied the hearse on its seventy-five mile journey from Manila to Aquino's home province of Tarlac. The body was then transported back to Manila, where hundreds of thousands, perhaps millions, joined the eighteen-mile funeral procession, singing "Ang Bayan Ko," or "My Country." The song describes a caged bird struggling to fly, expressing a yearning nationalist Filipinos have had to suppress throughout most of their history. At the funeral, attended by three thousand including U.S. Ambassador Michael Armacost, Cardinal Sin eulogized Aquino and criticized the Marcos regime but also appealed to Filipinos for peace. With only a limited number of unarmed police in attendance, the crowds complied.

The man who had once been disappointed at the silence accompanying his arrest in 1972 now, in death, launched a wave of protest marches and public rallies, as the Manila middle class became politicized. The growing sense was, as one Filipino in the funeral procession said, "If this, this outright murder can happen to a man of the national and international status of Aquino, then what can happen to ordinary people...what about the rest of us?" Fearing harsh reprisals for even moderate opposition, moderates and revolutionaries began to ally. In the sea of yellow worn by those in the funeral procession were dots of red as well.[1] From 1969 when the NPA formed through 1985, it expanded from a few hundred to roughly 16,000 regulars, a million active supporters, and a broader base under the leftist umbrella group's National Democratic Front (NDF) estimated at ten million nationwide, or roughly twenty percent of the population.[2] The movement sought removal of the U.S. bases, improved human rights, and a restructuring of the Philippine economy, involving land reform and restrictions on U.S. investments.[3] The left's strength was greatest in the countryside where roughly 70 % of all Filipinos lived in 1985. Inequality in land ownership, a long-standing source of conflict in the countryside, was a driving force in the left's rural popularity, with 1985 figures indicating that about 80 percent of the land belonged to only 20 percent of the population.[4] Land reform was a key rallying cry for the left.[5]

The left was also growing in response to human rights violations by the military. According to Stephen Bosworth, who succeeded Armacost as U.S. Ambassador to the Philippines, serving from April 1984 to April 1987, long-standing hard-line strategies were increasingly seen as fueling not quelling revolutionary fervor. This was particularly true in the countryside, where "the only effective presence the Philippine government had... was the military and the military's behavior was such that they were alienating people from the government."[6] In fact, strategic hamletting programs and aerial bombings, both partially financed by the United States, were being conducted in remote regions of the country, leaving thousands homeless or dead. Though statistics from the countryside are both difficult to find and unreliable, after 1977, human rights violations were recorded, due in part to encouragement from the U.S. State Department's human rights bureau and the embassy in Manila as well as Amnesty International and other nongovernmental international and Philippine human rights organizations. According to the Task Force Detainees of the Philippines, a leading Philippine human rights organization sponsored by the Catholic church, over 21,000 people were arrested for political reasons from 1977 through 1985, while over 700 had disappeared since 1975 and more than 2,400 had died, also since 1975, in extrajudicial killings known as "salvagings."[7] Two leaders from the left later acknowledged the link between human rights violations by the military and the growth of the NPA.[8]

The political instability following the Aquino assassination, as well as the rampant crony capitalism, also deepened an emerging economic crisis. Investor confidence plummeted, leading to massive capital flight estimated at more than $10 billion[9] and a downward spiral in the economy.[10] Under international scrutiny following the Aquino assassination, evidence surfaced in late 1983 that the

Philippine Central Bank had been falsifying estimates of its foreign debt, overstating the country's foreign reserves in order to cover the Marcos regime's mismanagement. This revelation further eroded investor confidence. To restore his standing with the International Monetary Fund and foreign banks, Marcos was forced to impose rigid import controls. By October 1983, he also devalued the peso 21 percent against the dollar. Soon after, the Philippine government was forced to suspend principal payments on its foreign debt of over $25 billion. With inflation reaching 60 percent by early 1984,[11] real GNP fell by 5.5 percent that year and by an additional 4 percent in 1985.[12] The Filipino business community was hard hit; urban land prices, stock markets, and corporate profits tumbled. As the economic crisis hit the urban middle class, which had long been insulated from the economic concerns in the countryside, moderate opposition burgeoned. The anger of the business community exploded in a "confetti revolution" on September 14, 1983, when over 100,000 well-dressed office workers marched through Makati, Manila's Wall Street, tons of shredded yellow paper falling from the windows of surrounding skyscrapers. This set the tone for subsequent weekly anti-Marcos rallies. Meanwhile, formerly pro-Marcos business leaders from Makati and from the Chinese community began secretly contributing funds to the opposition.[13]

U.S. officials, notably in the State Department, drew analogies to pre-revolutionary Nicaragua and Iran and worried about the possibility of a moderate-left alliance, with the growing possibility of a leftist revolution. Would Marcos, and so U.S. interests in the Philippines, go the way of Somoza and the shah, both of whom had enjoyed substantial U.S. support but failed to avert revolution?[14] Though State Department reports described the left as home-grown, nonaligned and seeking to remain so, the movement's opposition to the U.S. military bases sounded alarms in the United States.[15]

The U.S. Response

The State Department immediately called the Aquino assassination a "despicable act which the government condemns in the strongest possible terms,"[16] and then encouraged Reagan to cancel a scheduled trip to the Philippines for November.[17] Rather than make the "strongest possible" statement against Marcos by canceling the trip only to Manila, however, Reagan opted to cancel all of his stops in Southeast Asia including the Philippines. Softening the message further, Bush publicly promised on October 6, 1983, that the United States would not "cut away from a person who, imperfect though he may be on human rights, has worked with us."[18] Yet fissures were growing in the United States where the Filipino community mobilized a nationwide network of organizations to publicize their anger at Marcos and to lobby for a change in U.S. policy. These included the Ninoy Aquino Movement, the Movement for a Free Philippines formed by exiled opposition leader Raul Manglapus, and others. In addition, the long-standing efforts of the human rights lobby to expose the Marcos regime's venality now hit home, as Aquino's many friends from various sectors of elite society, from the media, academia, business, and politics, rallied against Marcos. Even Ambassador Armacost, who had hitherto enjoyed close relations with the Marcoses, attended Aquino's funeral and began to distance himself from Marcos. By April 1984, Armacost would return to the United States to serve under Shultz as undersecretary of political affairs. In this capacity, he would give crucial testimony to Congress and would otherwise help redirect U.S. support from Marcos to the moderate opposition, now led by Aquino's widow.[19]

Laying the groundwork for this policy shift, an interagency task force was established in late 1983 to monitor the situation, with the State Department playing the lead role in this. Assistant Secretary for East Asian and Pacific Affairs Paul Wolfowitz brought together Assistant Secretary of State for International Security Affairs Richard Armitage, NSC Asian specialists Gaston Sigur and Richard Childress, and others, "all Asian specialists by proclivity" for weekly meetings on the Philippines. According to Armitage, "There was an unusual unanimity of views at the assistant secretary level." Although all were loyal to Reagan, Armitage acknowledges that "...we gave testimony to congress which was uncleared by anybody but ourselves."[20] The congressional link would ultimately prove crucial in Marcos' downfall after the Aquino assassination, beginning in October 1983 when Solarz, a close personal friend of the Aquino family, shepherded through a "Sense of the House" resolution. The resolution called for a "thorough, independent, and impartial investigation of the Aquino assassination" as well as "genuine, free, and fair elections" to the Philippine National Assembly.[21] Approved by a vote of 413 to 3 on October 24, 1983, the resolution sent a bipartisan signal to Marcos supporters in the United States and in the Philippines. Bowing to the pressures, Marcos named in November 1983 an independent panel, known as the Agrava Board for chairwoman Corazon Agrava, to investigate the Aquino assassination.[22]

This stab at liberalization raised U.S. hopes that reforms could resolve the Philippine crisis while preserving the Marcos regime. In January 1984, there seemed to be agreement on a new State Department plan to seek a political solution to the instability, spurring Marcos toward reform. The approach, headed by Armacost, was designed to establish distance from Marcos, while pressuring him to initiate a limited power-sharing arrangement with the moderate opposition in order to stem its radicalization.[23] As part of the strategy, State Department officials urged Congress not to cut aid to Marcos, citing his achievements in managing the Aquino assassination trial.[24] Soon after, however, Marcos lost a key ally in the State Department when, in April 1984, Armacost was recalled to D.C., and was replaced by Stephen Bosworth. Where Armacost had been close to the Marcoses until the death of Aquino, Bosworth, more reserved and skeptical by nature than his predecessor, never succumbed to the Marcos charm, often lavishly proffered.[25] Maintaining his distance from the Marcoses, Bosworth forged stronger ties with Cardinal Sin and with the moderate opposition, which the United States had sidelined since 1972 in deference to Marcos.[26]

Bowing further to the pressures, Marcos announced plans for legislative elections to be held May 14, 1984. The Marcos administration then requested the presence of a U.S. observer delegation to monitor the elections, sparking a debate between Congress and the State Department. A month before the elections, Congressman Solarz canceled his plans to participate.[27] The State Department then exerted pressure on Congress, though hopes of official U.S. participation dimmed.[28] By early May, Congress announced its final decision not to participate, in part because they did not want to help legitimize fraudulent elections.[29] Anticipating fraud, the left called for a boycott hoping to ally again with the moderate opposition, as had been the case in the 1981 boycott. Instead, over 300,000 citizens revived the National Committee for Free Elections (NAMFREL), the independent citizen's watch group established with CIA assistance in 1951. Moreover, 85 percent of registered voters participated in the elections, signaling a resurgent faith in democratic processes while limiting the prospects of a moderate-left alliance.[30] The elections were, in fact, marred by fraud and violence as the boycott advocates projected; yet the opposition, led by UNIDO, nevertheless won 59 of the 183 eligible seats, nearly double the 30 seats the opposition had hoped to garner.[31] "I would presume," Marcos acknowledged in a May 15, 1984, interview on CBS News, "that our instructions to our people to allow the opposition to win some seats might have been taken too literally." Shultz notes: "It was an incredible statement for Marcos to have made, but there it was."[32]

Continuing Growth of the NPA

Despite the liberalizations, a June 1984 report from the U.S. embassy sent a grave warning about the continuing growth of the NPA. James Nach, the report's author, held a Master's in international relations from Columbia and had been in Vietnam from 1970 to 1974. His wife was Vietnamese, and he had a special sensitivity to communist insurgencies. He had studied the insurgency from the United States,[33] but when he arrived in Manila in August 1982, he found that very little attention had been given to the subject there. Nach traveled throughout the countryside and conducted extensive interviews to understand the insurgency. He finally concluded in his 1984 report that the Marcos regime's corruption, crony capitalism and human rights violations made it incapable of instituting the kind of economic, social and other reforms needed to stem the insurgency.[34] It was, if not the first at least the most influential, and documented, official U.S. argument calling for reform not repression to quell the insurgency since martial law had been declared in 1972. Moreover, Nach found that the insurgency, though Maoist, received little if any external support, particularly since Philippine communists had split from the Soviets in 1969 while Philippine government relations with China had normalized in 1975. The Philippine insurgents, Nach found, relied instead on a strategy of "agaw armas," or the stealing of arms from the Philippine military, most bought with U.S. aid. They also had an underground network of supporters in the United States who helped hide members, publish and distribute materials, while providing other relatively small scale assistance.[35] Thus, Nach concluded, Marcos must be seen as part of the problem. Without "new directions from the top," Nach predicted further, there would be an eventual "Communist takeover" with grave implications for U.S. interests.

Nach's report was initially considered alarmist; but when Admiral William Crowe, commander in chief of U.S. forces in the Pacific and a top contender for the Joint Chiefs of Staff, weighed in on the subject after a visit to the Philippines soon after, concluding as Nach had that the NPA posed a serious threat to U.S. interests in the Philippines, official Washington took notice. As he told journalist Stanley Karnow, Crowe believed "Things had to change. Marcos was not making the decisions that had to be made...and the country was sliding downhill. So, I felt, he had to go."[36] Moreover, Crowe had spoken with military sources and learned that the Philippine armed forces had become corrupt and demoralized under Marcos' cronyism. Crowe concluded that the military was at the time incapable of fighting the insurgency effectively and needed to be both professionalized and depoliticized.[37] Few top U.S. officials were prepared to defect from Marcos, however, and Crowe was unable to persuade Defense Secretary Caspar Weinberger, CIA Director William Casey, and others from Reagan's inner circle of foreign policy advisors. Only Shultz, though unprepared for such a drastic measure, nevertheless listened.[38] Meanwhile, two Senate Foreign Relations Committee staffers, Carl Ford and Frederick Brown, returned from two Philippine research trips in the spring and summer with the conclusion that a "disciplined, purposeful communist insurgency with sophisticated political infrastructure and growing military capability countrywide has become a major threat to the Philippine democracy."[39] Senator Richard Lugar (R-IN), as chair of the committee, took notice, and would play an increasingly central role in the drama.[40]

As the first anniversary of the Aquino assassination approached, mass demonstrations strengthened the perception among U.S. officials of the Philippines as the new Nicaragua or Iran, ripe for revolution. According to a confidential cable from Bosworth to the State Department, between 100,000 and 500,000 Filipinos marked the anniversary on August 21, 1984 in street demonstrations.[41] Two days later, Reagan accepted his party's nomination to run for a second term, while Walter Mondale won the Democratic nomination. And the campaign promised to revive the ideological feud between the foreign policy of Carter with its emphasis on human rights and the more militant anticommunism of Reagan. A particularly explosive aspect of the debate centered on U.S. policy toward Nicaragua, such that nearly 75 percent of those polled worried that the U.S. role in Nicaragua might lead to "another Vietnam." To avoid public criticism, and to circumvent congressional obstructions, policy toward Nicaragua went covert. Soon, evidence began to surface regarding CIA training and other U.S. support for the contras, despite an executive order Reagan had signed in 1981 prohibiting such tactics.[42]

Meanwhile, the Agrava Commission issued two separate reports on the Aquino Assassination. One report, issued by Agrava, cited military involvement but excluded Philippine Armed Forces Chief of Staff General Fabian Ver. The other report, however, was issued by the majority and cited Ver as well. When Marcos accepted the minority report, Corazon Aquino led the national outcry, condemning Marcos' treatment of her husband as well as his likely involvement in the assassination. While the moderate opposition rallied in protest, General Fidel Ramos formed a "special action committee" to review complaints of human rights violations by the military and to press military officers to strengthen relations with the church. Now, opposition from within the Marcos regime as well as the moderate opposition began to organize.[43]

Undaunted, official U.S. policy supported Marcos. In one presidential debate, when asked about the declining situation in the Philippines, Reagan held firm to the Kirkpatrick doctrine, reasoning that although "there are things there...that do not look good to us from the standpoint...of democratic rights...what is the alternative? It is a large Communist movement to take over the Philippines." The moderate opposition in the Philippines was outraged by the remark. One moderate opposition leader, Ramon Mitra, a former senator who was imprisoned during the first months of martial law in 1972, publicly stated that "Our alternative to Marcos is certainly not Communism. The alternative to Marcos is a democratic government. But if there is one thing that may lead to communism here, it is Marcos staying in power." The State Department tried to repair the damage from Reagan's remark, issuing a statement to the Associated Press that "there is certainly recognition on everybody's part that there are other forces working for democratic change in the Philippines." U.S. analysts began to fear, however, that unless a moderate opposition was allowed breathing space, Reagan might in fact prove to be right, particularly since the Philippine economy continued to plummet. Capital flight reached an estimated $1 billion; foreign banks refused to renew short-term credit; real GNP was down by 7.1 percent in 1984; and unemployment reached 25 percent of the labor force.[44] Testifying before the House Subcommittee on Asian and Pacific Affairs, Assistant Secretary of Defense for International Security Affairs Richard Armitage noted that the Pentagon was seeking alternative sites for U.S. bases should revolution in the Philippines require that.[45]

Though Reagan won a second term in a landslide, the State Department began formulating a new policy in November urging Marcos to reform. Drafted by John Maisto, a career foreign service officer who was married to a Filipina, had studied the Philippines closely for many years, and now headed the Philippine desk, the policy proposal urged a shift in policy to acknowledge the need for reform. Though the proposal identified Marcos as "part of the problem," it also continued to uphold him as "necessarily part of the solution."[46] This position acknowledged the need to reform the Marcos regime in order to stem the threat of revolution, but remained loyal to Marcos, viewing him not only as capable of such reforms but also as the most reliable protector of U.S. interests in the Philippines.

A New Direction

Now, U.S. officials agreed on the need to stem the revolutionary movement's growth, but disagreed on whether Marcos was part of the solution or part of the problem. Reagan, together with Weinberger, Casey and Chief of Staff Donald Regan were among those most influential in arguing for continued support of Marcos. Midlevel analysts, particularly in the State Department, however, argued that hard-line tactics had alienated so many Filipinos that many former moderates were allying with the left, with the increasingly real possibility of a Sandinista-like revolution. Reports from the embassy supported this view, as Maisto, Nach, and other analysts, with the support of Armacost, Wolfowitz, and Armitage argued for moderate change in order to avert revolution. In January 1985, consensus formed around Maisto's policy proposal, which Reagan signed as a new National Security Decision Directive (NSDD) designed to pressure Marcos to institute political, economic and military reforms. As Maisto's draft had done, the NSDD cited Marcos as "part of the problem" but also as a necessary part of any solution.[47] In mid-January, the Marcos regime seemed to respond to the pressure when government prosecutors indicted General Ver, one of Marcos' closest allies, as well as 25 others in the plot to assassinate Aquino. The *New York Times* hailed this decision in an article titled "Democracy Gains Steam in the Philippines."[48] Because Ver had become a symbol of the politicization and corruption in the military, his indictment was seen as a step toward military reform.

During a visit to Manila also in January, Wolfowitz applauded the indictments, publicly indicating that American aid programs for the Philippines would be aimed at strengthening democratic institutions and encouraging economic and social reforms to stem the "root causes" of the insurgency.[49] To strengthen the message, he also met with human rights monitors as well as opposition leaders, something U.S. officials had typically refrained from doing in deference to Marcos.[50] Wolfowitz then briefed Secretary of State George Shultz in preparation for a February 7 meeting with Bosworth on the current "quiet diplomacy." This diplomacy, Wolfowitz explained, urged Marcos to reform while defining procedures for a Marcos succession and a restructuring of the Philippines' foreign debt.[51] Subsequently, Shultz brought together William Casey, Caspar Weinberger, William Crowe, and Robert McFarlane to discuss the Philippine crisis. Shultz describes how a "rough consensus" emerged from the meeting, as all agreed to strengthen Philippine political, military, business, and financial institutions, hoping that Marcos would join the efforts to reform his regime. Though Shultz acknowledged that "critical decisions would have to emerge from a Philippine process," he and the others believed that the United States could help. He proposed that the U.S support business leaders who could press for open elections and a more free market economy; Catholic leaders concerned with the revolutionary trends within the church as well as with the human rights situation; military professionals who wanted to depoliticize their institutions; and moderate opposition leaders who, Bosworth believed, wanted to work "constructively" for democratic reforms. Shultz then notified Reagan, who agreed with the assessment but hoped as well that Marcos would "work with us" on reform.[52]

By February 22, just as witnesses were being called in the Aquino assassination trial in Manila,[53] Wolfowitz publicly urged the Philippine government to hasten progress on political, economic and military issues. He added further that a U.S. proposal for an extra $15 million in military assistance would be "premised on the full expectation that the incipient reforms we have seen will continue and expand."[54] Later, covert assistance was supplied, just in case, to the Reform the Armed Forces Movement (RAM) of the Philippine military.[55] Formed in March 1985 by reformist officers in the Philippine military, RAM members included two colonels from Enrile's security unit, who were concerned by the corruption, lack of professionalism, human rights violations, and low morale in a military where promotions were increasingly doled out on the basis of cronyism not merit. They also believed that corruption had helped usher in communist regimes in China, Vietnam, Laos and Cambodia, and hoped to avert such an event in the

Philippines via reform.[56] According to Armitage, "the defense attache's office had very good contacts in the RAM group," though "US policy was to discourage RAM from premature coups." He adds, "We were not so much disinclined to moving as we were about the timing." In short, the intelligence community believed that most senior Philippine military officers would back Marcos in the event of a coup.[57] Still, RAM leaders were brought to the United States to meet with State Department officials, members of Congress, journalists and others, both to discuss and by their very existence to demonstrate the prospects for military reform in the Philippines.[58]

The Senate Foreign Relations Committee also initiated hearings on foreign assistance legislation to the Philippines in March. Both Wolfowitz and Armitage testified, focusing on the "indispensable role of the military bases in the Philippines, the dangers of the communist insurgency threat, the deficiencies of President Marcos and the Philippine army in meeting that threat, and the reforms being pressed by the United States with only small signs of progress."[59] By May, the Senate, led by John Kerry (D-MA), passed 89 to 8 a foreign aid amendment to the 1986 foreign aid bill which expressed "the sense of the Senate" that the future of aid to the Philippines should be conditioned on progress toward political democracy and human rights.[60] The statement also called for free elections as well as a fair trial in the Aquino assassination case. Further, congressional and State Department reports acknowledged the need for a loosening of media censorship as well as freer media access for the opposition. Toward this end, the United States began secretly channeling funds to Radio Veritas, a Catholic radio station which would quickly become the voice of the moderate opposition. Though State Department officials have denied such support, Filipino activist Walden Bello attended a session at the Foreign Service Institute where Armacost gave a press briefing intended to be off the record. There, Armacost told the audience that Radio Veritas received U.S. funds channeled through the Asia Foundation. Priests affiliated with Veritas and a senior officer of the Asia Foundation have privately confirmed this.[61]

Hidden Wealth and the Implications for U.S. Aid

Meanwhile, the Philippine business community also got into the act, using transnational political strategies to undermine the credibility of the Marcos regime. In a particularly damaging July 1985 expose, the *San Jose Mercury News* ran a series of articles on Marcos' hidden wealth and possible diversion of U.S. aid. Since Marcos himself had acknowledged in his earlier campaigns that he did not come from a wealthy family, his massive fortune, estimated in the billions, raised questions about its source. The allegations of U.S. aid diversion had been made before, but now Philippine business leaders, including critical sources from the displaced oligarchy and former Marcos cronies disillusioned by the political and economic crises following the Aquino assassination, fed new, more substantive information to journalists Pete Carey and Lew Simons. Because the *San Jose Mercury News* is located in an area of California densely populated with Filipinos, it is likely that the Filipino businessmen leaking the information to Simons and Carey hoped that the U.S. press coverage would ignite anti-Marcos activism among Filipinos in the United States, while providing a non-censored channel for the information to flow back to the Philippines. In this, according to Carey, they also undoubtedly believed that it would thus have more credibility at home and would be more likely to be picked up in the heavily censored, Marcos-controlled Philippine press.[62] In fact, the story was picked up in the Philippines and helped feed opposition there, leading 56 of the 59 opposition members of the National Assembly who had won seats in 1984 to call for Marcos' impeachment. Though the motion, initiated in August, was swiftly rejected by a government panel, it was widely seen as an embarrassment and yet another spur that might lead Marcos to call presidential elections.[63]

Amid such challenges to the Marcos regime's credibility, the United States continued to urge Marcos to institute economic, political, and military reforms as well as to hold a fair trial on the Aquino assassination. Toward this end, U.S. Air Force personnel stationed in the Philippines were encouraged to provide affidavits revealing an attempted aircraft interception on the day of the assassination. Since only a select few had the power to deploy such a tactic, the affidavits implicated the highest levels of the Philippine command including Ver and possibly Marcos.[64] And the ground continued to slip beneath Marcos' feet. By mid-1985, the State Department's Philippine analyst for INR, Marjorie Niehaus, concluded that any notion of a reformist Marcos was an oxymoron. State's Philippine desk officer John Maisto agreed, as did Morton Abramowitz, head of INR. Analysts for the Senate Select Committee on Intelligence visited the Philippines in August and concluded also that the Marcos government was unlikely to institute the reforms needed to stem the economic hemorrhaging and the insurgency's growth.[65]

That same month, over sixty foreign policy analysts and officials from Defense, State, CIA and the NSC as well as from academia gathered at the National War College in Washington to discuss the situation. Even Edward Lansdale was there, though his primary observation was simply that the situation in 1985 was quite different from that in the 1950s. Also present was William Overholt, a vice president of Bankers Trust who had once worked on development projects in the Philippines. Some, led by President Reagan, Chief of Staff Donald Regan, CIA Director William Casey and Secretary of Defense Caspar Weinberger, still argued that only Marcos could defeat the NPA, and that he could be counted on to initiate what they now agreed were needed reforms. Others, however, including Overholt and Niehaus, with apparent concurrence from Wolfowitz, Armitage and Armacost, argued instead for continued pressure on Marcos to revive democratic processes. They argued as well for covert U.S. assistance to be provided to organizations like NAMFREL, RAM and Radio Veritas in order to cultivate a moderate, pro-U.S. alternative to Marcos.[66]

Still, Marcos understood the situation well enough to suggest on the *MacNeil/Lehrer News Hour* in August 1985 that a foreign leader needed two ambassadors in Washington: "one for Congress and another for the Executive Department." In fact, Marcos was right. Despite the pressures to reform, Marcos continued to enjoy the support of Reagan and his inner circle, notably Regan, Casey, and Weinberger. Commenting on the resulting tensions within the foreign policy community, Frederick Brown, the Senate Foreign Relations Committee staffer who had visited the Philippines in 1984 and subsequently reported on the NPA's growth, said: "The people in the State Department were using us...to get their point across to the White House...We shifted our focus from the President of the Philippines to the President of the United States."[67] From October 1985 to January 1986, the Senate Foreign Relations Committee held three hearings to review U.S. policy on the Philippines. In testimony before the committee, Wolfowitz, Armitage, Armacost and others cited the "unmistakable clear" signals the United States had sent Marcos on the need for "dramatic progress toward fundamental reforms." The House Subcommittee on Asian and Pacific Affairs, led by Solarz, further recommended that military sales credit be reduced from $50 million to $25 million and that economic aid be increased from the $95 million requested by the Reagan administration to $155 million. The Senate Foreign Relations Committee then added an amendment to the foreign aid bill linking aid to the Philippines with progress by the Philippine government in guaranteeing democratic processes and in prosecuting the Aquino assassination case. These changes were intended to facilitate political, economic and military reforms and to demonstrate to Filipinos that the aid was "not for the benefit of any particular leader or faction." [68]

By October, U.S. officials acknowledged that in order for Marcos to take the message for reform seriously, it would have to come more directly from Reagan, not just from the bureaucracy. In mid-October 1985, Senator Paul Laxalt (R-NV), a close personal friend of Reagan, was sent to the Philippines to meet with Marcos. He brought with him a handwritten letter from Reagan expressing the U.S. President's belief in Marcos and in his ability to reform. Marcos now had to understand that the call for reform came from the highest levels of the U.S. government. Flagrantly ignoring this, however, Marcos soon after threw out the U.S. Air Force affidavits that implicated Ver in the Aquino assassination trial.[69] Now,

U.S. concerns about Marcos' credibility deepened. With pressure building in both the Philippines and the United States, Marcos made a surprising decision.

On November 3, 1985, in an interview on David Brinkley's Sunday morning talk show, Marcos announced to the world that he would hold "snap" presidential elections. Marcos apparently assumed that the narrow time frame would prevent the deeply fragmented opposition from waging a successful campaign. That he made the announcement on U.S. television in the middle of the night in the Philippines, moreover, indicates that the elections were designed more for a U.S. than for a Philippine audience, as a State Department memo from Maisto to Wolfowitz acknowledged.[70] U.S. officials grew concerned, however, that a Marcos victory won through election fraud might lead moderates to support the NPA.[71] Marcos' own "kitchen cabinet," including Enrile, were caught off-guard by the announcement and criticized the election plans as "reckless." Marcos countered that because of the U.S. television coverage, it was too late to reconsider.[72] U.S. media attention to events in the Philippines and to the Marcos regime in particular did, in fact, increase. As the elections added news value to the Philippines,[73] the hidden wealth and other issues were now picked up by the *Village Voice*, the *Washington Post* and the *New York Times*.[74]

With approval from State, Solarz, as Chairman of the House Foreign Affairs Subcommittee on Asian and Pacific Affairs, initiated hearings in December on the hidden wealth issue and its implications for U.S. aid. Solarz had seen the articles on the hidden wealth issue and was now determined to hold hearings on the subject prior to the Philippine elections.[75] Solarz told a *New York Times* reporter that he "would not hang (his) head in shame" if the hearings affected the elections.[76] Solarz also invited NAMFREL Chairman Jose Concepcion Jr. to the United States in mid-November to meet with members of Congress and State Department officials in order to win U.S. backing for independent electoral monitoring in the up-coming elections.[77] Together with Senator Lugar of the Senate Foreign Relations Committee, Solarz also drafted a letter to Marcos, urging him to hold free and fair elections. The letter "received wide commendations from [Congress] and the administration."

And the Senate Foreign Relations Committee now opened hearings on the Philippines as well. Here, Armitage from Defense and State's Wolfowitz, Armacost, and Bosworth, in particular, advised that the survival of the U.S. bases was "ancillary" to the survival of democracy, that failure to reform the government now would mean the loss of the bases in five to ten years. In addition, the Senate Foreign Relations Committee requested the D.C.-based Center for Democracy, headed by Boston University professor Allen Weinstein, to go to the Philippines to assess the preparations needed for the elections, a signal as well to the opposition that the U.S. Senate was committed to Philippine democracy.[78] Five days before the team's departure, on

December 2, all 26 accused in the Aquino assassination, including General Ver, were acquitted. During his October visit, Laxalt had warned Marcos that such an apparent miscarriage of justice would likely unleash a "firestorm" of protests from the U.S. Congress. Marcos' open defiance of Laxalt now indicated that he was not only unlikely to reform, he was also no longer reliable.[79]

As Laxalt had predicted, Congress was now inflamed against Marcos. While Reagan wanted 1985 aid to exceed that for 1984 and wanted about half to go to the military, Congress questioned the aid levels and offered just 30 percent to the military. Reagan and his closest aides worked to rebuild support for Marcos in Congress and continued to hope that he would re-establish his legitimacy by holding fair elections. The acquittals, however, raised new concerns about Marcos among congressional leaders. By December 1985, following the Aquino assassination trial verdict, Congress ordered a $15 million reduction in security assistance to the Philippines.[80] Meanwhile, the Philippine left debated whether to participate in the elections or to boycott them in protest of anticipated fraud. And the moderates, however skeptical of the outcome, opted to participate, struggling to unite behind a single candidate.

The Moderate Challenge:
Laban Unites Under Aquino

By the time the team arrived in Manila, the acquittals had galvanized the hitherto fractious moderate opposition, comprised of an alphabet soup of cause-oriented groups with names like ATOM (August Twenty One Movement), ROAR (Running Organization for Aquino and Reconciliation, for joggers against Marcos) and even ACRONYM (Anti-Cronyism Movement), though these lacked both a coherent platform and leadership. On December 3, one day after the acquittals and after a month of fending off pressure from Filipino moderates to run, Corazon Aquino announced her candidacy. Cardinal Sin then helped to unite the moderates in the final hours before the deadline for the filing of slates, with Aquino in the presidential and Laurel in the vice presidential slots, both on Laurel's UNIDO ticket. This was a critical achievement, since a split opposition would likely have allowed a Marcos win. Soon after, Aquino granted *New York Times* reporter Seth Mydans, foreign editor Warren Hoge, and executive editor A.M. Rosenthal an exclusive interview. Though she had substantial experience with the press from her years as messenger for her husband, Aquino mishandled several questions on the U.S. bases and the communists. Not only did she ramble, she also changed position on these key issues during the course of the interview, vacillating between opposition to and support for the U.S. bases, and likewise with respect to the communists. "Abe and I were pretty much stunned," Hoge notes, adding "Both of us walked out of there thinking we could not remember talking to a public figure more naive about the responsibilities and uses of power."[81]

Aquino denies any attempt to subsequently refurbish her U.S. image, arguing that her campaign was solely for Filipinos;[82] yet her American allies, concerned by the bad press, soon afterwards hired the Democratic public relations firm D.H. Sawyer & Associates to shape Aquino's image as strong, reliable, and pro-U.S, particularly on communism and the U.S. bases. The firm worked closely with Aquino to prepare her for the hordes of U.S. journalists arriving in the Philippines.[83] Initially opposed to the bases and open to the possibility of talking with the communists, perhaps even admitting some into her prospective administration, as quoted at one point in the disastrous *New York Times* article, Aquino soon yielded to pressure from her U.S. advisors to publicly proclaim opposition to communism and support for the 1983 bases agreement, which allowed for the bases through 1991. In a speech just days later in Olongapo, site of the U.S. Naval base, Aquino did just that. This cost her backing from BAYAN, the political umbrella group for the Philippine left, which had offered to back her candidacy should she agree to call for a withdrawal of U.S. military facilities but threatened to boycott should she refuse to comply. The left, claiming roughly 20 percent of the Philippine population's support, now called for a boycott.[84] Aquino's comments aside, that her campaign forfeited BAYAN's offer rather than oppose the bases reveals the relatively greater weight assigned to U.S. versus domestic Filipino concerns, particularly given her own initial opposition to the bases as well as that of many of her moderate supporters. Nevertheless, Aquino's strategy worked. Golf course designer Robert Trent Jones Jr., the long-time friend of Corazon Aquino who had lobbied for her husband's release during his imprisonment, now lobbied his U.S. congressional friends such as Bill Bradley, Sam Nunn and Alan Cranston to back Aquino's candidacy.[85]

Meanwhile, the Center for Democracy team left on December 7 for the Philippines. On December 18, they reported their findings to the Senate Foreign Relations Committee, with Wolfowitz and Armitage both present. In their report, which became an immediate best-seller in Manila,[86] the team offered eight guidelines to insure free and fair elections. First, they urged accreditation by the Marcos-controlled electoral monitoring organization, COMELEC, of the independent, though implicitly oppositionist, citizen's watch group NAMFREL. They also urged Marcos to appoint two additional members to COMELEC to join the 1986 election deliberations; to recognize the Aquino-Laurel UNIDO ticket as the "dominant opposition party" (DOP) with all poll-watching and other rights legally accorded such a party under the electoral code; enforceable guarantees of access to media for the DOP, including the allocation of substantial free radio and television time, with similar provisions for newspapers; enforceable guarantees of reasonable access to paid media; supervision of all military to assure that they not be used for partisan purposes prior to the elections, intimidation during the elections, or fraudulent vote-counting following the elections; the quickest possible counting of ballots throughout the country; and the establishment of a coordinated international observer process beginning in January 1986.[87] When Senators John Kerry and Claiborne Pell expressed concerns that an observer team could not adequately monitor elections and might instead simply lend credibility to a fraudulent process, Weinstein responded that the opposition clearly wanted the observer team. He advised, however, that Congress not agree to send an observer team until the other conditions had been met.[88]

Following the hearing, Congress would be in recess until January 20, just eighteen days before the elections. To chart the progress in the Philippines during the recess, Lugar and other members of the committee relied on information from the embassy as well as from the press. On December 24, COMELEC accredited NAMFREL, a positive sign that Marcos might comply with the Center for Democracy's conditions.[89] At the same time, reports indicated a crescendo of support building for Aquino, as well as her new, more pro-U.S. positions on the key issues of communism and the bases. On December 26, for instance, Aquino held a rally in Olongapo and there told thousands of cheering supporters her plans to allow the United States to use the bases through 1991, after which she would "keep all of our options open." This was not enough, however, for U.S. hard-liners, who remained wary of Aquino, even as Marcos' credibility continued to fall. According to Shultz, when A.M. Rosenthal returned from the Philippines in mid-January, and reported to him, Reagan, Regan and others at an official White House dinner that Aquino was an "empty-headed housewife (with) no positions," his words made a "deep and lasting impact on them." Though Armacost countered that "Makati businessmen (were) advising Aquino, and they are sound," concerns about her viability remained, as the debate within the U.S. executive branch intensified. Adding a sense of urgency to the debate was an apocalyptic account of the NPA as "the new Khmer Rouge." Written by journalist Ross Munro, the article appeared in the December 1985 edition of *Commentary* and carried much weight in official circles.[90]

On January 13, 1986, Bosworth announced that the United States could work with any democratically elected government there, a statement the U.S. press heralded with headlines like "State Department Assails Marcos." NSC adviser John Poindexter subsequently warned Shultz that Reagan did not want to see any more such coverage. Shultz argued that U.S. support for free elections should not be equated with opposition to Marcos. As debate continued regarding Aquino as well as on the narrower question of whether or not to send an observer team, Shultz urged political impartiality among INR staff.[91]

On January 22, just two weeks before the elections, the *New York Times* added another nail to the Marcos coffin. A front page article exposed as fraudulent Marcos' claims that he had been an anti-Japanese guerrilla during World War II. Although questioned for years, the war record had long given Marcos a measure of public credibility as both a vital U.S. ally and as a military commander in the current fight against the NPA. The story was then picked up by several other influential papers, including the *Washington Post*. It was not just the exposure of fraud that harmed Marcos; it was the perception that once closely kept secrets were being leaked by former Marcos allies in the United States and the Philippines. Debate in the United States further intensified, with the Philippines now at the top of the CIA's "fever chart." Meanwhile, on January 23, the Senate Foreign Relations Committee met with Pacifico Castro, acting foreign minister of the Philippines. Present again were Wolfowitz, Armitage and members of their staffs. The debate centered on whether the committee should participate as observers in the upcoming elections. When Castro revealed confidentially that he had with him a letter from Marcos to Reagan with a strong plea for an official observer team, Lugar considered this crucial information. Lugar pressed Castro for assurances, which were given, that such an observer team would have adequate access to the voting. Lugar then deliberated, concerned that the senate had "staked our prestige and credibility that if Philippine democracy was violated on February 7, the Marcos regime should no longer get U.S. moral or material support." Though not all of the preconditions for fair elections had been met, Lugar opted to support the process.

On January 24, Lugar publicly urged Reagan to send an official observer team, offering as well to participate.[92] As late as January 26, Leslie Gelb, *New York Times* national security correspondent, wrote, however, that most U.S. officials "hoped that Marcos would win in elections that were not too unfair and then quickly step aside in favor of his running mate Arturo Tolentino." The article also outlined the efforts of U.S. officials, including Armacost, Bosworth, Abramowitz, Sigur, Armitage and Wolfowitz, to turn Reagan, Regan, Casey and Weinberger from continued support for Marcos. Gelb, who had served in the State Department and had also directed the Pentagon Papers study, now exposed the forces shaping U.S. policy toward the Philippines as well as the on-going debate between pro- and anti-Marcos factions within the United States. The administration dismissed Gelb as trying to make not report policy, a charge he, in turn, dismisses as "baloney."[93] Wolfowitz, a conservative, was particularly angered by the article, which presented him along with the "Carterites" as attempting to tilt U.S. policy in a liberal direction.[94] Gelb's story was, however, based on information leaked from State Department analysts to him and others, including Walden Bello, who wrote an article for the *World Policy Journal*.[95]

Behind the scenes, Shultz maintained contact with Lugar, who assured him of his continued willingness to participate in an official observer delegation. Four days after Gelb's article, on January 30, Reagan officially announced his decision to send an observer team, with the unexpected offer to significantly increase U.S. economic and military aid following the elections. Shultz then asked, at Lugar's request, all members of the Senate Foreign Relations Committee to participate; but only John Kerry of Massachusetts and Frank Murkowski of Alaska accepted. Lugar was named head of the bipartisan, 20-member delegation, and worked closely with the State Department to plan the observation process. The team arrived in Manila on February 5, two days before the balloting, amid hordes of U.S. journalists arriving in Manila as well. As a Lugar aide noted of the American media, "They covered (the Philippine elections) almost like it was an American primary out in the hinterlands." Or, perhaps, the "boondocks." In fact, U.S. media coverage was the most extensive ever accorded a foreign election, adding a crucial nonofficial observer presence to Lugar's 20-member team. Cognizant of this, Marcos had hired, like Aquino, a U.S. public relations firm—Manafort, Black & Stone (a Republican affiliate)—to refurbish his U.S. image. The firm had encouraged Marcos to increase his U.S. public appearances; but the strategy was backfiring. On the night before the elections, Marcos appeared on *Nightline* but, under fire from Koppel, threatened to terminate his appearance midshow should the hostile questioning continue. As the polls opened on February 7, the same day, ironically, that Baby Doc fled Haiti, U.S. journalists as well as the observer team fanned out across the country, together with 500,000 NAMFREL volunteers, and a team of RAM officers,[96] to monitor the voting.

Though U.S. officials denied backing NAMFREL, in the months prior to the elections, the U.S. Agency for International Development had given a $390,000 grant to the Asia Foundation,[97] which then channeled the funds through the 100-odd groups comprising NAMFREL.[98] During the elections, NAMFREL reported many incidents involving stolen ballot boxes, intimidation of voters and NAMFREL volunteers, and even killings. The U.S. observer team initially reported fraud but avoided sharp criticism. As the vote-counting proceeded, however, the observer team's reports of fraud became more strident, while the embassy sent a steady stream of reports to the State Department substantiating the claims of fraud.[99] The American Chamber of Commerce in Manila weighed in with the opinion that any attempt to whitewash the accounts of election fraud would "seriously damage American corporations and increase anti-Americanism in the Philippines," an opinion which increased U.S. vigilance in monitoring the elections.[100]

State Department analysts acknowledged that participation among the more than 26 million registered voters had been spectacular, an overwhelming defeat for the left's boycott campaign. Moreover, the analysts estimated that Aquino had actually won 60 to 70 percent of the vote.[101] Not only would Marcos have to cheat much more than in previous elections, he was also faced with greater barriers to cheating due to the presence of the observer teams and the international media. In fact, Marcos later conceded to *New York Times* reporter Seth Mydans that he had underestimated the role the U.S. media would play in the elections.[102] As the vote-counting proceeded, evidence of fraud mounted. In one incident, on February 8, thirty computer technicians working for Marcos fled COMELEC headquarters for the refuge of a nearby church and told a gathering crowd, including many international journalists, that the figures showing Aquino in the lead were being discarded. This sounded alarms among U.S. officials.[103] The *New York Times* and other U.S. media reported widespread abuses in the election, as the U.S. observer team became more critical as well. In Marcos' continuing appearances on U.S. television, American journalists played straight man to Marcos' antics. On the Sunday after the elections, for instance, David Brinkley asked how Marcos had received over 13,000 votes in one town while Aquino had received zero. The voters were "probably my relatives," Marcos explained. Later, when George Will asked Marcos about his war record, Marcos urged Will to read Emperor Hirohito's memoirs. "They've not been published, sir!" Will replied. Will later called the White House to say their man was an "inveterate liar." Coming from a conservative like Will, such an assessment carried weight in the White House.[104]

The U.S. Debate Intensifies

On February 11, despite the evidence as well as the advice of Lugar, a State Department task force, and others, all of whom urged Reagan not to endorse a Marcos victory,[105] Reagan held a rare televised news conference in which he praised the elections and indicated support for Marcos. While Reagan conceded to the "possibility of fraud," he asserted that "it could have been...occurring on both sides."[106] This unleashed a storm of protest in Manila as Aquino began preparing to take the election "to the streets." She also worked through Solarz' office to inform the White House that "wishy-washy" statements regarding election fraud would engender anti-Americanism. What she needed, she told her friends, was strong U.S. support in order to denounce election fraud and prevent further violence against her supporters.[107] At the same time, she fended off pressures to unite with BAYAN, which now reissued its offer of support; but Philippine analysts and U.S. officials worried that Aquino's position might soften if the Marcos regime were to be prolonged.[108] "We thought (Reagan) was dead wrong," U.S. Ambassador to the Philippines Stephen Bosworth now acknowledges, adding that there was concern among State Department analysts and others in the intelligence community that the moderate opposition, if robbed of its electoral victory, might ally with the left, with the increasingly real possibility of an anti-U.S. revolution.[109] That same day, a leading Aquino supporter, Evelio Javier, was gunned down and killed by six masked gunmen. Though human rights abuses had been rampant throughout the Marcos era, this incident, somewhat like the 1983 assassination of Ninoy Aquino, was so flagrant a violation of democratic processes that U.S. officials now saw the lengths Marcos was willing to go to in order to retain power.

On February 12, the State Department went public with its disapproval of Reagan's statements, with strategically-placed quotes in leading U.S. newspapers. A *New York Times* article, for example, cited State Department "anger," "embarrassment," "surprise" and efforts to "limit confusion and uncertainty." Lugar and others on the observer team, reacting in part to what they had seen and in part to their constituents' growing support for Aquino, returned to the United States and openly dismissed Reagan's allegations as "misinformed." Appearing on several talk shows, Lugar wanted to make sure that his "point of view was heard to frame the issues."[110] In addition to intensifying anger among Philippine moderates led by Aquino, popular and elite U.S. opposition to Reagan's position was growing. And the U.S. business community in the Philippines complained that Reagan's statements were jeopardizing their interests.[111] Likewise, Congress charged that aid to the Philippines would be terminated unless Aquino were accepted as the nation's new leader.[112] U.S. embassy officials in Manila now cultivated close contact with members of the moderate opposition, urging them to avoid violence, anti-Americanism, and contacts with the left, in tacit exchange for immediate support and future recognition.[113] At the same time, however, embassy officials devised plans to reduce personnel and destroy classified documents in preparation for anticipated anti-American demonstrations and possibly even a hostile transition from Marcos.[114]

By February 15, Reagan recanted, publicly acknowledging that the "widespread fraud and violence" had been "perpetrated largely" by Marcos and his supporters.[115] Lugar notes that "Once Reagan made a change in course, then the ball was in Marcos' court...Marcos was going to have to make a very tough decision as to how far he wanted to go to suppress the opposition."[116] Hours after Reagan's statement, however, the Marcos-controlled National Assembly declared him the victor. Opposition members protested by walking out of the session.[117] A hundred bishops from the relatively conservative Catholic Bishops Conference circulated a statement through the national and international media condemning Marcos and charging that his attempt to retain power had "no moral basis." Aquino then staged a rally in Luneta Park near a statue of Rizal, invoking an earlier era of resistance, and urged her growing ranks of supporters to use civil disobedience to unseat Marcos. Estimates from the U.S. Embassy placed the number of Filipinos in attendance at more than a million.[118] By February 20, Marcos sent a team of senior officials to D.C. to lobby for continued support from members of Congress and the Reagan administration.[119]

Meanwhile, the U.S. State Department sent Philip Habib as a special envoy to "assess the situation." For six days, Habib interviewed over a hundred politicians, priests, educators, business leaders, and U.S. journalists. He also met with Cardinal Sin, Corazon Aquino, NAMFREL volunteers, American citizens and others.[120] Before leaving on Saturday, February 22, Habib told one of these journalists, Stanley Karnow, that he was particularly impressed by Enrile, still Marcos' Minister of Defense, who "seemed to be distancing himself from Marcos" and might soon "reveal his hand." Habib also told a U.S. embassy officer to tell Bosworth, "Something's going to break." Bosworth reported "unusual military activity," citing the possibility of a coup or a countercoup, as well as statements from Ramos and Enrile declaring RAM preparedness to defend against military actions coordinated by Ver.[121]

Later that day, February 22 at 6:00 p.m., Enrile, together with Ramos and a few leading RAM officers holed up in a Manila military base called Camp Aguinaldo, invoking another hero from the earlier resistance to Spain. Here, they told a gathering mob of reporters that they recognized Aquino as the country's new president. In fact, the defectors had been planning a coup for almost a year, since their meetings in D.C. in March 1985. Marcos' decision to hold presidential elections had surprised them, however, and they decided not to act unless the elections were fraudulent, lest they be seen as thwarting the democratic process. Marcos' election fraud finally spurred the plotters to schedule a coup for the early morning hours of February 23. On February 20, however, Marcos arrested four military rebels, who subsequently revealed the coup plan. Two days later, on February 22, RAM leader Colonel Gregorio Honasan learned of the arrests and warned against the coup. Swiftly revising plans, Ramos and Enrile decided instead to secure themselves within Camp Aguinaldo, the site of Enrile's Ministry of Defense, and appeal to others in the military to support them, including the 200-man force Enrile had begun cultivating in 1981, which comprised the core of RAM's growing ranks.[122]

Whether or not the United States was directly involved in the RAM coup plot or subsequent defections, prior U.S. support for RAM and the discussions in U.S. official circles with RAM leaders in early 1985, as well as Habib's uncanny prescience, all indicate at least a modicum of U.S. involvement. Further, the entire U.S. seventh fleet was in Manila Harbor during the period, in addition to air and naval forces at Subic and Clark. Without U.S. backing or at least a pledge from the United States not to intervene militarily in support of Marcos, the coup attempt would have been little more than a suicidal bid for power. Neither Ramos, a West Point–trained military professional who had risen steadily through the ranks of the Philippine armed forces, nor Enrile, a Harvard-trained lawyer with years of political and military experience, is likely to have acted without considering the postcoup prospects of survival, nor without some understanding of the U.S. position.

Why, however, did Ramos and Enrile, both long-time Marcos allies, defect? As described in the previous chapter, both Ramos and Enrile, like the RAM officers, were concerned by Marcos' growing tendency to promote within the military on the basis of loyalty to Marcos rather than on merit, as exemplified by the continuing presence of General Ver, a Marcos relative and former chauffeur who had circumvented all traditional paths to the top position in the Philippine military. While both Ramos and Enrile had enjoyed Marcos' backing in the early years of martial law and had emerged as political powers in their own right, they were both sidelined in 1981 when Marcos named Ver to serve as Armed Forces Chief of Staff. Marcos later removed Enrile from the chain of command altogether. Fearing assassination, Enrile then created his security force to defend himself against a suspected assault from Ver.[123] And these forces now formed the core of RAM, playing a central role in the crisis that was to finally unseat Marcos. While personal incentives first encouraged Ramos and Enrile to ally against Marcos in 1981, their opposition gained broader support from other disgruntled sectors of the military thereafter, reaching organizational viability in the form of RAM by early 1985. RAM gained U.S. allies by March of that year, as the new NSDD calling for military and political reforms was put into effect. At the same time, institutional incentives for a transition emerged as well when the U.S. Congress threatened to cut military aid to the Philippines unless Marcos launched meaningful reforms. Given Marcos' apparent inability to comply, RAM leaders reasoned that in order to secure U.S. aid, a transition from Marcos was needed.

All the King's Horses and All the King's Men

At 9:00 p.m. on February 22, Cardinal Sin spoke on Radio Veritas, the U.S.-supported radio station of the Catholic Church which had been used by the moderate opposition during the campaign. Here, he appealed to Filipinos to support "our two good friends," Enrile and Ramos. In the next few hours, nuns, priests, students and other long-time opponents of the Marcos regime gathered at Camp Aguinaldo, holding an all-night vigil for a peaceful transition.[124]

While Marcos and his remaining loyalists worked around the clock plotting their counter move, Aquino, with urging from Cardinal Sin, rallied her supporters to back the military defectors. By early Sunday morning, February 23, loyalist tanks moved toward Camp Aguinaldo where over 40,000 had gathered in a vivid expression of "people power" and the mass desire among Filipinos for political change. Later that afternoon, hundreds of thousands of Filipinos filled the streets, wielding rosary beads, giving flowers to soldiers, singing nationalist songs, and otherwise pressuring Marcos loyalists not to fire upon them.[125] The U.S. White House urged Marcos not to use force, implying that he would lose subsequent U.S. support, with even Reagan's acceptance, should he do so.[126] As the day wore on, more and more troops defected from Marcos. The United States, meanwhile, allowed rebel helicopters to refuel at Clark Air Base while transmitting intelligence to the rebels. Bosworth also urged Marcos repeatedly not to use force. And Radio Veritas, dodging from one frequency to another in order to stay on the air, played the jubilant "Magsaysay Mambo" which recalled an earlier era of U.S. involvement in Philippine elections. The radio station also encouraged people power supporters, while allowing rebel troops to communicate helicopter landing instructions and other tactical information on air as a rapt nation listened.[127] Cornered, Marcos ordered at least one pilot to fire upon the demonstrators. After seeing the crowds in the streets below, however, the pilot turned around and defected to Enrile and Ramos. "Everybody," Lugar notes, "understood that this would not be played out on the basis of personal rapport. It was going to play out in public opinion, on who really had staying power."[128]

In D.C., Secretary of State George Shultz called a special meeting at his home on Sunday morning, evening in Manila, to discuss a message from Bosworth concluding that Marcos would not leave unless Reagan put it to him directly.[129] A surreal exchange on American television that same morning confirmed Bosworth's assertion, as the key players jousted, live, in the battle for public opinion. On *Meet the Press*, Ramos vowed to defeat Marcos "by sheer numbers" while Marcos retorted that he had been legally elected, adding, "I don't believe President Reagan would ask me to step down."[130] It was a remarkably candid revelation. Apparently, Marcos was unprepared to resign as long as he felt he still enjoyed Reagan's support, regardless of the "people power" display, now climbing above an estimated two million,[131] the defecting troops, or the disloyalty of his own senior staff. In fact, the message never did come directly from Reagan. Instead, the United States first issued a public statement via the media warning Marcos that he "would cause untold damage to the relationship between our two governments" if he used force. The United States also threatened to suspend Marcos' military aid unless he complied. The carefully crafted message sought to avoid two scenarios. One was that Marcos, in a last ditch effort to retain power, would hold to his televised statement to Philippine audiences to "fight to the last breath," with the possibility that he might attack rebel camps and the masses of civilians—on world television. The other scenario was that the rebel troops might capture and murder Marcos and his family, as had happened in the earlier U.S.-backed coup against Diem in Vietnam.[132] Marcos lobbyists arriving in D.C. were given the same message, urged by Shultz to tell Marcos to depart gracefully.

Still Marcos remained. By Monday afternoon, February 24, in D.C., evening in Manila, Reagan approved a public plea to Marcos to quit. "Attempts to prolong the life of the present regime by violence are futile," the statement read, adding, "A solution to this crisis can only be achieved through a peaceful transition to a new government." After some debate, the statement included the word transition, so that Marcos would have no doubt about U.S. intentions.[133] Marcos received the message at 3:00 a.m. Tuesday, February 25. Still Marcos wanted to speak directly with Reagan. Marcos phoned Laxalt at the Capitol Building, interrupting a secret briefing among Shultz, Habib and thirty key members of Congress, including Lugar, Kerry, Inouye, Laxalt and others, as well as Marcos' aide Melchor who had gauged the official D.C. reaction to martial law fourteen years earlier and now provided crucial advice. "Was the statement about a transition real or another State Department ploy?" Marcos asked. Laxalt confirmed the statement's veracity. Marcos then suggested several "power sharing" alternatives. Laxalt agreed to present these to Reagan and call back. Reagan, however, agreed with Shultz, who felt that the power sharing schemes were "impractical." At 5:00 a.m. Tuesday morning in Manila, Marcos answered the call he had been waiting for from Laxalt. Laxalt, having been coached by Shultz, told Marcos that Reagan had vetoed the power sharing suggestions but offered him asylum in the United States. Still Marcos wanted to know, did Reagan want him to resign. "Senator," Marcos asked, "what do you think? Should I step down?" Laxalt responded, "I think you should cut and cut cleanly. I think the time has come."[134]

Hours later, Marcos and his wife Imelda, stood on a balcony at Malacanang Palace and, for a throng of their closest supporters, sang a duet of the traditional Filipino love song "Dahil Sa Iyo," "Because of You." Soon after, the Marcoses and their entourage fled by U.S. helicopter to Clark Air Base, where they boarded a plane for an ignominious exile to Hawaii. And Imelda's now infamous shoes came to represent all that was corrupt, even rapacious, about the Marcos era. Meanwhile, Corazon Aquino, in her signature yellow, took the oath of office as the new president of the Philippines.[135] The conditions of the transition required Aquino to form an uneasy pact with Ramos, Enrile, and large segments of the military, including those like Enrile who had been among her husband's tormentors. This would ultimately undermine her subsequent attempts to consolidate the democratization process, with recurrent coup attempts by a still politicized military. For the moment, though, Aquino and her allies in the United States and the Philippines succeeded in ousting a similarly transnational alliance that had too long supported Marcos. It was also a victory for the human rights movement that Corazon Aquino, whose husband had long been a symbol of the cause, should now replace Marcos. The U.S. congressional human rights caucus cheered the occasion with a letter of congratulations to the new Philippine president.[136]

Resurgent Democracy:
A Transnational Explanation

In sum, Marcos enjoyed substantial U.S. technical, political, and economic support throughout his regime, primarily because of his reliability in protecting U.S. interests, notably the U.S. military bases. As U.S. investment in the Philippine bases increased, particularly during the Vietnam War and later after the loss of Cam Ranh Bay to the Soviets, so too did U.S. dependence on Marcos increase. At the same time, Marcos' dependence on U.S. support increased after his 1972 declaration of martial law. From that point, opposition spread in the form of both moderate and revolutionary movements, as well as within his regime, particularly in the military. To address such opposition, Marcos relied upon U.S. military aid, using this to expand his armed forces from 60,000 in 1972 to over 200,000 by 1986. And these were designated purely for internal security. Far from silencing opposition, however, the repression fueled both revolutionary and moderate opposition, particularly after the 1983 assassination of Benigno Aquino Jr., an act for which many held Marcos or those close to him responsible. If such a violation could occur to someone as powerful as Aquino, many Filipinos reasoned, what might happen to anyone voicing even moderate opposition to Marcos. Church, business, military, political and other sectors of the established oligarchy began defecting from Marcos after 1972, but they defected in droves after 1983. Soon, the political crisis spurred an economic crisis which further fed the political crisis in a vicious cycle.

In the United States, reports from congressional and embassy sources on the growth of the communist insurgency sparked concern in official circles. By early 1985, U.S. official policy in the form of the NSDD shifted from full support of Marcos to support conditioned upon his ability to reform the economic, military and political systems, with the Marcos regime's corruption now seen as contributing to the Philippine crisis. Amid growing pressures from the U.S. executive, led by Armacost, Wolfowitz and others at State, with support from Armitage and others at Defense and from Sigur at the NSC, Congress began holding hearings on the Philippines, linking, by May, aid to Marcos with his efforts to rebuild democracy. Now opposition Filipinos leaked to U.S. reporters information on Marcos' hidden wealth and alleged diversion of U.S.

aid. The coverage, which began in August 1985, further intensified congressional debates on aid. Reagan and his inner circle sought to refurbish Marcos' image by pressing him toward reforms. Still, Marcos did not comply, arguing on U.S. television that he believed the criticism came from Congress not from Reagan. Marcos apparently believed that the U.S. President's support was enough to fend off growing opposition to his regime at home and abroad. By mid-October, Reagan sent Laxalt as his personal emissary to Marcos, to assure the Philippine president that the message for reform came from the White House as well as from the bureaucracy and congress. Days later, Marcos, in an attempt to comply, called for "snap" presidential elections for early 1986. Now Congress emerged as a central forum for U.S. critics of Marcos from the executive, notably Wolfowitz and Armitage, while Lugar eventually served a critical role as head of the bipartisan official observer delegation for the elections.

Here, Marcos seriously miscalculated the strength of the opposition, as well as the role the international media and U.S. observer teams would play in limiting his ability to steal the election. As evidence of electoral fraud mounted and Corazon Aquino threatened to "take the elections to the streets," the debate in the United States intensified. Reagan, Regan, Weinberger, Casey and others in the president's inner circle urged continued support of Marcos; but Shultz, Bosworth, Armacost, Armitage and others, mainly from State together with congressional foreign policy leaders such as Lugar, Solarz and Kerry, urged support for a democratic transition from Marcos to Aquino. Lugar argued that by agreeing to participate as observers in the elections, the congressional foreign policy leaders had staked their reputations on "free and fair" Philippine elections and were now determined to protect the democratic process there, as were their allies in the executive, who were waging a more narrow political battle with Reagan and his inner circle. By February 22, when Ramos and Enrile defected from Marcos, bringing with them the U.S.-backed RAM officers, Cardinal Sin called to Aquino and her supporters to back the defectors. Now, the "people power" revolution erupted on the streets of Manila. Still Marcos clung to power. Only when Reagan finally agreed to press Marcos, via Laxalt, to "cut and cut cleanly," offering as well asylum in the United States, did Marcos leave. Clearly, it mattered less who had won the elections in the Philippines, than where the United States placed its support. Thus, while domestic Philippine revolutionary and moderate opposition created the impetus for change, opponents from within the Marcos regime together with those in the United States created the political space for a moderate alternative to both the left and the right to gain power by supporting RAM, NAMFREL, Radio Veritas, the election observer team and other key actors in the transition.

Domestic Philippine politics then determined the nature of the transition. For instance, that the moderates united behind Aquino in the elections, that Ramos and Enrile backed her as president rather than seeking power for themselves, that Aquino's supporters heeded Cardinal Sin's call for non-violence, and, finally, that Marcos ultimately left peacefully, are all of the domestic Philippine contingencies that allowed for a moderate, nonviolent transition from Marcos to Aquino. Even here, however, the prospects of U.S. support or opposition seem to have strongly influenced the behavior of all the key players. One needed only to look out at Manila Harbor where the entire U.S. seventh fleet was positioned to remember all that stood in the balance. Marcos, for instance, knew that without U.S. backing, his regime could not survive. Similarly, Enrile and Ramos might have lacked sufficient U.S. as well as Filipino popular and military backing had they attempted a coup, while a moderate-left revolution might not have had the capacity to withstand the likely opposition from the United States, as the Sandinistas faced after 1979. Thus, domestic Philippine politics created the impetus for change by threatening U.S. and elite Philippine interests; while the transnational strategies used by Filipino moderates to first undermine Marcos, as in the hidden wealth story, and then to redirect U.S. support away from Marcos, allowed for a moderate transition. Philippine domestic politics, within the context of U.S. pressures, then determined the outcome and the contingencies, particularly Aquino's uneasy alliance with the military, which would affect subsequent efforts to consolidate the archipelago's resurgent democracy.

Notes

1. The above information is a compilation from Simons, 1-44, and from selected declassified U.S. Embassy cables from Manila to the State Department during the period surrounding the funeral, notably Secret Cable #22047, August 25; Confidential Cable #22655, August 30; hourly cables sent on the day of the funeral, August 31; and one describing Cardinal Sin's eulogy criticizing the Marcos government, #22696, also sent August 31, 1983. See also Confidential Cable #21920 for Armacost's decision to attend the funeral despite strong pressure not to from Marcos. All from the National Security Archive collection.

2. Compiled from Ibon Data Bank figures.

3. From personal interviews in the Philippine countryside with peasants and NPA organizers, May 1984 to February 1986. See also Jones' excellent account of the NPA from the inside (1987), as well as William Chapman (1987) and Kessler (1989).

4. From rough estimates made by the Philippine Department of Agrarian Reform as cited in Ibon Primer Series (1988:15).

5. From lectures by Jose Marie Sison, founder of the Philippine Communist Party, and Dante Buscayno, former head of the New People's Army, in April 1986 after their release from prison.

6. Personal interview with Bosworth, March 1989.

7. From Kessler, 137, from Task Force Detainees of the Philippines.

8. Personal conversations with Father Edicio de la Torre, Spring 1987, and Dante Buscayno, April 1986.

9. The figure is a rough estimate for the period surrounding the assassination and is from Dr. Bernardo Villegas, a leading Philippine economist, as cited in Simons, 172.

10. In Secret Cable #23099 sent from the U.S. Embassy in Manila to the State Department on September 6, 1983, a withdrawal of foreign investments from the Philippines was predicted. From the National Security Archive collection.

11. Thompson, 166.

12. Kline and Worthen, 6-7.

13. According to Corazon Aquino, as quoted in Sandra Burton's *Impossible Dream*, 277.

14. The analogies with Nicaragua and Iran are described in Shultz, 634.

15. Personal interview with Bosworth, March 1989.

16. Shultz, 610-611.

17. U.S. embassy officials in Manila urged Reagan to cancel his planned visit to the Philippines unless Marcos instituted political reforms and carried out a credible investigation of the Aquino assassination. When Marcos threatened that such a cancellation might undermine the security of the bases agreement, a debate within the United States executive ensued, leading to the decision to cancel Reagan's entire Southeast Asian itinerary. See Confidential Cable #24646, sent September 20, 1983, from the National Security Archive collection.

18. Bonner, 355.

19. Kline and Worthen.

20. Armitage, as quoted in Kline and Worthen, 12-13.

21. Bello, "Edging Toward the Quagmire," 33.

22. For information on the Agrava Commission's formation and purpose, see Confidential Cables #29310, #29526, and #29919, from November 8, 9, and 15, 1983, respectively. From the National Security Archive collection.

23. Bello, "Edging Toward the Quagmire," 32.

24. See, for example, an unclassified memorandum from within the State Department to Shultz describing relations with congress, sent March 6, 1984, reprinted in the National Security Archive collection.

25. Interview with Bosworth, March 1989, and from Karnow, *In Our Image*, 407-409 and Bonner, 279, 369-71.

26. Martial law diplomacy had fostered too great a reliance on Marcos' assessments of his opposition, because U.S. officials were loathe to offend Marcos by maintaining contacts with the opposition. As a response to this "clientitis," the Philippine opposition then sought out the U.S. media as an alternative channel to express their views and influence policy in the United States, as well as to circumvent the Marcos-controlled Philippine media. From Bonner, 369-71.

27. Confidential Cable #108309, April 13, 1984, from the National Security Archive collection.

28. Confidential Memorandum from Wolfowitz to Armacost, April 19, 1984, from the National Security Archive collection.

29. See Limited Official Use Cable #129405 from Shultz to the U.S. Embassy in Manila, May 3, 1984, reprinted in the National Security Archive collection.

30. Lugar (1988).

31. Staff report for the Senate Foreign Relations Committee by Carl Ford and Fred Brown, 7.

32. Shultz, 611.

33. See, for example, Confidential Briefing Memorandum, October 14, 1981, U.S. Department of State, from the National Security Archive collection.

34. Secret Cable #15403, June 9, 1984 from the U.S. Embassy to the Department of State, reprinted in the National Security Archive collection.

35. See, for example, Secret Cable #262789 sent from Kissinger to Ambassador Sullivan and Sullivan's response in Secret Cable #16413, both sent October 22, 1976, reprinted in the National Security Archive collection.

36. Karnow, *In Our Image*, 407.

37. Bonner, 361 and Shultz, 612.

38. Karnow, *In Our Image*, 407.

39. Report to congress by Ford and Brown, September 1984, reprinted in the National Security Archive collection.

40. Kline and Worthen, 11-12, and personal interviews with Lugar and Semmel, April 1993.

41. Confidential Cable #22776, August 21, 1984, from Ambassador Bosworth to the State Department, reprinted in the National Security Archive collection.

42. The above is from Mayer and McManus, 15-16.

43. Unclassified Cable #29301, October 25, 1984, reporting on Corazon Aquino's reaction and that of the moderate opposition, and Unclassified Cable #32195, November 23, 1984, reporting on Ramos' steps to curb military abuses, both reprinted in the National Security Archive collection.

44. The above is from Shultz, 611, and 16.

45. Trumbell, *New York Times*, April 21, 1985, describing debates on proposed military bases in Micronesia.

46. Bonner, 367.

47. Bonner, 347.

48. Lohr, "Democracy Gains Steam in the Phillipines," *New York Times*, January 27, 1985.

49. Ibid.

50. Secret Cable #09564 sent April 1, 1985, reprinted in the National Security Archive collection, provides details of the Wolfowitz visit.

51. Secret Memorandum, from Wolfowitz to Shultz, February 6, 1985, reprinted in the National Security Archive collection.

52. Shultz, 612-613. Bosworth's position on the moderate opposition is from a personal interview in March 1989 and from a Confidential Cable #05814 sent to the State Department following the meeting, on February 27, 1985, reprinted in the National Security Archive collection.

53. Confidential Cable #05470 from Ambassador Bosworth to the U.S. Department of State, February 22, 1985, reprinted in the National Security Archive collection.

54. "U.S. Official Prods Manila," *New York Times*, February 23, 1985.

55. According to Bonner, based on confidential interviews, the United States also secretly channeled funds to RAM via other Philippine organizations. Bonner, 372.

56. Cable #37446, December 2, 1985, from the U.S. Embassy in Manila to the U.S. Defense Intelligence Agency describes the RAM position, as outlined in a RAM newsletter. Both the cable and the newsletter are reprinted in the National Security Archive collection.

57. Armitage quotes and intelligence assessment from Kline and Worthen, 20.

58. Personal interview with Butcher in December 1994, cited in the previous chapter. Butcher is currently the director of the East Asia and Pacific Affairs Bureau of the State Department, and participated in U.S. debates on policy toward the Philippines during the period of analysis. Information on RAM's U.S. relations is also from a personal interview with Lugar, April 1993, and from Bonner, 372.

59. Lugar, 103.

60. "Votes in Congress," *New York Times*, May 19, 1985.

61. Personal interview with Bello and with an Asia Foundation officer as well as secondary interviews with priests conducted by Bonner, 524.

62. The above is from a personal interview with Carey, November 1993.

63. Lohr, "Impeachment Bill," *New York Times*, August 13, 1985.

64. Secret Cable #283732, September 15, 1985, reprinted in the National Security Archive collection, provides background on the as it emerged in mid-1985 and then evolved through the release of U.S. Air Force affidavits in September 1985.

65. Kline and Worthen, 21.

66. The above is from Bonner, 379-80.

67. Karnow, *In Our Image*, 407.

68. The above is from Kline and Worthen, 12.

69. The U.S. Air Force affidavits described above revealed that two Philippine air force fighter planes were activated on the day of the assassination. Further, airport controllers observed a scrambling of information on the day Aquino's flight arrived in Manila, possibly for an interception of the aircraft. Only the highest level of military authorization could have accomplished this. From Secret Cable #283732, op. cit. The Philippine court's deliberations on the affidavits is described in Secret Cable #28419, September 13, 1985, reprinted in the National Security Archive collection.

70. Secret Memorandum from Maisto to Wolfowitz, November 5, 1985, reprinted in the National Security Archive collection.

71. Secret Briefing Paper by INR, November 9, 1985, from the National Security Archive collection.

72. The account of the response from the "kitchen cabinet" is from Lugar (1988), based on his August 1986 discussions with Enrile, 108.

73. Personal interview with Hoge, March 1989.

74. One August 8, 1985 *New York Times* editorial "On Escaping the Marcos Embrace," discusses aid to the Philippines. It briefly refers to the recommendation by some in Congress

to channel food aid through private groups due to the "problem of diversion" and "damaging charges of extensive overseas investments by senior Marcos officials."

75. Bonner, 394.

76. Roberts, Steven, "Investigation of Marcos by Solarz Is Issue in United States as well as Manila," *New York Times*, February 7, 1986, Section I, 10.

77. Confidential Cable #35525, November 14, 1985, from the National Security Archive collection describes the planned visit.

78. Lugar (1988), 107-113, and personal interview, April 1993. A text of the letter is reprinted in the National Security Archive collection, in Confidential Cable #361339 from the State Department to the U.S. Embassy in Manila, November 26, 1985.

79. Shultz, 615. Also, Unclassified Cable #337854, November 3, 1985, from the National Security Archive collection, describes Laxalt's warning to Marcos regarding any plans to reinstate Ver.

80. Secret Cable #39432, December 18, 1985, from Bosworth to the State Department, reprinted in the National Security Archive collection.

81. Personal interview, March 1989. See also Shultz on Rosenthal's influence among U.S. officials regarding Corazon Aquino, 617 and 636.

82. Personal interviews with Aquino, October 1992.

83. Based upon secondary interview with D.H. Sawyer staff conducted by Bonner, cited 522; Karnow, *In Our Image*, 412; and from a personal interview with a confidential source from the firm, May 1993.

84. Information on the left's position and negotiations with Aquino is from Secret Cable #391261, December 26, 1985, reprinted in the National Security Archive collection.

85. Bonner, 401-403; Karnow, *In Our Image*, 412.

86. Lugar (1988), 111.

87. Center for Democracy report submitted to Congress, December 1985. The executive summary of the report is reprinted in Unclassified Cable #386766 from Shultz to the U.S. Embassies in the region, sent December 20, 1985, from the National Security Archive collection.

88. Lugar (1988), 111-113, and personal interview, April 1993.

89. Confidential Cable #39879, December 24, 1985, from Bosworth to the State Department, reprinted in the National Security Archive collection.

90. See Munro's article "The New Khmer Rouge" in the December 1985 issue of *Commentary*. See also Bonner, 397-98, for his account of the impact of the article on official views toward the Philippine situation and toward Aquino, in particular. Confidential Cable #002932 written by Shultz January 4, 1986, reprinted in the National Security Archive collection, describes U.S. Embassy endorsement of the article, as well as the heightened concern regarding the NPA among U.S. officials.

91. The above is from Shultz, 616-619.

92. The above is from Lugar (1988), 117-18.

93. Personal interview with Gelb, March 1989, and his front page *New York Times* article, "Marcos Reported to Lose Support in Administration," January 26, 1986.

94. Bonner, 438.

95. Personal interview with Bello, November 1993, and his 1985–1986 article.

96. Cable #00327, January 6, 1986, describes RAM's election activities under the aegis of its "Kamalayan 86" project, reprinted in the National Security Archive collection.

97. Secret Cable #38088, December 7, 1985, cited in Bonner, 523.

98. Bonner, 415. See also Secret Cable #38320 from Philip Kaplan to the State Department regarding the Asia Foundation's support for communications systems and electoral monitoring for the Philippine elections, December 10, 1985, reprinted in the National Security Archive collection.

99. See coverage in the *New York Times* during the period for evidence of the observer team's increasingly strident reports, documented in Blitz (1990). See the National Security Archive's collection during the period for evidence of the embassy's efforts to convince their colleagues in the United States that the claims of fraud by Marcos were accurate.

100. Confidential Cable #04421, February 10, 1986, from Bosworth to the U.S. Pacific Commander-in-Chief, reprinted in the National Security Archive collection.

101. Lugar (1988), 131, on number of voters. Secret Cable #041479, February 10, 1986, on the failure of the boycott campaign and the resurgent faith in democratic processes, reprinted in the National Security Archive collection. The estimated percentage of votes cast for Aquino is from a personal interview with Bosworth based upon State Department estimates at the time, March 1989.

102. Personal interview with Mydans, March 1989, based on his own personal conversation with Marcos after the events of 1986.

103. Confidential Cable #04422, February 10, 1986, from Bosworth to the State Department, reprinted in the National Security Archive collection.

104. The account of Will's call to the White House is from Bonner, 423.

105. Information on the advice to Reagan is from a personal interview with Lugar in April 1993 and from a Secret Memorandum sent February 10, 1986, from Wolfowitz to Shultz containing the text of a post-election briefing strategy for Reagan, reprinted in the National Security Archive collection.

106. Karnow, *In Our Image*, 414. Philippine reactions to Reagan's statement, particularly the concern that the United States cared more about its bases than about democracy, are summarized in a review of anti-American Philippine press coverage and editorials in Confidential Cable #05338, February 15, 1986, and in a letter from the American Chamber of Commerce in Manila to the State Department urging a shift in U.S. support from Marcos to Aquino, in Unclassified Cable #05341, February 15, 1986, both reprinted in the National Security Archive collection.

107. Unclassified Cable #04878, February 12, 1986, describes Aquino's response to Reagan's statement. Confidential Cable #04680, February 11, 1986, describes Aquino's dealings with Solarz, both from the National Security Archive collection.

108. Confidential Cable #05064, February 13, 1986, describes official U.S. concerns. Secret Cable #05294, February 14, 1986, describes military fortifications underway to protect Marcos, and Confidential Cable #05296, February 14, 1986, describes growing pressures on the moderates to ally with the left, all reprinted in the National Security Archive collection.

109. Personal interview with Bosworth, March 1989.

110. Personal interview with Lugar, April 1993.

111. Confidential Cable #05234, February 14, 1986, from the National Security Archive collection.

112. Non-Classified Memorandum of letter from Senator Nunn as well as a Dole/Lugar/ Nunn Action statement, February 13, 1986, reprinted in the National Security Archive collection.

113. Confidential Cable #05186, February 14, 1986, from the National Security Archive collection.

114. Secret Cable #048670, February 15, 1986, from the National Security Archive collection.

115. The text of Reagan's statement is reprinted in Unclassified Cable #049446, February 15, 1986, from the National Security Archive collection.

116. Personal interview with Lugar, April 1993.

117. Confidential Cable #05363, February 16, 1986, from the National Security Archive collection.

118. Confidential Cable #05323, February 15, 1986, and Confidential Cable #05362 a day later, both reprinted in the National Security Archive collection.

119. Confidential Cable #05893, February 20, 1986, from the National Security Archive collection.

120. Secret Cable #05365, February 16, 1986, describes Habib's itinerary, reprinted in the National Security Archive collection.

121. Secret Cable #06192, February 22, 1986, from the National Security Archive collection.

122. The above is from Karnow, *In Our Image*, 415-17 and from personal interviews with journalists and clergy present in the early hours of the so-called "People Power revolution."

123. Thompson, 149.

124. Personal interviews and Radio Veritas broadcasts, February 1986.

125. Confidential Cable #06196, February 23, 1986, from the National Security Archive collection, and personal interviews with journalists and clergy who participated in the show of support.

126. Secret Cable #055988, February 23, 1986, from the National Security Archive collection.

127. Ibid.

128. Personal interview with Lugar, April 1993.

129. Shultz, 624.

130. *Meet the Press* transcript and interviews with Marvin Kalb, April 1989.

131. Confidential Cable #06292, February 24, 1986, from the National Security Archive collection.

132. Personal interview with Lugar, April 1993.

133. Speakes.

134. The information here is a compilation from accounts by Shultz, Speakes, Bonner, and Karnow, *In Our Image*.

135. As reported on CNN, among other Philippine and U.S. news outlets, February 1986. Note that Walden Bello alleges that the Marcoses left armed, believing they were headed not into exile but for a last stand in Marcos' home province of Ilocos Norte. If this is so, and Marcos did not *choose* to step down, then the United States played an even more crucial, leadership role in the transition.

136. Nonclassified letter sent February 25, 1986, reprinted in the National Security Archive collection.

Chapter 7

The Contested State:
Transnational Sources
of Regime Change

W e now return to our original questions. What causes regime transition? What determines the direction of change—revolutionary, author-itarian or democratic? And what broader lessons can we learn from the Philippines? This chapter summarizes the findings of each of the cases of regime change in the Philippines and describes some of the implications for theory and practice.

1898: From Spanish to U.S. Colonial Rule

From the first armed conflict between the forces of Lapu Lapu and those of Humabon and Magellan, Filipinos have cultivated international alliances as a strategy for dealing with domestic conflict. At the same time, international groups have cultivated alliances with Filipinos as a strategy of conquest within the Philippines. And such attempts at conquest have been used, in turn, in the service of larger international strategic objectives.

During the Spanish colonial period from 1565 through 1898, Spain cultivated a Filipino cacique, granting them privileged access to land, international trade and other economic resources. In exchange, the caciques carried out the colonial policies of Spain, extracting labor, taxes, church tributes and other resources Spain needed to enhance its position with respect to such international competitors as Portugal and Holland. In the process, the caciques established a grossly inequitable land tenure system that remains largely intact today. Because land has traditionally been the primary source of wealth and power in the Philippines, the inequalities in land tenure have long extended from the economic to the social and political realms. And because the vast majority of Filipinos have traditionally resided in the countryside and relied on the land for their livelihoods, the land tenure issue has been an ongoing source of revolutionary opposition from Spanish times to the present. To combat this, Spain deployed its "sword and cross" strategies to contain an increasingly restive peasant population. Forming an alliance with the Macabebes to address militarily the peasant opposition, Spain also introduced some moderate approaches for handling peasant anger. While the Church sometimes contributed here, it was the rise of democracy in Europe, particularly with the revolution in France, that led Spain to institutionalize political and economic approaches to peasant revolutionary opposition at home and in the colonies.

This soon contributed to growing schisms in Spain, leading to frequent changes in government throughout the 1800s. The governmental changes weakened Spain at home and abroad, and reverberated, in turn, throughout Spain's colonies. A surge of revolts in the periphery left Spain with just Cuba, Puerto Rico, and the Philippines by 1826, ushering in a backlash from the ultraconservative King Ferdinand VII. Instead of quelling opposition, however, the hard-line policies fueled a new wave of revolutionary agitation in the Philippines and Cuba, as elites and peasants, moderates and revolutionaries began to ally against Spain. In the Philippines, this alliance solidified after the 1896 execution of moderate opposition leader Jose Rizal, just as a new international competitor challenged Spain. By 1898, the United States had already acquired extensive former Spanish colonies on the North American continent, including the Louisiana Territory in 1803, which Napoleon had forced Spain to retrocede to France; West Florida in 1810; and all of Florida by 1819. After Mexican independence in 1821, the United States faced down a new foe, acquiring by 1848 Texas and what are now New Mexico, Colorado, Utah, Arizona, Nevada and California. Now, American expansionists saw in the Cuban and Filipino uprisings against Spain an opportunity for additional territory. Following a heated debate in the U.S. Congress, however, the Teller Amendment passed, allowing for American intervention in Cuba to help liberate the revolutionaries from Spain while prohibiting the taking of Cuba thereafter for the United States. Pressing the expansionist cause regardless, Theodore Roosevelt, as Assistant Secretary of the Navy, deployed American ships to attack Spanish garrisons in the Philippines.

On May 1, 1898, Commodore Dewey sailed into Manila Harbor and routed Spanish forces there. The Spanish put up a better fight to hold the city of Manila from the United States, now allied with Filipino revolutionaries who understood from the Teller Amendment that the United States would not take the Philippines as a colony. When the fighting ended and the United States and Spain excluded the Filipinos from peace talks, however, tensions between the American troops and Filipino revolutionaries flared. This intensified after December 10, 1898, when the United States acquired the right to purchase the Philippines from Spain under the terms of the Paris Peace Treaty, which also granted Cuban independence as well as U.S. control of Guam and Puerto Rico. During an intense debate within the United States between expansionists and anti-imperialists over whether or not to ratify the treaty, war between the Filipinos and Americans broke out on February 4, 1899. The treaty was now ratified and overseas American imperialism was launched. The United States quickly learned, however, that seizing territory and holding it were two distinct enterprises, the former requiring merely military superiority, the latter requiring political capacity to control captive populations. Working on both fronts, the United States established a military alliance with Macabebe soldiers, using them as the Spanish before them had. Meanwhile nonmilitary U.S. advisors cultivated alliances with moderate and elite factions of the Philippine opposition. This nascent transnational alliance set up health, education, and other public projects while laying the foundation for a postconquest democratic colonial regime involving essentially the same Filipinos who had earlier collaborated with Spain.

Thus, the causes of the transition from Spanish to U.S. colonial rule are primarily international, centered on the broader, long-standing conflict between Spain and the United States for territory. Domestic opposition in the Philippines and Cuba, however, created the opportunity for American intervention by weakening Spain's hold over its colonies. Further, domestic opposition within Spain toward liberal approaches to revolutionary opposition forced Spain to pursue hard-line policies, even when it was clear that these policies were encouraging former caciques, elites and moderates to ally with revolutionaries. Similarly, domestic opposition within the United States prevented American expansionists from taking Cuba and nearly prevented them from taking the Philippines as well. Still, neither purely domestic nor purely international explanations take into account the crucial role played by the transnational alliance comprised of American forces and Macabebes. Moreover, the eventual transition from United States occupation to colonial rule required the involvement of Filipinos willing to collaborate in building the political, economic, social as well as military institutions that would form the foundation of the new regime. While a combination of international and domestic factors help explain the transition, emerging transnational alliances were also essential during the Philippine–American War and were then crucial to the ultimate success of the transition following the war.

1946: From Colony to Independent Nation

The war was to last until 1902, involving roughly 126,000 Americans and exacting a toll in lives lost of over 4,000 Americans and as many as half a million Filipinos. The war also ignited an intense, albeit little-known debate on foreign policy in the United States, indicating the domestic American limits to overseas imperialism while presaging as well similar debates decades later over policy toward Indochina.

Using transnational strategies to manage its new colony, the United States established a Philippine Police Force, comprised largely of Macabebes, institutionalizing in the process a transnational military alliance. The United States also maintained a troop presence of 50,000. On the political front, an American governor appointed by the U.S. president was installed and given veto power over an elected bicameral Philippine legislature. In addition, two Filipinos, one appointed by the American governor, the other by the Philippine assembly, were to sit in the U.S. House of Representatives, where they had the right to speak but not to vote. These representatives came to understand U.S. debates on the issue of Philippine sovereignty, wherein Democrats generally favored independence and Republicans generally favored continued colonial rule. Throughout the early years of colonization, the Republicans held the White House. In 1912, however, the election of Woodrow Wilson created an opportunity for change. And Philippine representative to the United States Manuel Quezon quickly capitalized on this, lobbying successfully to have anti-imperialist New York Congressman Francis Harrison named the new governor of the Philippines. Harrison quickly abolished the veto powers of the governor, and then greatly reduced the number of Americans in Philippine government while increasing the number of Filipinos. Quezon next lobbied successfully for what was to become known as the Jones Act, passed in 1916 and pledging eventual independence for the Philippines.

World War I soon reasserted, however, U.S. dependence on the Philippines for raw materials as well as Philippine dependence on trade with the United States. The war also exposed the threat to American military facilities posed by Japan and other contenders for control of the Philippines. In the United States, the issue of sovereignty languished through the Republican-dominated 1920s. In the Philippines, however, a new era of religious-based peasant revolutionary opposition was burgeoning amid the post–World War I collapse in agricultural markets. The collapse, together with new U.S. immigration laws, also led to a sudden spurt of Filipino migration to the United States, notably to the labor-intensive sugar cane fields of Hawaii and fruit farms of California. But the Filipino farm workers soon proved politically active, fueling by the late 1920s intense racism against them. This deepened in the early 1930s when the Depression brought new waves of white farm laborers to California from the dust-bowl states. In an attempt to protect American farmers during the Depression, powerful farm lobbies now revived protectionist arguments and pressed for Philippine independence. These lobbies gained an ally in the White House with the 1932 election of Democrat Franklin Roosevelt. Under pressure from Filipino and American lobbyists, Roosevelt helped push through the Tydings–McDuffie Act in 1934, which allowed for a commonwealth regime for ten years followed by a transition to full independence thereafter. Just as the commonwealth regime was inaugurated, however, the growing external threat posed by Japan together with a resurgence of domestic revolutionary opposition in the Philippines, again reasserted the interdependencies between the United States and its Asian colony.

Now, General Douglas MacArthur was charged with creating a Philippine army capable of defending against external as well as domestic threats, particularly to protect the increasingly important American naval base at Subic and the air base at Clark, by then home of America's largest air armada anywhere overseas. MacArthur would, however, fail in this, as American and Philippine forces were swiftly overcome by Japan in December 1941, just hours after the attack on Pearl Harbor. MacArthur fled soon after, vowing to return. Many elite Filipinos now collaborated with the Japanese while other Filipinos maintained a network of support for the United States, including a shadow government as well as American-trained military bands waging guerrilla warfare against the Japanese. Peasant-based revolutionary forces under the aegis of the Soviet-inspired Philippine Communist Party also formed a military arm in 1942 known as the Huks. Following Soviet protocols, the Huks set aside their opposition to American colonialism and allied with the United States in the war against Japan, hoping in the process to secure an eventual role for themselves in an independent Philippines. Following MacArthur's return in October 1944 and the subsequent Japanese withdrawal in 1945, however, the Huks were quickly betrayed amid growing Cold War tensions. And it soon became clear that the United States would allow only for an "independent" Philippines willing to maintain American economic and strategic interests in the archipelago. So it was that the United States met in name the promises of the Tydings–McDuffie Act, granting the Philippines its independence on July 4, 1946, while safeguarding American economic and strategic interests there. One month later, the Huks would pick up their arms again, waging full-scale civil war in central Luzon by 1948.

As in 1898, neither purely international nor purely domestic factors can fully explain the 1946 transition to independence, nor the steps leading to it, including the 1916 Jones Act and the 1934 Tydings–McDuffie Act. While domestic American factors centering on political and economic competition between Republicans and Democrats contributed to the debates on the question of Philippine independence and created openings for this when Democrats held the White House, it was the transnational lobbying by Filipinos that pushed the issue toward a conclusion. Similarly, international factors such as World War I contributed to the collapse of Philippine agricultural markets, with implications for domestic Philippine agitation. It was, however, Filipino migration to the United States that sparked antagonism from American growers and white farm workers during the Depression, reviving U.S. debates on the question of Philippine independence. Finally, the international crisis of World War II exposed Philippine vulnerability to other colonial contenders, in this case the Japanese, while fostering as well the rise of new, more organized peasant revolutionary opposition led by the Huks. Meanwhile, the combination of external and domestic threats to their bid for control of Philippine politics encouraged elite Filipinos to seek continued military support from the United States even after independence. And U.S. interests were aligned with this, given that the war had intensified U.S. strategic ties to the Philippines. As a result, Philippine independence was compromised from the outset.

In short, a combination of domestic, international and transnational factors account for the transition while the international context, this time the Cold War, played a key role in determining the direction of change.

1972: The Transition to Authoritarian Rule

The postwar interdependence between the United States and the Philippines was institutionalized with a 1947 agreement that committed the United States to provide the Philippines with external security while domestic Philippine forces were to provide for the new nation's internal security. The interdependence increased further during the Huk rebellion, as Cold War "containment" policies, formalized in 1950 with NSC-68, placed the Huk threat within the broader conflict with the Soviets.

Seeking to use native rather than American forces in order to avert domestic opposition in the United States, American military advisors led by Colonel Edward Lansdale cultivated Philippine military as well as political and economic institutions in the service of silencing the Huk challenge. Though some transnational attempts were made to introduce reforms, notably in land tenure, these were a mere sideshow to the main transnational military policies. Lansdale did, however, intervene in politics as well, promising increased aid to the corrupt regime of Elpidio Quirino in exchange for naming Ramon Magsaysay Defense Minister in 1950. Lansdale also helped the CIA establish a citizen's group, the National Committee for Free Elections (NAMFREL), to monitor 1951 legislative elections. Magsaysay, with directives from Lansdale, supported NAMFREL by preventing the military from stealing ballot boxes and by stationing troops to prevent violence in what turned out to be relatively honest elections in which Quirino suffered heavy losses. Truman then applauded Magsaysay and, with continued American backing, Magsaysay won by a huge margin in 1953 presidential elections. That same year, the Huks formally surrendered, though sporadic uprisings would continue for the next two decades.

In addition to the domestic Philippine Huk crisis and the rise of the transnational U.S.–Philippine military alliance it prompted, international events soon increased the value to the United States of its Philippine bases. During the Korean War, Clark and Subic proved strategically useful. The bases would be used again in the Quemoy-Matsu crises of the late 1950s; but it was not until the Vietnam War, particularly after the massive escalation in 1965, that the bases would become vital to the regional and global projection of U.S. power. That year, just as Ferdinand Marcos and his wife Imelda were moving into Malacanang Palace, President Johnson increased U.S. military presence in Vietnam from the 16,000 advisors sent by Kennedy to more than 23,000, followed by a rapid escalation in troop presence. Facing growing opposition at home and abroad, Johnson was desperate for a "more flags" campaign to give the impression of international support for the war. Marcos shrewdly used this need for Philippine support as well as for the bases to procure ever-higher levels of economic and military aid from the United States. Earlier regimes had also used the bases to leverage U.S. aid but Marcos brought this to new heights, using much of the aid to establish a network of cronies and to cultivate the Philippine military as a viable instrument for repressing opposition to his regime. Opposition spread anyway, particularly after 1969 elections when Marcos' 2,000,000-vote margin of victory was profoundly challenged by rioting students and others in what was to become known as the "First Quarter Storm." Only with Philippine and American military intervention was Marcos able to restore order.

But this would not hold. Legislative elections in 1971 brought victory to the moderate opposition, with an increasingly likely win for opposition leader Benigno Aquino Jr., in upcoming 1973 presidential elections. By 1972, his regime more threatened than ever, Marcos considered martial law. Given heavy doses of U.S. aid from 1946 to 1972, totaling about $1.85 billion in economic aid and about $672.5 million in military aid as well as the growth in the Philippine armed forces from 37,000 to 62,000 over the same period, Marcos had the capacity to carry it out. By doling out rewards to a network of cronies within the military, he also had their loyalty. The American position was vague but Marcos gambled that as long as a communist threat loomed, the United States would back him. A new Maoist insurgency had in fact formed in 1969 on the foundations built by the Huks before them, but this insurgency, known as the New People's Army (NPA) was only in its infancy by 1972. U.S. officials knew this but they went along with Marcos primarily because he promised to safeguard U.S. economic and strategic interests. Of particular importance were Subic, now America's largest overseas naval base, and Clark among America's top five largest overseas air bases. So it was that on September 22, 1972, Marcos declared martial law. Although the United States was not directly involved in the Marcos-led transition to authoritarian rule, the United States had played a central role in cultivating the political, economic, and military foundations for it throughout the first half of the Cold War. And now, in 1972, the United States backed Marcos, maintaining aid, trade and other forms of crucial support that would continue up to the last moments of the Marcos regime in 1986.

The 1972 transition must then be understood in the international context of the Cold War and the rise in power during the period of the transnational U.S.– Philippine authoritarian alliance born during the initial war of colonial conquest and now fully mobilized.

1986: The Transition to Democracy

The period of martial law was a brutal one for Filipinos, but it promoted the resurgence of a complex, broad-based transnational pro-democratic alliance ultimately capable of overthrowing Marcos.

Under martial law, political killings or "salvagings" as well as torture, imprisonment and other human rights violations became so widespread after 1972 that even formerly moderate oppositionists, including members of the traditional oligarchy, were displaced. Marcos then supplanted them with a network of his friends, family and other cronies. This soon created deep opposition within the military, church, oligarchy and other traditional sources of Philippine power, as well as in the countryside, as both moderate and revolutionary opposition grew. Silenced at home, exiled opposition leaders mobilized opposition to Marcos among the roughly one million Filipinos living in the United States, the even larger Filipino-American community, cultivating as well a network of anti-Marcos allies in American official, business, academic, media and other elite circles. They used such strategies in part to circumvent Marcos' domestic restrictions on political expression, in part because of the crucial role played by the United States in sustaining the Marcos regime, and in part because of long-standing personal, professional, and institutional ties in the United States established since 1898. Still, Marcos retained control and enjoyed substantial support from the United States due to a combination of American dependence on Marcos for access to the bases, a dependence that rose after the 1975 loss of Cam Ranh Bay, as well as Marcos' inventiveness in capitalizing on this dependence. In fact, Marcos secured ever more aid from the United States and then used the aid to tighten his control of economic and political structures while expanding the military's capacity as an instrument for containing opposition to his increasingly unpopular regime.

Despite official U.S. support, however, opposition to the hard-line strategies that had dominated U.S. foreign policy since 1946 and had helped create the military capacity for authoritarian rule in several allied countries including the Philippines, was gaining ground in the United States in response to events in Indochina, Watergate, Chile and elsewhere. In 1973, Congress initiated hearings on human rights in allied regimes. By 1974, Congress wrote new laws linking human rights with U.S. foreign aid and then institutionalized the issue in 1977 with the establishment of a human rights bureau within the State Department just as President Carter came to power. Ideological and bureaucratic tensions now arose between the hard-liners and their increasingly powerful opponents in Congress, the State Department and other centers of foreign policy, notably the Defense Department, the White House, and the CIA, as well as among nonofficial elites in business, academia, the media, etc. Central to the debate was whether hard-line tactics of repression fueled or quelled revolutionary threats to United States interests abroad. After the 1979 revolutions in Iran and Nicaragua and the threat of revolution in El Salvador, the debate intensified. Even with Carter in the White House, however, the hard-liners retained control of foreign policy towards the Philippines and then in 1981 saw the ultra-hard-line Kirkpatrick Doctrine gain predominance under Reagan. Nevertheless, one apparently minor concession to the human rights advocates would soon change that. In May 1980, moderate opposition leader and pre-martial law senator Benigno Aquino Jr. was released from prison and allowed to travel to the United States for heart surgery. Aquino stayed for three years and established during that time a broad network of powerful friends in government, academia, business, the media, the American-Filipino community and other sectors where Filipino oppositionists had been building anti-Marcos allies. And these friends quickly mobilized after Aquino's August 21, 1983, assassination.

Filipino moderates, human rights advocates, other opponents of hard-line tactics in and out of the U.S. government, and disillusioned former Marcos allies in and out of the Philippine government now began to coalesce into a transnational alliance actively seeking a nonrevolutionary, democratic alternative to Marcos. This transnational alliance urged economic, political, and military reforms, arguing that Marcos and his abusive tactics were part of the problem, not part of the solution.[1] By early 1985, coordinated opposition emerged from within the Marcos regime, notably military officers in the Reform the Armed Forces Movement (RAM). And opposition within the United States intensified after August 1985, when Filipino elites leaked to American journalists information substantiating claims that Marcos had diverted U.S. aid to benefit himself and his cronies. Under pressure to reform, Marcos announced "snap" presidential elections on American television. That the announcement came on American television in the middle of the night in the Philippines is but one indication of its target audience. While the left opted to boycott the elections, the moderate opposition united behind Benigno Aquino Jr.'s widow, Corazon. And her American allies quickly redirected her initially left-leaning platform on the bases and the communists toward a pro-American stance. Congress then sent political analysts to help Filipinos insure democratic procedures, helped revive NAMFREL to monitor the elections, and sent a bipartisan observer delegation for the elections to be held February 7, 1986. The media descended as well, with U.S. coverage eventually exceeding that for any foreign election up to that time.[2]

With so many observers, Reagan faced intense public opposition at home when he publicly stated that election fraud might have occurred on both sides. Still, Reagan and his inner circle continued to support Marcos, but others, mainly from the State Department and Congress, now urged support for a democratic transition from Marcos to Aquino. On February 22, the situation finally exploded, as RAM leaders Ramos and Enrile defected from Marcos and the "people power" revolution burst onto the streets of Manila. Still Marcos clung to power, leaving only when pressed by Reagan to do so. Hours later, Aquino took the oath of office and formed an uneasy pact with the RAM leaders, an arrangement that would undermine subsequent democratization while posing a recurring threat to her regime of a military coup. In those surprising moments of February 1986, however, the increasingly strong transnational U.S.–Philippine alliance opposing the Marcos regime created the political space for a moderate alternative to both the left and the right to gain power. Domestic Philippine politics then determined the nature of the transition. That the moderates united behind Aquino, that Ramos and Enrile agreed to back her rather than seek power for themselves, and that Marcos ultimately left peacefully, are among the domestic Philippine contingencies that allowed for a moderate, peaceful transition. Even these contingencies, however, were influenced by the specter of the United States, vividly demonstrated by the entire seventh fleet's presence on the horizon not far from Manila. For instance, without American backing, Marcos knew he would not long survive. Similarly, Ramos and Enrile understood that without American support, their attempted coup, even if successful, would be suicidal.

In short, domestic Philippine politics created the impetus for change and the contingencies surrounding it, while key U.S. officials, strengthened vis-à-vis hard-liners by revolutions in Indochina, Nicaragua, Iran, etc., enabled the direction of change from Marcos to Aquino. And again, neither purely domestic nor purely international but rather transnational efforts by a complex, broad-based coalition of Marcos opponents seeking a moderate transition explain the transition in 1986. Finally, the 1986 transition must be understood in its historical context. Indeed, Marcos nearly succeeded in his attempt to "salvage" democracy, and the political, economic, and military legacies of his regime continue to threaten democratization. Yet Filipino democratic processes cultivated throughout the American colonial and post-colonial period survived martial law, the fragile democracy of the early Aquino years, as well as the potentially unstable period following the U.S. withdrawal of its military bases after 1992. At the same time, however, the sources of revolutionary opposition have persisted. Sidelined in the 1986 elections and in the subsequent "people power" uprising because of their decision to boycott, the revolutionary opposition was similarly sidelined by the Aquino administration, as their continuing calls for land reform and other structural changes, echoing centuries of peasant anger, went unanswered.

Lessons Learned:
Implications for Theory and Practice

Lessons learned from the Philippine experience can be applied more broadly to the question of regime change—authoritarian, democratic or revolutionary—in chronically contested states elsewhere. The lessons are particularly applicable to the many Latin American countries with similar legacies of Spanish then U.S. ties. The lessons are relevant as well, however, to regime change in any chronically contested state, where domestic structures are shaped by strategic, economic or political interdependencies with foreign powers. Thus the model has relevance as well to questions regarding the international causes and consequences of civil war. Further, the model contributes to our understanding of the transnational sources of U.S. foreign policy. In this case, while U.S. foreign policy has affected Philippine regime type, Filipinos have likewise affected U.S. foreign policy. And the long-standing debate in the United States regarding policy toward the Philippines sheds light on how consensus among U.S. officials can break down and then be reestablished. Finally, because much of the U.S. foreign policy debate surrounding the 1986 transition, as well as the one in 1898, took place in the media, the study also contributes to the surprisingly scant body of literature on the role of the media in the U.S. foreign policy making process. The contributions of the Philippine experience to these enduring questions are described below.

Regime Transition

Extensive research and policy debates have attempted to understand the causes of transitions to democracy[3] and transitions to authoritarian rule.[4] Most analyses to date have, however, treated diverse types of regime change in isolation, overlooking the historical connections linking one regime with its successors, overlooking as well the similar root causes driving the various transitions. In order to understand transitions to democracy, the Philippine experience demonstrates, it is essential to understand earlier transitions to authoritarian rule—the sources of the authoritarian regime's power, the strategies used to maintain that power, and the impact of these strategies on key sectors of society. Most analyses have also emphasized either purely domestic or purely international sources of regime change, overlooking the transnational factors so important in many contested states, particularly those conditioned by long-standing interdependence with foreign powers.

The Philippine experience establishes an historically grounded, transnational framework for understanding the causes and direction of regime transition. In this framework, regime change is essentially a manifestation of the contest over time among authoritarian, democratic and revolutionary forces seeking control of the Philippines. And this contest has, since the Spanish period, been a transnational one, with foreign powers intervening in the domestic politics of the Philippines as part of their international strategies and Filipinos allying with foreign groups as a competitive strategy at home. As such, diverse regime changes in the Philippines over time must also be understood in their historical contexts as linked outcomes of the same essential contest. The Philippine cases of authoritarian change in 1972 and democratic change in 1986, in particular, demonstrate that these two transitions were related, the outcome of conflict between two competing transnational alliances, both seeking to contain revolutionary opposition but using different strategies, one emphasizing bullets the other ballots. Even the recurring revolutionary opposition, which has been primarily Philippine-based, must also be placed in the context of broader international competition, given the support revolutionary groups have received from foreign powers as part of broader international conflicts. Such support has come from the United States during its war against Spain in 1898, Japan prior to World War II in the 1930s, the Soviets via the United States Communist Party also in the 1930s, Libya to Muslim separatists in the 1970s, and China after 1969 until the rapprochement with the Marcos regime in 1975.

Finally, the direction of regime change is determined by the relative strength of each competing transnational group at critical moments, and this relative strength is determined in turn by the interplay of domestic and international factors. Here, the framework that emerges from the Philippine experience integrates structural sources of regime change such as class conflict and the position of key political actors or groups within the international system with voluntarist sources emphasizing historical contingencies and elements of choice.[5] While ongoing structural sources of conflict within the Philippines include the land tenure system as well as the presence of American military bases from about 1905 through 1992, the Philippine experience demonstrates the link between structural explanations of interests with voluntarist explanations centering on contingencies. Specifically, domestic Philippine structures such as land tenure or international structures such as the bases have created the interests driving competing groups to seek control of the state; but the outcomes of these structurally based conflicts have depended on the strategies various actors chose at key moments and the relative success of these. That is, the choices political actors make during crises of regime transition may be structurally constrained, but they are not predetermined. Rather, they evolve as events unfold, often in dramatic, interactive, contingent processes of debate, action and response—in short, politics. Moreover, the structures themselves—the military bases, land tenure system, as well as authoritarian and democratic institutions—are not predetermined but evolve through time, out of political competition at the domestic, international and ultimately transnational levels.

Revolutionary Movements

At the heart of the debate on how best to contain peasant revolutionary movements is the underlying question: what, in brief, are the root causes and prime motivations of such groups? Different ideological, even philosophical answers to this question yield different strategies. Initially, "moral" economists predicted that peasants would revolt to restore the traditional order when the penetration of capital broke down their bonds with landlords, undermining traditional subsistence rights. This approach provided a useful alternative to earlier modernization theories emphasizing urban industrialization as the solution to rural poverty. Subsequent political economists, however, argued that this offered an overly romantic view of village life as egalitarian, mutually supportive, and essentially conservative. The political economists emphasized instead rural class stratification and the effects of this on "rational" peasants assessing the anticipated costs and benefits of joining revolutionary movements.[6] Both approaches, however, emphasize relatively recent commercialization of agriculture as the source of peasant anger, overlooking long-standing conflicts stretching far back in time, as in the Philippine case. A further limitation later identified was the focus on the peasant alone, overlooking the role of the state and its place in the international system as sources of peasant militancy. When the state's ability to contain or coerce peasant opposition is weak, this approach argued, revolutionaries can succeed.[7]

While these analyses are useful, they all fail to address a far more basic, far more human question concerning peasant militancy. Whatever we hold to be the economic, political or social factors that create the *incentive* for peasants to seek dramatic changes, we must ask what might make a peasant, whether conservative as the moral economists believe, utility maximizing as the political economists hold, or opportunistic as the latter model suggests, risk his or her life? This question is particularly important given that constraints to effective collective action are operative in most peasant revolutionary situations. Why would they not simply pursue "everyday forms of resistance?"[8] Contrary to the expectation that increased militarization will prompt a *decrease* in revolutionary activity, as the last of the models described above suggests, the Philippine experience and other evidence from low intensity conflict elsewhere, indicates that the reverse may also be true.[9] As American and Filipino officials, and even the revolutionaries acknowledged by the mid-1980s, the hard-line tactics used by the Marcos regime with U.S. assistance not only failed to stem the growth of the revolutionary opposition but actually provided the movement with most of its arsenal. Moreover, the hard-line tactics helped the revolutionary movement recruit new members.[10] While peasants had long sought reforms in such areas as land tenure, political access, elite control of the economy, and other sources of peasant anger, it was the regime's human rights violations against peasant revolutionaries and nonrevolutionaries alike that encouraged many otherwise risk-averse peasants to support the revolutionaries, as much for protection as for political expression. Thus, the Philippine experience supports arguments that repression can actually stir, not silence, revolutionary opposition.

Moreover, while most analysts have emphasized successful peasant revolutionary movements, the Philippine experience demonstrates the impact even unsuccessful movements can have over time. Such movements create, for example, a need for institutions that will combat them and so play a key role in a contested state's political development. When such movements gain enough strength, they can also prompt regime change even if they themselves do not gain power. This approach to understanding even unsuccessful revolutionary movements is particularly relevant where structural sources of revolutionary opposition, such as land tenure, remain unresolved through successive regime transitions. While revolutionary opposition has contributed to each of the regime transitions discussed here, it has also prompted the development of both authoritarian and democratic institutions. Further, contrary to the prevailing view of revolutionary opposition as a recent response to the influx of foreign capital, the Philippine case demonstrates that neither peasant opposition nor foreign investment is a recent invention; rather, both have evolved over centuries. Up to the present, the Philippine peasantry can, in fact, be seen as a creation of Spanish colonial policies that granted colonists and Filipino collaborators privileged access to land, the primary source of political and economic power in the Philippines, as well as to state resources and military protection.

Despite repeated attempts at land reform since Spanish times, however, roughly 70 percent of all Filipinos remained, through the 1986 transition, landless peasants. Although increased urbanization since 1986 has reduced this figure, attempts to resolve the problem of political order in the Philippines either through authoritarian or democratic measures will likely fail until this and other structural inequalities are addressed.

The Causes of War

What causes war? This question is at the core of international relations theory and policy debates. Most of the attention, however, has emphasized interstate rather than civil war.[11] Yet civil wars, wherein competing forces battle for control of a contested state, have been far more prevalent throughout time than interstate wars have been, and have often had a broader international context. In the ongoing battle for control of the Philippines, for example, the international context emerges as a key cause of civil war. Because Philippine revolutionary movements have long been anti-imperialist, first Spain then the United States cultivated indigenous authoritarian institutions to carry out colonial policies and militarily combat the revolutionaries. American concerns about revolutionary opposition continued after Philippine independence in 1946, when the United States greatly expanded its bases there during the Korean and Vietnam Wars as part of the broader Cold War. To manage its war effort in each of those civil conflicts, the United States needed to secure its Philippine bases from nationalist opposition within the Philippines. Caught in a web of international civil wars, the United States contributed substantially to the build-up of armed forces in allied regimes in the region and elsewhere. And in the civil conflict that helped bring Marcos down, the New People's Army (NPA) relied almost exclusively on weapons stolen from the Philippine military, as noted above. Here it becomes clear that the influx of American military aid fed the armed conflict on both sides and so was a key cause of civil war.

Beyond understanding the international causes of civil wars, it is also essential to understand their international consequences. These consequences can be far-reaching, particularly when a civil war creates new states as with the Soviet, Chinese, Cuban, Iranian, Nicaraguan and other revolutions, or when civil war otherwise alters international alliances and the global balance of power. For example, had the NPA succeeded in 1986, the consequences for the international system would likely have been even more destabilizing than either the Iranian or Nicaraguan revolutions had been due to the loss of major American military bases. Because the transition was moderate, it had instead a "demonstration effect," spawning similar "people power" uprisings in the region and elsewhere, including Korea and South Africa.[12] Moreover, while the NPA made it a policy to rely on stolen weapons and so remain independent of foreign influence, earlier revolutionary movements in the Philippines received support, as noted above, from foreign powers competing with the United States for control of the Philippines. As international conflicts from the Spanish–American War, World War II and the Cold War have all played out in the rice paddies, villages and mountains of the Philippines, the international causes and consequences of civil war have become vividly apparent.

Although some interesting works have probed the international causes and consequences of civil war,[13] further analysis is needed to develop a more dynamic model of the state than realist theories offer. Such a model would emphasize the state and its role in the international system as historically created, frequently contested, and ultimately shaped by the interplay of domestic and international forces. This, the Philippine experience suggests, is particularly useful in understanding civil war in contested states faced with widespread domestic opposition and entrenched elites whose power derives largely from external sources. In viewing the international system from this perspective, we might then redefine security to encompass interdependence between *segments* of states, anticipating the kind of transnational cooperation, conflict and political strategies segments of the American and Philippine state and society have exhibited, particularly since the latter's independence in 1946. Building on the idea that small states might "bandwagon" with a more powerful state like the United States as an alternative to balancing,[14] the Philippine experience suggests such states might not be unitary actors. Rather, an historically based, transnational understanding of such behavior and the domestic conflicts and contingencies out of which it arises is needed. Finally, while neorealist work on interdependence and cooperation is useful, more research is needed to understand the continuing effects of centuries of colonization on the domestic development and external relations not only of formerly colonized but also formerly colonizing states.

American Foreign Policy

The approach to the state as divided, facing ongoing political competition, extends beyond the Philippines to the United States. While officials may agree on the goals of foreign policy, they often disagree on the best means of achieving those goals. For long stretches, such disagreements may play out in congressional hearings, executive debates and other arenas for rebuilding consensus. During crises, however, the disagreements may lead to open conflict if one coalition attempts to redirect policy against the plans of the coalition in control. The Philippine transition in 1986 offers a particularly useful example of such a crisis, given the revolutionary threat to U.S. interests and the conflict between those advocating continued support of Marcos vis-à-vis those advocating moderate change as strategies for managing the revolutionary threat. This conflict, the Philippine story instructs, is deeply rooted in competing strategic and philosophical approaches to protecting U.S. interests abroad. Since the beginning of U.S. expansionism, especially since 1898 and the subsequent war to subdue nationalist opposition in the Philippines, the United States has used "bullets and ballots" to control foreign populations. While the two approaches have sometimes been complementary, they have frequently vied for control of U.S. foreign policy.

This competition plays out in the form of "policy currents"[15] running through the U.S. government, media, business community, foundations, think tanks and academia. These policy currents agree on the goal of defending elite U.S. interests abroad but favor different strategies for containing threats to these interests both at home and abroad. Further, these policy currents are often transnational. In the Philippine case, immigrant, later ethnic, communities of Filipinos and Philippine-Americans have since 1898 worked through the American political system to influence U.S. policy toward the Philippines. For another example of this, American-based Chinese supporting Chiang Kai-shek advanced their cause back home by allying with U.S. Republicans and, via this alliance, played a key role in shaping U.S. policy against Mao in the 1940s and 1950s.[16] This approach to understanding the international sources of U.S. foreign policy is relevant to other countries with large, politically active ethnic communities in the United States. Witness, for example, the Polish influence on policy toward the Soviet Union during the onset of the Cold War or Jewish influence on policy toward Israel since 1948. Ethnic communities will be most likely to try to influence U.S. foreign policy when the U.S. role in their "home" countries is significant. This is expected to increase further when "home" country politics restrict political participation and create large numbers of political refugees who are forced to seek change at home from abroad. Future research might identify the various strategies and their relative effectiveness ethnic communities have used, distinguishing as well between the role played by immigrants and that of ethnic minority citizens with voting privileges.

Other transnational sources of U.S. policy toward the Philippines included a human rights movement that emerged in the 1960s but burgeoned in the early 1970s as a result of the Vietnam War, Watergate and the Chilean coup, and then expanded further in the 1980s amid opposition to U.S. policy in Central America.[17] Not discussed here but also influential in shaping U.S. foreign policy have been the transnational civil rights, women's, nuclear freeze, anti-war, anti- and pro-abortion and environmental movements, among others.[18] In the Philippine case, after 1972, anti-Marcos Filipinos in the United States worked with human rights activists in church and other nongovernmental organizations as well as Congress and, eventually, the State Department to expose the moral flaws in U.S. support for Marcos. This suggests another important source of American foreign policy and bureaucratic conflict. Specifically, during the Carter administration, human rights activists gained a toehold in the foreign policy bureaucracy. Reagan tried in 1981 to rid his administration of the "Carterites"; but enough remained in the bureaucracy with ties to displaced "Carterites" outside of government and to transnational human rights organizations. Together these groups provided enough documentation of human rights violations to challenge the Reagan administration's policies. Thus, the Philippine story adds as well an ideological, societal and transnational dimension to our understanding of foreign policy, building on studies that have emphasized such issues as individual personality, perception and bureaucratic interests as sources of conflict.[19]

In short, although realist strategies have dominated U.S. foreign policy toward the Philippines since 1898, these strategies have consistently been challenged by Philippine opposition, both moderate and revolutionary, and by the ethical and strategic issues such opposition has raised in the United States.

The Media and Foreign Policy

Finally, although it is often difficult to establish a direct impact of the media on foreign policy, research on the topic tends to fall into two camps, from a view of the media as watchdogs with liberal biases who pressure politicians toward reform, as in Vietnam and Watergate, to a view of the media as lapdogs with conservative biases toward guarding the status quo. Politicians and journalists comprise the bulk of analysts in the former category while media critics, leftist analysts[20] and others comprise the bulk of the latter category.[21]

In keeping with the metaphor, the Philippine case, particularly during the 1986 transition, suggests instead a sled team analogy, wherein competing transnational groups cultivated anti- versus pro-Marcos journalists, essentially watchdogs versus lapdogs, to "pull their sleds." Those seeking a transition from Marcos were most effective in leaking information to displaced "Carterites" and other Marcos opponents in the media, and in creating enough attention to the Philippine elections to restrict Marcos' ability to cheat, a point Marcos himself later conceded.[22] Moreover, the Philippine experience indicates that the American media serve as a forum for conflict resolution between competing coalitions, especially during crises. In the Philippine case, the media was particularly effective as an alternative channel of communication for the anti-Marcos coalition in and out of government as it sought to wrest control of Philippine policy from Marcos, Reagan and Reagan's inner circle. When they were no longer being heard via official channels, key members of the coalition leaked information on Marcos and on the inner policy debates to the media in order to discredit Marcos, embarrass Reagan, and so undermine U.S. support of the Marcos regime. In this way, they also helped create political space for a moderate alternative to gain credibility among American officials. Further, as the moderate alternative began to emerge, the American media, with American public relations advisors and campaign strategists, helped redirect Aquino's campaign platform from an initial openness to nationalist critiques of the American bases, toward a more pro-American pledge of support for the bases. In the process, the media also helped define the boundaries within which a new leader might expect to gain American support.

Reinventing the Future

The Philippine experience demonstrates that regime change in contested states is connected to broader conflicts at the level of the international system. This suggests, in turn, that the waves of regime change experienced at different times throughout history are indeed linked outcomes of systemic conflicts and the associated transnational strategies competing groups have used over time.

Viewing nearly a century of U.S. foreign policy and international relations through the prism of the Philippines thus provides an unusual vantage point for re-examining the forces that have shaped our world in the past and are likely to continue to shape it into the future. Indeed, the old maxim that history repeats itself has here been shown to be true—not because of some coincidence or quirk of fate but because when the basic sources of a conflict remain unresolved, the competing interest groups surrounding that conflict will continue to do battle through time. The battles may seem different on the surface, and may well have different outcomes, but the essential nature of the battle will be similar. Further, such battles may seem small, remote, even insignificant, but they can have dramatic and lasting effects throughout the international system. Imagine again Mount Pinatubo—the once unknown volcano, long thought dormant, suddenly exploding with such force that global climate was affected for more than a year. Buried under the volcano's ashes, Clark Air closed, setting in motion the eventual withdrawal of all of the American military bases from Philippine soil. The eruption of Mount Pinatubo provides a useful metaphor for understanding the potential global impact of apparently dormant, unseen and remote civil conflicts abroad. And while global connectedness has been important in the past, it is likely to increase dramatically in coming years as the Internet and other core elements of the so-called Information Revolution intensify globalization of communications, commerce, trade and international as well as transnational interactions in general.

Whatever the future holds, however, the Philippine experience instructs that whether a strategy of repression or reform, bullets or ballots, is used, a state will likely remain contested as long as structural inequality and so the conditions for revolutionary opposition persist.

Notes

1. Despite an American-backed expansion of the Philippine armed forces from 60,000 in 1972 to over 200,000 by 1986, the revolutionary opposition had grown steadily from a few hundred at the outset of martial law to roughly 16,000 regulars, a million active supporters, and a broader base under the leftist umbrella group's National Democratic Front (NDF) estimated at ten million nationwide, or roughly twenty percent of the population.

2. Roberts, Steven, "The Global Village," *New York Times*, 20 February 1986, Section II, p. 8. See also Blitz, "The Press and Foreign Policy."

3. Significant contributions on democratic transitions include Huntington (1991), who helped identify and explain the "third wave" of democratization but overlooked the transnational dimension as well as the historical links to earlier transitions. Also significant is Whitehead's work on American efforts to build democratic institutions abroad. This work describes the conflict with realist strategies but misses the transnational interests, alliances and strategies beyond morality underlying such efforts. See the O'Donnell, Schmitter, and Whitehead (1986) collection. Finally, of particular significance to this work is the O'Donnell and Schmitter essay on Argentina in the same collection. They identify the conflict between hard-liners and soft-liners at the domestic level, a framework extended

here to the United States and the Philippines, and the transnational conflict that evolved over time between similarly oriented groups.

4. Early analysts, notably Gerschenkron (1962), emphasized the effects of the international economy on "late" industrializers, on their greater need for central authority to compete effectively with countries that had industrialized early. Though such transitions may be linked to the international economy, to shocks like OPEC or stages of industrialization, they are not, however, predetermined by it. In more recent analyses, the emphasis moves to the domestic level and the contingencies surrounding authoritarian transitions in Europe in the 1920s and 1930s. This domestic focus becomes problematic in cases conditioned by the Cold War, as in the Chilean transition in 1973. While many analysts have described the American influence in this and other similar transitions elsewhere, more analysis is needed to explain the transnational sources of transitions to authoritarian rule and the impact such transitions have on subsequent political development, particularly attempts to democratize.

5. For a description of the evolution of the literature on this, see for example Herbert Kitschelt's article in the *American Political Science Review* (December 1992) and David Levine's in *World Politics* (April 1988).

6. The "moral" economists include Scott (1976), Wolf (1969) and Migdal (1974), while the political economists include Popkin (1979), Paige (1975), and Bates (1981).

7. Skocpol (1979).

8. Scott (1985).

9. Jones (1989), Kessler (1989), and this author's own field research.

10. See in particular Jones, as corroborated by declassified United States government documents in the National Security Archive collection, and personal interviews with Philippine peasants and with United States Ambassador to the Philippines Stephen Bosworth.

11. See Levy's survey of the literature on the causes of war.

12. Huntington, 76.

13. See, in particular, the collection of essays in Brown, ed. (1996).

14. Walt (1987)

15. Joseph (1981)

16. See Koen (1974) for an excellent analysis of the influence on American foreign policy of Nationalist Chinese during this period.

17. Sikkink (1993).

18. Robinson and Sheehan (1983), Haas (1992).

19. See Jervis (1968), George (1969), and Allison (1972) pieces in the collection edited by Ikenberry.

20. See, for example, Chomsky and Herman (1988), and Bagdikian (1987).

21. Surprisingly little scholarly attention has been given to the influence of the media on foreign policy since Cohen's (1963) watershed analysis of the interaction among American foreign policy officials and journalists, and the influence of this interaction on the foreign policy making process. Almond (1966) argued, like Cohen, that the media most affected public opinion via media "opinion leaders." Linsky (1986) sought to identify

a more direct link between media coverage and policy outcomes, and cited the elite press as a kind of bulletin board for officials to exchange ideas. He found as well that officials in foreign policy spent substantially more time cultivating media coverage than did their counterparts in the rest of government. O'Heffernan (1991) builds on this, to create an "insider's model" wherein the media are used by foreign policy actors in conflict resolution processes.

22. Personal interview with Mydans, February 1989.

References

Interviews

Abrams, Floyd, attorney for the *New York Times* on the Pentagon Papers case, in a lecture at Harvard Law School, November 1989.

Aquino, Corazon, former Philippine President, October 1992.

Asia Foundation source, confidential, November 1993.

Bello, Walden, Executive Director, Institute for Food and Development Policy, November 1993.

Bosworth, Stephen, former U.S. Ambassador to the Philippines, March 1989.

Buscayno, Dante, Tarlac Province Huk leader, later the leader of the New People's Army, lecture following his release from prison, April 1986.

Butcher, Scott, Director, East Asia and Pacific Affairs Bureau, U.S. State Department, December 1994.

Carey, Pete, investigative reporter for the *San Jose Mercury News*, August 1992 and November 1993.

Daughton, Tom, Philippine Desk Officer, State Department, December 1994.

De La Torre, Edicio, revolutionary priest, lecture in April 1993.

D.H. Sawyer source, confidential, May 1993.

Filipino CIA Operative during the Vietnam War, confidential, February 1986.

Gelb, Lesley, former national security correspondent, *New York Times*, March 1989.

Gershman, John, human rights activist and analyst at the Institute for Food and Development Policy, November 1993.

Hoge, Warren, former foreign editor, *New York Times*, March 1989.

Huntington, Samuel, Harvard Professor of Government and personal friend of Benigno Aquino Jr., October 1991.

Karl, Terri Lynn, Stanford Professor of Political Science, November 1993.

Lister, George, long-time State Department human rights analyst, December 1994.

Lugar, Richard, U.S. Senator and former Chairman of the Senate Foreign Relations Committee, April 1993.

Manahan, Manuel, Magsaysay aide during the Huk negotiations, October 1983.

Mydans, Seth, former Philippine correspondent, *New York Times*, March 1989.

Noble, Lela Garner, San Jose State University Professor of Political Science and an expert on Muslim Filipinos, November 1993.

O'Brien, Tom, American Maryknoll priest stationed for many years in the Philippines, December 1985.

Pye, Lucian, M.I.T. Professor of Political Science and personal friend of the Aquino family, August 1992.

RAM Officer, confidential, April 1989.

Schmitter, Philippe, Stanford Professor of Political Science, November 1993.

Schirmer, Daniel, scholar, activist and leader of the U.S.-based Friends of the Filipino People, which has supported Filipino leftists in opposing the presence of U.S. military bases in the Philippines, and other causes, various conversations from April 1986 to August 1994.

Semmel, Andy, foreign policy analyst and aide to Senator Lugar, April 1993.

Sison, Jose Maria, founder of the Philippine Communist Party, lecture following his release from prison, April 1986.

Selected Bibliography

Agency for International Development, *Overseas Loans and Grants and Assistance from International Organizations*, 1961-1988, Special Report Prepared for the House Foreign Affairs Committee, Office of Statistics and Reports, Bureau for Program and Policy Coordination, A.I.D.

Allison, Graham and Morton Halperin, "Bureaucratic Politics: A Paradigm and Some Policy Implications," in Raymond Tanter and Richard Ullman, *Theory and Policy in International Relations*, Princeton University Press, Princeton, NJ, 1972.

Anderson, Benedict, "Cacique Democracy and the Philippines: Origins and Dreams," *New Left Review*, Number 169, May/June 1988.

Aquino, Belinda, ed., *Cronies and Enemies: The Current Philippine Scene*, Philippine Studies Occasional Paper No. 5, Philippine Studies Program, Center for Asian and Pacific Studies, University of Hawaii, Honolulu, Hawaii, 1982.

Bacani, Teodoro C., Bishop, *The Church and Politics*, Claretian Publications, Quezon City, 1987.

Bagdikian, Ben, *The Media Monopoly*, Beacon Press, Boston, MA, 1987.

Bates, Robert H., *Markets and States in Tropical Africa: The Political Bias of Agricultural Policies*, University of California Press, Berkeley and Los Angeles, CA, 1981.

Bello, Walden, David Kinley and Elaine Elinson, *Development Debacle: The World Bank in the Philippines*, Institute for Food and Development Policy and the Philippine Solidarity Network, San Francisco, CA, 1982.

Bello, Walden, "Edging toward the Quagmire: The United States and the Philippine Crisis," *World Policy Journal*, Winter 1985-1986.

Bello, Walden and Severina Rivera, ed., *The Logistics of Repression and Other Essays*, Friends of the Filipino People, Washington, D.C., 1977.

Berry, William E., Jr., *U.S. Bases in the Philippines: The Evolution of the Special Relationship*, Westview Press, Boulder, CO, 1989.

Blair, Emma Helen and Robertson, James Alexander, eds., *The Philippine Islands: 1493-1898*, 55 Vols., A.H. Clark, Cleveland, Ohio, 1903, reprinted by Cachos Hermanos, Mandaluyong, Rizal, 1973.

Blaug, Mark, *Economic Theory in Retrospect: Third Edition*, Cambridge University Press, Cambridge, England, 1978.

Blitz, Amy, "The Press and Foreign Policy: A Case Study of *New York Times* Coverage of the Philippines, 1985-1986, Master's thesis, Massachusetts Institute of Technology, 1990.

Bloomfield, Lincoln, *The Foreign Policy Process: A Modern Primer*, Prentice-Hall, Inc., Englewood Cliffs, NJ, 1982.

Bogardus, Emory S., "The Filipino Press in the United States," *Sociology and Social Research*, Vol. 19, 1934.

Bogardus, Emory S., "American Attitudes Towards Filipinos," *Sociology and Social Research*, Vol. 19, 1934.

Bogardus, Emory S., "Filipino Labor in Central California," *Sociology and Social Research*, Vol. 20, 1935.

Bonner, Raymond, *Waltzing with a Dictator: The Marcoses and the Making of American Policy*, Vintage Books, New York, NY, 1988.

Brands, H.W., *Bound to Empire: The United States and the Philippines*, Oxford University Press, New York, NY and Oxford, England, 1992.

Braudel, Fernand, *Capitalism and Material Life, 1400-1800*, translated from the French by Miriam Kochan, Harper and Row, New York, NY, 1973.

Bresnahan, Roger J., *In Time of Hesitation: American Anti-Imperialists and the Philippine-American War*, New Day Publishers, Quezon City, 1981.

Bresnan, John, ed., *Crisis in the Philippines: The Marcos Era and Beyond*, Princeton University Press, Princeton, NJ, 1986.

Broad, Robin, *Unequal Alliance: The World Bank, the International Monetary Fund, and the Philippines*, University of California Press, Berkeley and Los Angeles, 1988.

Brown, Frederick Z., and Carl Ford, "The Current Situation in the Philippines," Committee on Foreign Relations Report to Congress, September 1984.

Brown, Michael, ed., *The International Dimensions of Civil Conflict*, CSIA Studies in International Security, MIT Press, Cambridge, MA, 1996.

Bulosan, Carlos, *America is in the Heart*, Harcourt, Brace and Company, New York, NY, 1945.

Burton, Sandra, *Impossible Dream: The Marcoses, the Aquinos, the Unfinished Revolution*, Warner Books, New York, 1989.

Buss, Claude A., *Cory Aquino and the People of the Philippines*, Stanford Alumni Association, Palo Alto, CA, 1987.

Carr, Raymond, *Spain: 1808-1975*, Oxford University Press, New York, NY, 1982.

Caspar, Gretchen, "Civil-Military Relations in the Philippines: The Legacy of Authoritarianism for the Aquino Administration," paper presented at the Latin American Studies Association meeting, April 4-6, 1991.

Caspar, Gretchen, "Catholicism and Politics in the Philippines," paper presented at the American Political Science Association conference, September 3-6, 1992.

Cayongcat, Al-Rashid I., *Bangsa Moro People: In Search of Peace*, The Foundation for the Advancement of Islam in the Philippines, Manila, 1986.

Central Intelligence Agency, Office of Current Intelligence, "Significance of the Philippine Elections," OCI No. 1026, November 20, 1953.

Central Intelligence Agency, National Intelligence Survey, NIS 99, "The Philippines," Section 46: Welfare, June 1963.

Chapman, Edward Charles, *A History of Spain*, Free Press, New York, NY, 1965.

Chapman, William, *Inside the Philippine Revolution*, W.W. Norton & Company, New York, NY, 1987.

Chomsky, Noam and Edward Herman, *Manufacturing Consent: The Political Economy of the Mass Media*, Pantheon Books, New York, NY, 1988.

Clarke, H. Butler, *Modern Spain: 1815-1898*, AMS Press, Inc., New York, NY, 1906, reprinted 1969.

Cohen, Bernard, *The Press and Foreign Policy*, Princeton University Press, Princeton, NJ, 1963.

Collier, Ruth Berins and David Collier, *Shaping the Political Arena: Critical Junctures, the Labor Movement, and Regime Dynamics in Latin America*, Princeton University Press, Princeton, NJ, 1991.

Combs, Jerald, *The History of American Foreign Policy*, Alfred A. Knopf Publishers, New York, NY, 1986.

Constantino, Renato, *The Philippines: A Past Revisited*, Renato Constantino, Quezon City, Manila, 1975.

Constantino, Renato and Letizia R., *The Philippines: The Continuing Past*, The Foundation for Nationalist Studies, Quezon City, 1978.

Crabb, Cecil V., Jr. and Pat M. Holt, *Invitation to Struggle: Congress, the President and Foreign Policy*, Congressional Quarterly, Washington, D.C., 1984.

Daniels, Cletus, *Bitter Harvest*, Cornell University Press, Ithaca, NY, 1981.

Daniels, Roger, *Racism in California*, The MacMillan Company, New York, NY, 1972.

Diamond, Larry, Juan J. Linz, and Seymour Martin Lipset, *Democracy in Developing Countries: Volume Three, Asia*, Lynne Rienner Publishers, Boulder, CO, 1989.

Dominguez, Jorge, *Insurrection or Loyalty: The Breakdown of the Spanish American Empire*, Harvard University Press, Cambridge, MA, 1980.

Donnelly, Jack, *Human Rights in Theory and Practice*, Cornell University Press, Ithaca, NY, 1989.

Doty, Roxanne Lynn, *Imperial Encounters*, University of Minnesota Press, Minneapolis, MN, 1996.

Doyle, Michael, *Empires*, Cornell University Press, Ithaca and London, 1986.

"On Escaping the Marcos Embrace," editorial, *New York Times*, 8 August 1985.

Ethier, Diane, ed., *Democratic Transition and Consolidation in Southern Europe, Latin America, and Southeast Asia*, MacMillan Press, Hampshire, 1990.

Evans, Peter, Harold Jacobson, and Robert Putnam, eds., *Double Edged Diplomacy: International Bargaining and Domestic Politics*, University of California Press, Berkeley, CA, 1993.

Fact-Finding Commission, *The Final Report, Pursuant to R.A. No. 6832*, Bookmark, Inc., Manila, 1990.

Farkas, Charles, "Partido Federal: The Policy of Attraction," Bulletin of the American Historical Collection, Manila, October-December 1978.

Farkas, Charles, "Relieving the White Man's Burden: President Wilson and the Philippines," Bulletin of the American Historical Collection, January-March 1978.

Fernandez, Pablo, O.P., *History of the Church in the Philippines (1521-1898)*, National Book Store, Manila, 1979.

Fieldhouse, D.K., *The Colonial Empires: A Comparative Survey from the Eighteenth Century*, Delacorte Press, New York, 1965.

Forsythe, David, *Human Rights and U.S. Foreign Policy*, University Presses of Florida, Gainesville, 1988.

Fox, Jonathan, "The Challenge of Rural Democratisation: Perspectives from Latin America and the Philippines," *Journal of Development Studies*, Vol. 26, No. 4, July 1990.

Francisco, Luzviminda Bartolome and Jonathan Fast, *Conspiracy for Empire: Big Business, Corruption and the Politics of Imperialism in America, 1876-1907*, Foundation for Nationalist Studies, Quezon City, 1985.

Friend, Theodore, *Between Two Empires: The Ordeal of the Philippines, 1929-1946*, Yale University Press, New Haven and London, 1965.

Gaddis, John Lewis, *Strategies of Containment: A Critical Appraisal of Post-war American National Security Policy*, Oxford University Press, New York, NY, 1982.

Gaddis, John Lewis, *The United States and the Origins of the Cold War, 1941-1947*, Columbia University Press, New York, NY, 1972.

Garcia, Ed and Francisco Nemenzo, *The Sovereign Quest: Freedom from Foreign Military Bases*, Claretian Publications, Quezon City, 1988.

Gates, John Morgan, *Schoolbooks and Krags: The United States Army in the Philippines, 1898-1902*, Greenwood Press, Inc., Westport, CT and London, 1973.

Gelb, Lesley, "Marcos Reported to Lose Support in Aministration," *New York Times*, 26 January 1986.

Gerschenkron, Alexander, *Economic Backwardness in Historical Perspective*, Harvard University Press, Cambridge, MA, 1976.

Gitlin, Todd, *The Whole World Is Watching: Mass Media in the Making and Unmaking of the New Left*, University of California Press, Berkeley, CA, 1980.

Gleeck, Lewis E., Jr., *The American Governors-General and High Commissioners in the Philippines: Proconsuls, Nation-Builders, and Politicians*, New Day Publishers, Quezon City, 1986.

Gleeck, Lewis E., Jr., *Americans on the Philippine Frontiers*, Carmelo & Bauermann, Inc., Manila, 1974.

Gourevitch, Peter, "Second Image Reversed: International Sources of Domestic Politics," *International Organization*, Autumn 1978.

Greene, Fred, ed., *The Philippine Bases: Negotiating for the Future, American and Philippine Perspectives*, Council on Foreign Relations, New York, NY, 1988.

Greene, Graham, *The Quiet American*, W. Heinemann, London, England, 1955.

Gregor, A. James and Virgilio Aganon, *The Philippine Bases: U.S. Security at Risk*, Ethics and Public Policy Center, Washington, D.C., 1987.

Grenville, John A.S. and George Berkeley Young, *Politics, Strategy and American Diplomacy: Studies in Foreign Policy, 1873-1917*, Yale University Press, New Haven, CT, 1966.

"The Growing Lobby for Human Rights," *Washington Post*, 12 December 1976.

Guerrero, Amado, *Philippine Society and Revolution: Specific Characteristics of Our People's War*, International Association of Filipino Patriots, Oakland, CA, 1979.

Guillemard, Francis, *Life of Magellan*, Hakluyt Society, London, England, 1890.

Haas, Peter, ed., *Knowledge, Power, and International Policy Coordination*, special issue of *International Organization*, Vol. 46, Winter 1992.

Halle, Louis J., *The United States Acquires the Philippines: Consensus vs. Reality*, University Press of America, Lanham, MD, 1985.

Hawes, Gary, *The Philippine State and the Marcos Regime: The Politics of Export*, Cornell University Press, Ithaca, NY, 1987.

Healy, David, *U.S. Expansionism: The Imperialist Urge in the 1890s*, University of Wisconsin Press, Madison, WI, 1970.

Hirschman, Albert O., "The Rise and Decline of Development Economics," *Essays in Trespassing*, Cambridge University Press, Cambridge, England, 1981.

Hoeffel, Paul Heath and Peter Kornbluh, "The War at Home: Chile's Legacy in the United States," *NACLA Report on the Americas*, Volume 17, September-October 1983.

Huntington, Samuel, *The Third Wave: Democratization in the Late Twentieth Century*, University of Oklahoma Press, Norman and London, 1991.

Hutchcroft, Paul D., "Oligarchs and Cronies in the Philippine State: The Politics of Patrimonial Plunder," *World Politics*, Vol. 43, No. 3, April 1991.

Ibon Data Bank, *Ibon Facts and Figures*, Volumes VII and VIII, Ibon Data Bank Philippines Inc., Manila, Philippines, 1984 and 1985.

Ibon Primer Series, *The Philippine Financial System*, Ibon Databank Phil., Inc., Manila, 1983.

Ikenberry, G. John, *American Foreign Policy: Theoretical Essays*, Scott, Foresman and Co., Glenview, IL, 1989.

Interdepartmental Committee, State, DOD, JCS, USIA, CIA, and AID, "U.S. Overseas Internal Defense Policy," approved as policy by National Security Action Memorandum 182/24, August 1962.

Javate-De Dios, Aurora, Petronilo Daroy, and Lorna Kalaw-Tirol, ed., *Dictatorship and Revolution: Roots of People's Power*, Conspectus Foundation Inc., Quezon City, 1988.

Jenkins, Shirley, *American Economic Policy Toward the Philippines*, Stanford University Press, Stanford, CA, 1954.

Johnson, Bryan, *The Four Days of Courage: The Untold Story of the People Who Brought Marcos Down*, The Free Press, A Division of Macmillan, Inc., New York, NY, 1987.

Jones, Gregg R., *Red Revolution: Inside the Philippine Guerrilla Movement*, Westview Press, Boulder, CO, 1989.

Joseph, Paul, *Cracks in the Empire: State Politics and the Vietnam War*, Columbia University Press, New York, NY, 1981.

Karl, Terri Lynn, "After La Palma: The Prospects for Democratization in El Salvador," *World Policy Journal*, Spring 1985.

Karnow, Stanley, *In Our Image: America's Empire in the Philippines*, Random House, New York, NY, 1989.

Karnow, Stanley, *Vietnam, A History: The First Complete Account of Vietnam at War*, Penguin Books, New York, NY, 1984.

Keck, Margaret and Kathryn Sikkink, "Transnational Issue Networks in International Politics," unpublished, September 16, 1994.

Kennan, George as Mr. X, "The Sources of Soviet Conduct," *Foreign Affairs*, Summer 1947.

Keohane, Robert, *NeoRealism and its Critics*, Columbia University Press, New York, NY, 1986.

Keohane, Robert and Joseph Nye, Jr., eds., *Transnational Relations and World Politics*, Harvard University Press, Cambridge, MA, 1970.

Kerkvliet, Benedict, *The Huk Rebellion: A Study of Peasant Revolt in the Philippines*, University of California Press, Berkeley, 1977.

Kerkvliet, Benedict, and Resil Mojares, *From Marcos to Aquino: Local Perspectives on Political Transition in the Philippines*, University of Hawaii Press, Honolulu, Hawaii, 1991.

Kerkvliet, Benedict, "Contested Meanings of Elections in the Philippines," paper presented at the Conference on Elections in Southeast Asia: Meaning and Practice, Woodrow Wilson International Center, Washington, D.C., September 16-18, 1993.

Kessler, Richard, *Rebellion and Repression in the Philippines*, Yale University Press, New Haven, CT, 1989.

Kindleberger, Charles P., *The World in Depression, 1929-1939*, University of California Press, Berkeley, CA, 1973.

Kirk, Donald, *Looted: The Philippines after the Bases*, St. Martin's Press, New York, NY, 1998.

Kirkpatrick, Jean, "Dictatorships and Double Standards," *Commentary*, November 1979.

Kitschelt, Herbert, "Review Essay: Structure and Process Driven Explanations of Regime Change," *American Political Science Review*, December 1992.

Kline, William E. and James Worthen, CIA Research Fellows at the Kennedy School of Government, "The Fall of Marcos," Harvard University, 1988.

Koen, Ross, *The China Lobby in American Politics*, Harper & Row Publishers, New York, NY, 1974.

Komisar, Lucy, *Corazon Aquino: The Story of a Revolution*, George Braziller, Inc., New York, NY, 1987.

Lachica, Eduardo, *Huk: Philippine Agrarian Society in Revolt*, Solidaridad Publishing House, Manila, 1971.

LaFeber, Walter, *The New Empire: An Interpretation of American Expansion, 1860-1898*, Cornell U. Press, Ithaca, NY, 1963.

Lederer, Jim, *The Ugly American*, W.W. Norton & Company, New York, NY, 1965.

Lee, Henry, *The War Correspondent and the Insurrection: A Study of American Newspaper Correspondents in the Philippines, 1898-1900*, Senior Thesis, Harvard College, Cambridge, MA, 1968.

Levine, Daniel, "Paradigm Lost: Dependency to Democracy," *World Politics*, Vol. XL, No. 3, April 1988.

Levy, Jack S., "The Causes of War: A Review of Theories and Evidence," in *Behavior, Society, and Nuclear War, Vol. I*, edited by Philip E. Tetlock et al., Oxford University Press, New York, NY, 1989.

Linn, Brian McAllister, *The U.S. Army and Counterinsurgency in the Philippine War, 1899–1902*, University of North Carolina Press, Chapel Hill and London, 1989.

Linsky, Martin, *Impact: How the Press Affects Federal Policymaking*, W.W. Norton & Co., New York, NY, 1986.

Linz, Juan J. and Alfred Stepan, ed., *The Breakdown of Democratic Regimes*, Johns Hopkins University Press, Baltimore and London, 1978.

Livermore, Harold, *A History of Spain*, Ruskin House, George Allen and Unwin, Ltd., London, 1958.

Lohr, Steve, "Democracy Gains Steam in the Philippines," *New York Times*, 27 January 1985.

Lohr, Steve, "Impeachment Bill," *New York Times*, 13 August 1985.

Lugar, Richard G., *Letters to the Next President*, Simon and Schuster, New York, NY, 1988.

Madison, Christopher "Foreign Policy: Human Rights—Again," *National Journal*, Vol. 18, May 1, 1982.

Magno, Alexander, "Elections as Political Fulcrum: The Place of Electoral Struggles in Filipino Politics," public speech, London, 1994.

Malefakis, Edward, *Agrarian Reform and Peasant Revolution in Spain: Origins of the Civil War*, Yale University Press, New Haven and London, 1970.

Man, W.K. Che, *Muslim Separatism: The Moros of Southern Philippines and the Malays of Southern Thailand*, Oxford University Press, Singapore, 1990.

Manglapus, Raul, *A Pen for Democracy*, Washington Office, Movement for a Free Philippines, Washington, D.C., 1986.

May, Ernest, *American Imperialism: A Speculative Essay*, Atheneum, New York, NY, 1968.

May, Glenn Anthony, *Social Engineering in the Philippines: The Aims, Execution, and Impact of American Colonial Policy, 1900-1913*, Greenwood Press, Westport, CT and London, England, 1980.

Mayer, Jane and Doyle McManus, *Landslide: The Unmaking of the President, 1984-1988*, Houghton Mifflin Company, Boston, MA, 1988.

McFarlane, Robert C. and Zofia Smardz, *Special Trust*, Cadell & Davies, New York, NY, 1994.

McLane, Charles B., *Soviet Strategies in Southeast Asia: An Exploration of Eastern Policy under Lenin and Stalin*, Princeton University Press, Princeton, NJ, 1966.

McWilliams, Carey, *Factories in the Field: The Story of Migratory Farm Labor in California*, Little, Brown & Co., Boston, MA, 1939.

McWilliams, Carey, *Brothers Under the Skin*, Little, Brown, and Co., Toronto, Canada, 1942.

McWilliams, Carey, *Race Discrimination and the Law*, National Federation for Constitutional Liberties, New York, NY, 1945.

Migdal, Joel, *Peasants, Politics, and Revolution: Pressures toward Political and Social Change in the Third World*, Princeton University Press, Princeton, NJ, 1974.

Mills, Daniel Quinn, *Labor-Management Relations*, McGraw-Hill Book Company, New York, NY, 1986.

Morales, Francisco Lara, Jr., and Horacio Morales, Jr., "The Peasant Movement and the Challenge of Democratisation in the Philippines," *The Journal of Development Studies*, Vol. 26, No. 4, July 1990.

Munro, Ross, "The New Khmer Rouge," *Commentary*, December 1985.

Nadel, George H. and Perry Curtis, *Imperialism and Colonialism*, The Macmillan Company, New York, NY, 1964.

National Security Archive, all declassified U.S. documents from 1965 through 1986, available on microfilm at Harvard University, and more recent, unpublished declassified documents on file at the National Security Archive in Washington, D.C.

National Security Council 84/2, "Statement of Policy Proposed by the National Security Council on the Philippines," November 9, 1950. (from NSA)

National Security Action Memorandum No. 182, "Counterinsurgency Doctrine," The White House, Washington, D.C., August 24, 1962.

Nemenzo, Francisco, "Rectification Process in the Philippine Communist Movement," in Lim Joo-Jock, ed., *Armed Communist Movements in Southeast Asia*, Institute of Southeast Asian Studies, Hampshire, England, 1984.

New York Times, New York, NY, all articles from 1 January 1985 through 28 February 1986. (Articles cited in text are listed by author or title.)

Noble, Lela Garner, "The Philippines: Muslims Fight for an Independent State," *Southeast Asia Chronicle*, No. 75, October 1980.

O'Donnell, Guillermo, Philippe Schmitter and Laurence Whitehead, eds., *Transitions from Authoritarian Rule: Prospects for Democracy*, Johns Hopkins University Press, Baltimore and London, 1986.

Ofreneo, Rene, *Capitalism in Philippine Agriculture*, Foundation for Nationalist Studies, Quezon City, 1980

O'Heffernan, Patrick, *Mass Media and American Foreign Policy: Insider Perspectives on Global Journalism and the Foreign Policy Process*, Ablex Publishing Corporation, Norwood, NJ, 1991.

Paez, Patricia Ann, *The Bases Factor: Realpolitik of RP–US Relations*, Center for Strategic and International Studies of the Philippines, Manila, 1985.

Paige, Jeffrey M., *Agrarian Revolution, Social Movements, and Export Agriculture in the Underdeveloped World*, The Free Press, New York, NY, 1975.

Paredes, Ruby R., ed., *Philippine Colonial Democracy*, Yale University Southeast Asia Studies, New Haven, CT, 1988.

Paterson, Thomas G., J. Garry Clifford, and Kenneth Hagan, *American Foreign Policy: A History to 1914*, D.C. Heath, Lexington, KY, 1983.

Payer, Cheryl, *The World Bank: A Critical Analysis*, Monthly Review Press, New York, NY, 1982.

Phelan, John Leddy, *The Hispanization of the Philippines: Spanish Aims and Filipino Responses, 1565-1700*, University of Wisconsin Press, Madison, WI, 1967.

The Philippine Commission Report to the President, Volumes 1 and 2, Government Printing Office, Washington, D.C., 1900.

Pomeroy, William J., *The Philippines: Colonialism, Collaboration, and Resistance*, International Publishers Co., Inc., New York, NY, 1992.

Pomeroy, William J., *American Neocolonialism: Its Emergence in the Philippines and Asia*, International Publishers, New York, 1970.

Popkin, Samuel L., *The Rational Peasant: The Political Economy of Rural Society in Vietnam*, University of California Press, Berkeley, CA, 1979.

Pringle, Robert, *Indonesia and the Philippines: American Interests in Island Southeast Asia*, Columbia University Press, New York, NY, 1980.

Rand Corporation, Memorandum RM-3652-PR, "Symposium on the Role of Airpower in Counterinsurgency and Unconventional Warfare: The Philippine Huk Campaign," June 1963.

Rizal, Jose, *Noli Me Tangere,* trans. Leon Ma. Guerrero, Longman Group Limited, Quarry Bay, Hong Kong, 1961.

Roberts, Steven, "Investigation of Marcos by Solarz is Issue in United States as well as Manilla," 7 February 1986.

Robinson, Michael J. and Margaret Sheehan, *Over the Wire and on TV*, The Russell Sage Foundation, New York, NY, 1983.

Saito, Hiro, *Filipinos Overseas: Bibliography*, Center for Migration Studies, New York, NY, 1977.

Sand-30 (pseud) "Trench, Parapet, or 'the Open'" *Journal of the Military Service Institution*, July 1902.

Schirmer, Daniel B., *Republic or Empire: American Resistance to the Philippine War*, Schenkman Publishing Co., Cambridge, MA, 1972.

Schirmer, Daniel B. and Stephen Rosskam Shalom, eds., *The Philippines Reader: A History of Colonialism, Neocolonialism, Dictatorship, and Resistance*, South End Press, Boston, MA, 1987.

Schoultz, Lars, *Human Rights and United States Policy toward Latin America*, Princeton University Press, Princeton, NJ, 1981.

Schudson, Michael, *Discovering the News: A Social History of American Newspapers*, Basic Books, Inc., New York, 1978.

Schumacher, John N., S.J., *Readings in Philippine Church History*, Ateneo de Manila University Press, Manila, 1979.

Schumacher, John N., S.J., *Revolutionary Clergy: The Filipino Clergy and the Nationalist Movement, 1850-1903*, Ateneo de Manila University Press, Manila, 1981.

Scott, James, *The Moral Economy of the Peasant*, Yale University Press, New Haven, CT, 1976.

Scott, James, *Weapons of the Weak: Everyday Forms of Peasant Resistance*, Yale University Press, New Haven, CT, 1985.

Selochan, Viberto, "The Armed Forces of the Philippines: Its Perceptions on Governing and the Prospects for the Future," Working Paper, Strategic and Defense Studies Centre, Research School of Pacific Studies, The Australian National University, 1988.

Shalom, Stephen, *The United States and the Philippines: A Study of Neo-Colonialism*, Institute for the Study of Human Issues, Philadelphia, 1981.

Shafer, D. Michael, *Deadly Paradigms: The Failure of U.S. Counterinsurgency Policy*, Princeton University Press, Princeton, NJ, 1988.

Shultz, George P., *Turmoil and Triumph: My Years as Secretary of State*, Charles Scribner's Sons, New York, NY, 1993.

Sikkink, Kathryn, "Human Rights, Principled Issue-Networks, and Sovereignty in Latin America," *International Organization*, Volume 47, No. 3, Summer 1993.

Simons, Lewis, *Worth Dying For*, William Morrow and Company, Inc., New York, NY, 1987.

Skocpol, Theda, *States and Social Revolutions*, Cambridge University Press, New York, NY, 1979.

Smith, Hedrick, *The Power Game: How Washington Works*, Random House, New York, NY, 1988.

Smith, James Burkholder, *Portrait of a Cold Warrior*, G. P. Putnam's Sons, New York, NY, 1976.

Snyder, Richard, "Explaining Transitions from Neopatrimonial Dictatorships," *Comparative Politics*, Vol. 24, No. 4, July 1992.

Speakes, Larry, *Speaking Out*, Avon Books, New York, NY, 1988.

Stanley, Peter W., ed., *Reappraising an Empire: New Perspectives on Philippine–American History*, Harvard University Press, Cambridge, MA, 1984.

Stepan, Alfred, *Rethinking Military Politics: Brazil and the Southern Cone*, Princeton University Press, Princeton, NJ, 1988.

Sussman, Gerald, David O'Connor, and Charles W. Lindsey, "The Philippines, 1984: The Political Economy of a Dying Dictatorship," *Philippine Research Bulletin*, Friends of the Filipino People, Durham, NC, Summer 1984.

Swanson, David L. and Dan Nimmo, *New Directions in Political Communication: A Resource Book*, Sage Publications, Inc., Newbury Park, CA, 1990.

Taruc, Luis, *Born of the People*, Greenwood Press, Westport, CT, 1973, c1953.

Thompson, Mark, *Democratic Opposition to "Sultanistic" Rule: The Anti-Marcos Struggle and the Troubled Transition in the Philippines*, Ph.D. diss., July 1993, and forthcoming from Yale University Press.

Trumbell, Robert, "U.S. Plans for Guam Run into Snags," *New York Times*, 21 April 1985.

U.S. Congressional Documents Prepared for Hearings before the Committee on Foreign Relations and the Subcommittee on East Asian and Pacific Affairs.

U.S. Department of the Army General Staff, "Intelligence Research Report: The Philippine Constabulary," Project No. 7557, December 15, 1952.

U.S. Department of State, unpublished historical overview of the Bureau of Human Rights and Humanitarian Affairs, now called the Bureau of Democracy, Human Rights and Labor, prepared by Margaret F. Gourlay, Office of the Historian, March 1984.

U.S. Government Document, The Election Law, Manila Bureau of Printing, 1907, reproduced at the National Archives, Maryland.

"U.S. Official Prods Manila," *New York Times*, 23 February 1985.

U.S. Senate Committee on Foreign Relations, *Korea and the Philippines: November 1972*, Committee Print, 93rd Congress, 1st session, February 18, 1973.

Vives, Jaime Vicens, *An Economic History of Spain*, Princeton University Press, Princeton, NJ, 1969.

"Votes in Congress," *New York Times*, 19 May 1985.

Walt, Stephen, *The Origins of Alliances*, Cornell University Press, Ithaca, NY, 1987.

Waltz, Kenneth, *Man, the State, and War*, Columbia University Press, New York, 1979.

Whiting, Allen, *China Crosses the Yalu: The Decision to Enter the Korean War*, Macmillan, New York, NY, 1960.

Wilkie, James W. and Albert L. Michaels, *Revolution in Mexico: Years of Upheaval, 1910-1940*, Alfred A. Knopf, New York, NY, 1969.

Wolf, Eric R., *Peasant Wars of the Twentieth Century*, Harper & Row, New York, NY, 1969.

Worcester, Dean C., "The Non-Christian Peoples of the Philippine Islands, With an Account of What Has Been Done for Them under American Rule," The National Geographic Magazine, Vol. XXIV, Washington, D.C., November 1913.

Wurfel, David, *Filipino Politics: Development and Decay*, Cornell University Press, Ithaca, NY, 1988.

Yearbook of International Organizations, 1980 and 1990.

Youngblood, Robert L., *Marcos Against the Church: Economic Development and Political Repression in the Philippines*, Cornell University Press, Ithaca, NY, 1990.

Yu, Rolando and Mario Bolasco, *Church–State Relations*, St. Scholastica's College, Manila, RP, 1981.

Index

Abramowitz, Morton, 168
Abrams, Creighton, 148n35
Abrams, Elliott, 139-40
Acheson, Dean, 88, 92
ACRONYM (Anti-Cronyism Movement), 171
Agrava Commission, 161, 164
Agrava, Corazon, 161
Aguinaldo, Emilio, 15-16, 21-23, 33-36, 40, 67
Aldrich, Nelson, 46
Ali, Muhammad, 128
Allende, Salvador, 124
allies, and regime transitions, 4-5
American Chamber of Commerce, and martial law, 109
American Communist Party (CPUSA), 62, 68, 89
Amnesty International, 119, 124, 128, 140-41
Anti-Cronyism Movement (ACRONYM), 171

Anti-Imperialist League, 24, 34-35
anti-imperialists, 16-21
Anti-Martial Law Coalition (Philippines), 141
April 6 Movement, 137-38
Aquino, Benigno, 67
Aquino, Benigno, Jr. "Ninoy": arrest and imprisonment of, 118-19, 126-29, 132; assassination of. *See* assassination of Aquino; expatriation to U.S., 137; and Huks, 106, 148n53; and martial law, 107-8; and Taruc, 94; transnational politics and, 126-29
Aquino, Corazon, 121, 129, 132, 137, 158; election of, 171-82; transition to era of, 157-91; and transnational politics, 126-27
Aquino, Kris, 132
Aquino, Lupita, 127, 144
Armacost, Michael, 143, 158, 161, 165, 169-70, 173
Armas, Carlos Castillo, 95

227

Armitage, Richard, 161, 165, 167, 169-70
Asia Foundation, 91, 167, 175
Asia, U.S. foreign policy and, 95-99
assassination of Aquino, 118, 144-45;
    investigation of, 165-66; public
    response to, 158-60; U.S. response
    to, 160-62
Atkinson, Fred, 44
ATOM (August Twenty-One Movement),
    171
atomic weapons, 73, 86, 104
August Twenty-One Movement (ATOM),
    171
authoritarian groups: and allies, 4-5; on
    bullets vs. ballots, 4; factors
    affecting, 5-6; United States and, 136
authoritarian rule in Philippines, 117-55;
    end of, 157-91; transnational politics
    and, 198-200
Ayala family, 68

Bao Dai, emperor of Vietnam, 96
Barrio United Defense Corps (BUDC),
    69-70
Barrows, David, 44
Bataan, 66-67
BAYAN, 172, 176
Bay of Pigs invasion, 99
Beecher, William, 123
Bell, Daniel, 88
Bell, Franklin, 42
Bell, Jasper, 71
Bello, Walden, 124-25, 167, 174
Bell Trade Act, 71-72, 76-77; renegotiation
    of, 96-97
Benedicto, Roberto, 143
Blair, William, 104
bombings in Manila, 107-8
Bonaparte, Joseph, 13
Bonaparte, Napoleon, 13, 17
Bonifacio, Andrews, 15-16
Bonker, Donald, 140
boondocks, definition of, 34
Bosworth, Stephen, 159, 162, 170, 173,
    176-78
Bradley, Bill, 172
Brinkley, David, 170, 176

Britain, 11-12, 72, 84
Brown, Frederick, 163, 169
Bryan, William Jennings, 25, 35, 40, 48
BUDC. *See* Barrio United Defense Corps
Bundy, McGeorge, 100
Burgos, Jose, 14
Burke, Yvonne, 134
Burton, Sandra, 144
Buscayno, Dante, 106, 148n53
Bush, George, 139, 160
business community: and Marcos' hidden
    wealth, 167-71; opposition by, 160;
    and U.S. policy, 18-19
Byrnes, James F., 73
Byroade, Henry, 107-8

cacique, 9; definition of, 27n12
California, 8; Filipinos in, 60-62, 102, 168
Calosa, Pedro, 60
Cambodia, 123-24
Cam Ranh Bay, 136
carabaos, 43
Carey, Pete, 168
Carnegie, Andrew, 18, 24, 34
Carter, Jimmy, 129-36
Casey, William, 122, 163, 165-66, 168
Castillo, Mateo del, 87
Castro, Fidel, 98-99
Castro, Pacifico, 174
Catholic Bishops Conference of the
    Philippines (CBCP), 120
Catholic church: and authoritarian forces,
    13; in El Salvador, 135, 138; and
    Marcos, 119-20, 132-33, 143, 166-
    67, 177, 179; and Spanish, 6, 10, 12-
    14; and United States, 45-46, 55n61
CBCP (Catholic Bishops Conference of
    the Philippines), 120
CEA (Civilian Emergency Administra-
    tion), 68
Center for Democracy, 172-73
Central Intelligence Agency (CIA), 87-88,
    93-94, 97, 112n62, 131, 174
Chaffee, Adna R., 42
Chamorro, Pedro Joaquin, 135
Charles III, king of Spain, 12
Charles V, king of Spain, 7, 9

Chiang Kai-shek, 72-73, 85-86
Childress, Richard, 161
Chile, 124-25
China, 17, 66, 85-86, 97, 136
Chinese in Philippines, 11-13, 23, 68, 88, 99
Christopher, Warren, 150n72
Churchill, Winston, 72
CIA. *See* Central Intelligence Agency
Citizens' Assemblies, 120
Civilian Emergency Administration (CEA), 68
civil war, causes of, 207-9
Clark Air Force Base, 57-58, 66, 102, 104, 170, 181; Aquino and, 171-73; and Korean War, 89; lease on, 83, 128, 134
Clarke, James, 49-50
Cleveland, Grover, 18, 24, 34
Cojuangco, Eduardo, Jr., 109, 121-22
Cold War, 81-116; seeds of, 72-74
Collins, Robert, 34
Colorums, 59-60
COMELEC, 172-73, 176
Committee for Free Asia, 91
commonwealth status, 62-65
communism: and Aquino, Corozon, 171-72; in China, 85-86, 97; in Philippines, 62; and U.S. foreign policy, 81-116, 118, 162-65
Communist Party of the Philippines (CPP), 106, 132
Concepcion, Jose, Jr., 170
Confederation of Mexican Labor Unions, 61
confetti revolution, 160
Congress: and human rights, 124-26; and Marcos, 171,
containment, 85, 88-89
Cooper Act, 45
Corregidor Island, 66-67
corruption: in elections, 87-88, 94, 103, 106; Marcos and, 109, 161; in military, 91, 121; Sin on, 141; in World Bank, 141
Cortes, Hernan, 9
counter-insurgency, 99-102
CPP. *See* Communist Party of the Philippines

CPUSA. *See* American Communist Party
Cranston, Alan, 172
cronyism, 142-45, 159
Crowe, William, 163, 166
Cuba, 16, 19-20, 23, 98-99
Cuenca, Rodolfo, 143
Czolgosz, Leon F., 42

Dee, Dewey, 143
democracy in Philippines, 81-116; faith in, 91, 162; reestablishment of, 157-91; road to, 57-80; transnational politics and, 200-203
Democratic Alliance, 71, 74
democratic groups/institutions: factors affecting, 5-6; U.S., in Philippines, 41-43
Denby, Charles, 36-38
Derian, Patricia, 130-31
Dewey, George, 16-17, 21, 36
Disini, Herminio, 122, 143
Drinan, Robert, 119, 134
Dulles, Allen, 94-95
Dulles, John Foster, 92-93, 95-96

Eastern Construction Company, 97
education, 44
Eisenhower, Dwight, 65, 83, 92-96
Eliot, Charles, 24
Elizalde family, 68
Ellsberg, Daniel, 123
El Salvador, 135, 138, 153n124
encomienda system, 9-10
Enrile, Juan Ponce, 106-9, 121, 131, 134, 140, 143, 170, 178-79
expansionists, 16-21
Export-Import Bank, 143

fascism in Philippines, 68
Federalista Party, 40-41
Feleo, Juan, 87
Ferdinand VII, king of Spain, 13-14
Filipinos: in California, 60-62, 102, 168; in colonial government, 45; definition of, 26n6; in Hawaii, 102
First Quarter Storm, 106
Forbes, Cameron, 46, 48

Ford, Carl, 163
Ford, Gerald, 125, 127
Fordham University, 92
Foreign Assistance Act, 125, 129
France, 13, 89, 95
Franco, Francisco, 68
Fraser, Donald, 124, 127, 130
Freedom Company, 97
Friar Lands Act, 55n61
Frye, senator, 35
Fulbright, William, 109
Funston, Frederick, 35, 41

galleon trade, 10-13
Ganaps, 67
Garcia, Carlos, 98
Gelb, Leslie, 123, 174
Geneva Conference, 95
George, Harrison, 62
Germany, 58, 72
Gomez, Mariano, 14
Grayson, William, 32
Green Berets, 100
Greene, Francis, 22
Greene, Graham, 89
Guam, 23, 25
Guatemala, 95
Guzman, Jacobo Arbenz, 95

Habib, Philip, 128, 142, 178
haciendas, 12
Haig, Alexander, 141-42
Haldeman, H. R., 123
Hall, Tony, 135
hard-liners, 39; and 1980 U.S. elections, 136-
    38; and Cold War, 84, 86; effects of,
    117-18, 159, 165; and Marcos, 168-69;
    and martial law, 129; and Philippine–
    American War, 31-32; Roosevelt and,
    42; on Vietnam War, 126
Hare–Hawes–Cutting Act, 63
Harkin, Tom, 125
Harriman, E. H., 44
Harrison, Benjamin, 18
Harrison, Francis, 48-50
Harvard, 137
Havemeyer, Henry, 45

Hawaii, 18, 25
Hawes, Harry, 63
Hayden, Joseph Ralston, 74
Hearst, William Randolph, 20
Herrera, Trinidad, 130-31
Hirohito, emperor of Japan, 73
Hiroshima, 73
Hiss, Alger, 86, 88
history, study of, and regime transitions, 2
Hoar, George Frisbie, 24, 34, 42
Hobbes, Leland, 89
Ho Chi Minh, 95
Hoge, Warren, 171
Holbrooke, Richard, 130-31, 134, 150n72
Holdridge, John, 109
Holland, 11
Hoover, Herbert, 62-63
Hoover, J. Edgar, 123
House Committee on Un-American
    Activities, 86
Huerta, Victoriano, 56n73
Huks: and elections of 1946, 76;
    Marcos and, 106; and military
    bases, 84; and postwar administra-
    tion, 70-71, 74; United States and,
    69-71, 74, 87-93; in World War II,
    68-70
Humabon, 6-7
human rights: Carter and, 129-37; Catholic
    church and, 119-20; Congress and,
    124-26; Marcos and, 128, 140-43; and
    transnational politics, 126-29, 144
Humphrey, Hubert, 103
Huntington, Samuel, 137
Hutchinson, Walter, 76

Ickes, Harold, 74
IDA. *See* International Development
    Association
Ide, Henry, 39
ilustrados, 15; and Federalista Party, 41;
    and Philippine–American War, 36;
    and Schurman Commission, 37
Immigration Act, 60
Indochina, 89, 95-99, 124
Inouye, Daniel, 109, 134
Insular Police Force, 42, 58

International Development Association (IDA), 131-32
International Monetary Fund, 160
Intramuros, 22
Iran, 93

James, William, 34
Japan, 17, 62, 73, 75; in Philippines, 66-72, 76n23-24, 79n26; United States and, 58, 64-66
Javier, Evelio, 177
John Paul II, pope, 138, 140-41
Johnson, Henry, 24
Johnson, Lyndon B., 101-3
Joint U.S. Military Advisory Group (JUSMAG), 84
Jones Act, 31, 49-50; transnational politics and, 50-52
Jones, Robert Trent, Jr., 127, 172
Jones, William Atkinson, 49
JUSMAG (Joint U.S. Military Advisory Group), 84

Kalibapi, 67
Kaplan, Gabriel, 91
Karnow, Stanley, 163, 178
Kashiwahara, Ken, 144
Katipunan, 15, 36
Kattenberg, Paul, 127-28
Katubusan ng Bayan (Redemption of the People), 69
KBL (Kilusang Bagong Lipunan), 139
Kennan, George, 82, 85
Kennedy, John F., 99-101
Kerry, John, 167, 173, 175
Khanh, Nguyen, 101
Khomeini, Ayatollah Ruhollah, 135
Kilusang Bagong Lipunan (KBL), 139
King, Martin Luther, Jr., 105
Kirkpatrick Doctrine, 136, 138-40, 164
Kirkpatrick, Jeane, 136
Kissinger, Henry, 85, 123-25, 128-29
Koppel, Ted, 175
Korea, 88-89, 92, 95

Laban, 171-76
Lakas ng Bayan Party, 132

Lamadrid, sergeant, 14
land distribution: Huks and, 70; Magsaysay and, 90; National Democratic Front and, 159; Spain and, 8; United States and, 45-46, 64; in Vietnam, 97-98
Langley, James, 96
Lansdale, Edward, 89-92, 94, 97, 168
Lapu Lapu, 6-7
Laurel, Jose, 67, 87, 96-97, 102
Laurel–Langley Agreement, 96-97
Laurel, Salvador, 139, 171
Laurie, Jim, 144
Lawyers Committee for International Human Rights, 140
Laxalt, Paul, 169, 171, 181
Lefever, Ernest, 139
Legazpi, Miguel Lopez de, 7-9
Leo XIII, pope, 45
Liberal Party, 76, 87, 107, 119
Liga Filipina, 15
"Light A Fire Movement," 133
Lister, George, 139
Lodge, Henry Cabot, 19, 23, 25
Long, John, 21
Lopez, Eugenio, Jr., 122
Lopez, Fernando, 102
Lord, Wilston, 127
Lugar, Richard, 163, 170, 175

Macabebes, 9-11, 25, 33, 41-42
Macapagal, Diosdado, 98-99, 101-2, 135
MacArthur, Arthur: and Philippine–American War, 22, 33, 35, 42; and Taft Commission, 39-40
MacArthur, Douglas, 62, 64-65; and postwar policy, 74, 89; in World War II, 66, 70
Madison, James, 17
Magellan, Ferdinand, 6-7
Magsaysay, Ramon, 90-91, 98; and Bell Trade Act, 96-97; Eisenhower and, 93-95
Mahan, Alfred, 18
Maisto, John, 165, 168
Manahan, Manuel, 94
Manchuria, 62

Manglapus, Raul, 119, 137, 161
Manila Falange, 68
Manila Pact, 96
Mansfield, Mike, 109, 131
Mao Zedong, 72, 85, 106
Mara, Ernesto, 103
Marcos, Ferdinand, 99; assassination
    attempts on, 107; authoritarian rule
    by, 117-55; election of, 102-5, 176-
    78; hidden wealth of, 167-71; and
    human rights, 128, 140-43; institu-
    tion of martial law, 106-10; and
    Reagan, 169-70, 180-81; transition to
    authoritarian rule by, 81-116;
    unseating of, 157-91; U.S. foreign
    policy and, 165-67; and Vietnam,
    101; visits to United States, 103-4,
    142-43
Marcos, Imelda, 102-3, 122, 134, 142-43,
    181
Maria Cristina, queen of Spain, 16
Marshall, George C., 85
martial law in Philippines, 117-55; lifting
    of, 138; transition to, 106-10; United
    States and, 109-10
McCarran Internal Security Act, 89
McCarthy, Eugene, 105
McCarthy, Joseph, 86
McDuffie, John, 63
McFarlane, Robert, 166
McIntyre, Frank, 56n78
McKinley, William, 19-20, 25; assassina-
    tion of, 42; and Philippine–American
    War, 32-34; and Schurman Commis-
    sion, 36-37; and Taft Commission,
    38-40
McLane, James, 127
McNamara, Robert, 105, 109
McNutt, Paul, 75-76, 83
media: Aquino and, 126-27, 171-72; CIA
    and, 94; and elections, 170, 175-76;
    and hidden wealth, 168; Magsaysay
    and, 92; Marcos and, 103, 133, 175,
    177, 180; and martial law, 109; and
    Ninoy Aquino, 144; and papal visit,
    141; and Philippine–American War,
    34-35, 53n9; and transnational

politics, 210-11; and Vietnam, 105;
    and World War II, 66
Meet the Press, 180
Melby, John, 88
Melchor, Alejandro, 109, 181
Merchant, Livingston, 90
messiah movements, 59-60
Metcalf, Wilder, 32
Metropolitan Area Command, 108
Metzenbaum, Howard, 136
Mexicans in California, 61
Mexico, 8, 17; revolution in, 48, 56n73
middle class, politicization of, 158
Miller, Orville, 32
Mitra, Ramon, 164
MNLF. *See* Moro National Liberation Front
moderates: and 1985 election, 171-76; and
    Catholic church, 120, 166; and
    revolutionaries, 119, 144, 159, 177
Mondale, Walter, 133-34, 164
Moorer, Thomas, 109
Morales, Horacio, 153n126
More Flags crusade, 103-4
Morgan, J. P., 44
Moro National Liberation Front (MNLF),
    128, 149n60
Moses, Bernard, 39
Mossadegh, Mohammed, 93
Movement for a Free Philippines, 119, 161
Munro, Ross, 173
Murkowski, Frank, 175
Murphy, Richard, 134
Muslims in Philippines, 106-7, 128, 140,
    149n60
Mutual Defense Treaty, 92, 95
Mydans, Seth, 171, 176

Nach, James, 162-63, 165
Nacionalista Party, 47-49, 67, 76; Marcos
    and, 99, 106-7
Nagasaki, 73
NAMFREL. *See* National Committee for
    Free Elections
National Assembly, 120
National Committee for Free Elections
    (NAMFREL), 91, 94, 162, 170,
    172-73, 175

National Committee for the Restoration of Civil Liberties, 125
National Democratic Front, 138, 153n126, 159
National Security Council, 88
Natzke, Herbert, 131
Naval War College, 58
New People's Army (NPA), 106, 118, 127, 159, 173; growth of, 162-65
New Society Party, 132
Newsom, David, 131
New York Times, 109, 123-24, 133, 153n124, 165-66, 170-71, 174, 176-77
Ngo Dinh Diem, 93, 95-98
Nicaragua, 135, 164
Niehaus, Marjorie, 168-69
Nitze, Paul, 88
Nixon, Richard, 86, 92, 99, 105, 123-26; and Marcos, 107, 120
noise barrage, 132, 137
North Korea, 88-89
NPA. *See* New People's Army
Nunn, Sam, 172

Olaguer, Eduardo, 133
oligarchy: and Japanese, 67; and Marcos, 122-23; and opposition, 143
opposition: and 1985 elections, 170; authoritarianism and, 122-23; to Marcos, 108-9, 121, 143, 159-67, 177; to Spanish rule, 12; in United States, 42-43
Orange Plan, 58, 65
Organic Act, 45
Osmena, Sergio, 47, 62-63, 70, 74, 76, 107
Otis, Elwell, 32-35, 37
Overholt, William, 168-69

Pahlavi, Mohammad Reza, Shah of Iran, 93
Paris Peace Treaty, 23, 32, 46
Partido Progresista, 47
Payne–Aldrich Act, 46-47
Payne, Sereno, 46
peasant revolts, 64: in China, 86; in Vietnam, 97-98. *See also* Huks

Pell, Claiborne, 173
Pentagon Papers, 123-24
Philip II, king of Spain, 7-8
Philippine–American War, 16, 21-26, 31-43
Philippine Central Bank, 160
Philippine Communist Party (PKP), 62, 87, 98; and Huks, 68-69, 106
Philippine Constabulary, 58
Philippine economy: Korean War and, 97; Marcos' hidden wealth and, 167-71; Marcos years and, 159-60, 165; in Spanish colonial era, 8-9; U.S. conquest and, 44-45; World War I and, 59; World War II and, 88
Philippine elections: 1907, 47; 1961, 99; 1971, 106; 1978, 132-33; 1981, 138-39; 1984, 162; 1985, 170-76; fraud in, 87-88, 94, 103, 106, 132-33; MacArthur and, 75-76
Philippine independence, 75-77; before Marcos, 81-116; transnational politics and, 196-98
Philippine military, 64-65, 91, 140; and Aquino, 181; and Marcos, 108, 121, 178-79;and opposition, 143, 159; reform of, 166-67
Philippine nationalism, 15-16
Philippine News, 119, 122
Philippines: Cold War and, 72-74, 81-116; as commonwealth, 62-65; constitution of, 64, 71, 106, 120; flag of, 77; naming of, 7; Spanish colonialism in, 6-29; and Vietnam War, 101, 103-4; and World War I, 57-59; and World War II, 66-72. *See also* U.S.–Philippine relations
Philippine Security Council, 132
Philippine Solidarity Network, 141
Pigafetta, Antonio, 6
PKP. *See* Philippine Communist Party
Poindexter, John, 173
political approaches, versus military, 74
Pomeroy, William J., 93
Portugal, 7
Potsdam Conference, 73
Psinakis, Steve, 137

Puerto Rico, 23, 25
Pye, Lucian, 137

Qaddafi, Muammar, 128, 149n60
Quemoy-Matsu crisis, 97
Quezon, Manuel, 47-50, 56n78, 75; and
    commonwealth, 62-64, 66; and
    World War II, 67-68
Quirino, Elpidio, 87-89, 91, 94

Radio Veritas, 167, 179-80
RAM. See Reform the Armed Forces
    Movement
Ramos, Benigno, 67
Ramos, Fidel, 109, 121, 129, 134, 140,
    164, 179-80
Reagan, Ronald: and assassination of
    Aquino, 160-61; election of, 136-38,
    164; and foreign policy, 138-40; and
    Marcos, 142-43, 164-65, 168-70,
    175-77, 180-81
Recollects, 14
reconcentrado policy, 19-20
Recto, Claro, 97
Redfield, William, 48
reformist groups, 4-5
Reform the Armed Forces Movement
    (RAM), 166-67, 178-79
Regan, Donald, 165, 168
regime transitions, 1-2, 204-5; effects of,
    6; future of, 211-12; historical
    contexts of, 4; transnational politics
    and, 3-6, 193-214
Remington, Frederic, 20
revolutionary groups: factors affecting, 5-
    6; martial law and, 119; and
    transnational politics, 59-62, 205-7
Rizal, Jose, 15-16
ROAR (Running Organization for Aquino
    and Reconciliation), 171
Rogers, William, 125
"Rolex Twelve," 109
Romero, Oscar, 135
Romualdez, Benjamin "Kokoy," 122, 142
Romulo, Carlos, 67, 129, 131
Roosevelt, Franklin D., 62-65, 70, 72
Roosevelt, Theodore, 19, 21, 23, 25, 42, 58

Root, Elihu, 34, 39
Rosenthal, A. M., 171
Roxas, Manuel, 62-63, 75-77, 83-84, 87
Running Organization for Aquino and
    Reconciliation (ROAR), 171
Russia, 59
Ryan, Leo, 134

Sakdalistas, 64
salvagings, 117, 159
Salzberg, John, 150n72
Samar massacre, 42-43, 141
Sandanistas, 135
Sandiko, Teodoro, 49
San Jose Mercury News, 167
Santayana, George, 24, 34
Schurman Commission, 36-38
SDS (Students for a Democratic Society),
    105
SEATO (Southeast Asia Treaty Organiza-
    tion), 96
Sedition Law, 42
Senate Foreign Relations Committee, 167,
    170-73
Sheinbaum, Gilbert, 142
Shultz, George, 142, 161, 166, 173, 175, 180
Sigur, Gaston, 161
Simons, Lew, 168
Sin, cardinal, 120, 133, 141, 158, 171, 179
Sison, Jose Marie, 106
Smith, Joseph Burkholder, 98
Social Justic Program, 64
soft-liners, 39; and conquest, 36-38; and
    Philippine–American War, 31-32; on
    Vietnam War, 126
Solarz, Stephen, 141, 169-70, 176
Soriano family, 68
South Africa, 139-40
Southeast Asia Treaty Organization
    (SEATO), 96
South Korea, 89
South Vietnam, 93, 97
Soviet Union, 59, 72; and Cuba, 98-99;
    and Vietnam, 136. See also Cold War
Spain: and Cuba, 19-20; pressures on, 11-
    14; relations with Philippines, 1-29,
    46, 193-96; United States and, 17

Spanish–American War, 20-26
Spooner bill, 38-39, 41
Spooner, John, 38
Stalin, Joseph, 72
Stark, Fortney, 134
state capitalism in Philippines, 142-45, 159
State Department: purge of, 93; and
    Reagan administration, 165, 173-77
Stimson, Henry, 62, 73
Stonehill, Harry, 99
Students for a Democratic Society (SDS),
    105
Subcommittee on Human Rights and
    International Organizations, 124
Subic Bay naval station, 57-58, 66, 102,
    104, 170; Aquino and, 171-73; lease
    on, 83, 128, 134
Sullivan, William, 128
Symington, Stuart, 104
Synod of Manila, 10

Taft Commission, 38-41
Taft, William Howard, 39-41, 56n73; as
    governor of Philippines, 42, 44-47
Taiwan, 86
Tajika, Togo, 144
Taruc, Luis, 68, 70, 87, 94
Task Force Detainees of the Philippines, 159
Tavera, Pardo de, 41
Teller, Henry, 20
Tet Offensive, 105
Thomasites, 44
Thorpe, Claude, 69
Tolentino, Arturo, 174
Tonkin Gulf Resolution, 101
transnational, definition of, 26n1
transnational politics, 3-6, 193-214; and
    Aquino, Corazon, 182-84; and
    authoritarian rule, 198-200; and
    commonwealth status, 62-65;
    counter-insurgency policy, 100; and
    democracy, 200-203; future of,
    211-12; Huks and, 90-93; human
    rights lobby and, 126-29, 144; and
    independence, 196-98; and Jones Act,
    50-52; practical/theoretical
    implications of, 203-12; revolutionary

groups and, 59-62; and U.S. conquest,
    193-96
Truman Doctrine, 83-85
Truman, Harry S., 72-75, 77, 83, 89, 92
trusts, and U.S. policy, 18-19
Tupas, 7-8
Twain, Mark, 24, 34
"Twelve Apostles," 109
Tydings–McDuffie bill, 63-64
Tydings, Millard, 63, 71-72

Ueda, Katsuo, 144
Underwood-Simmons Act, 47
UNIDO. *See* United Nationalist Demo-
    cratic Organization
United Fruit Company, 95
United Nationalist Democratic Organiza-
    tion (UNIDO), 139, 171
United States: and Huks, 69-71, 74, 87-93;
    and Japan, 58, 66; and martial law,
    109-10; post-World War II, 71-74;
    and Spain, 17; and World War I, 57-
    59; and World War II, 66-72
Urdaneta, Andres de, 7-8
U.S. economy, 46-47
U.S. foreign policy: anti-imperialists vs.
    expansionists and, 16-21; on Asia, 95-
    99; communism and, 81-116, 118,
    162-65; on containment, 85, 88-89; on
    counter-insurgency, 99-102; debate
    on, 176-79; Eisenhower and, 93-95;
    human rights concerns and, 124-26,
    140-42, 144; Kirkpatrick Doctrine
    and, 136, 138-40; media and, 210-11;
    new direction in, 165-67; and
    revolution, 159; transnational politics
    and, 209-10; Watergate and, 123-26
U.S. military: Cold War and, 82; in
    Philippines, 41-43, 57-59, 65-66, 83;
    versus political approaches, 74
U.S.–Philippine relations: assassination of
    Aquino and, 160-62; conquest, 16,
    21-26, 31-43; early colonialism, 31-
    56, 193-96; economic aid, 88, 120-
    21, 129, 131-32, 143, 167-71; late
    colonialism, 57-80; Spanish
    colonialism and, 1-29

U.S. presidential elections: 1900, 35-36; 1980, 136-38

Vance, Cyrus, 135
Vandenberg, Arthur, 63
Vanzi, Max, 144
Velasco, Segundo, 103
Ver, Fabian, 103, 109, 134, 140, 164, 169, 171, 179
Vietnam, 93, 95, 97-98, 136; counter-insurgency policy and, 100-101
Vietnam War, 101-5; interpretations of, 126, 135; and Watergate, 123
Village Voice, 170
Virgin Islands, 25

Wakamiya, Kiyoshi, 144
Waller, Littleton Waller Tazewell, 42-43
war, causes of, 207-9
War Powers Act, 125
Washington Post, 142, 170, 174
Watergate, 123-26

Weinberger, Caspar, 163, 165-66, 168
Weinstein, Allen, 170
Westinghouse plant, 122, 143
Westmoreland, William, 101
Wheaton, Lloyd, 33
Will, George, 176
Wilson, Woodrow, 48-50, 56n73
Wisner, Frank, 90
Wolfowitz, Paul, 143, 161, 165-67, 169-70
Worcester, Dean, 36-39
World Bank, 131-32, 141, 150n80
World War I, 57-59
World War II, 66-72
Wright, Luke, 39

Yalta Conference, 72-74
Yamashita, Tomoyuki, 75
Yulo, Jose, 98

Zamora, Jacinto, 14
Zobel family, 68

About the Author

A my Blitz has a doctorate in political science from the Massachusetts Institute of Technology and has studied at the London School of Economics and Harvard University. Blitz spent two years in the Philippines conducting research on land tenure issues. While there, she witnessed firsthand the final tumultuous years of the Marcos regime.

Recently, she has turned her attention to producing multimedia materials for television broadcast, on-line learning and corporate training. She is currently with Harvard Business School where she directs a program to develop multimedia on the subject of entrepreneurship.

about the author